Child Neglect & Emotional Abuse

SAGE has been part of the global academic community since 1965, supporting high quality research and learning that transforms society and our understanding of individuals, groups, and cultures. SAGE is the independent, innovative, natural home for authors, editors and societies who share our commitment and passion for the social sciences.

Find out more at: **www.sagepublications.com**

Child Neglect &
Emotional Abuse

Understanding, Assessment & Response

Celia Doyle & Charles Timms

Los Angeles | London | New Delhi
Singapore | Washington DC

Los Angeles | London | New Delhi
Singapore | Washington DC

SAGE Publications Ltd
1 Oliver's Yard
55 City Road
London EC1Y 1SP

SAGE Publications Inc.
2455 Teller Road
Thousand Oaks, California 91320

SAGE Publications India Pvt Ltd
B 1/I 1 Mohan Cooperative Industrial Area
Mathura Road
New Delhi 110 044

SAGE Publications Asia-Pacific Pte Ltd
3 Church Street
#10-04 Samsung Hub
Singapore 049483

Editor: Kate Wharton
Editorial Assistant: Laura Walmsley
Production editor: Katie Forsythe
Copyeditor: Sarah Bury
Proofreader: Neil Sentance
Marketing manager: Tamara Navaratnam
Cover design: Jen Crisp
Typeset by: C&M Digitals (P) Ltd, Chennai, India
Printed in Great Britain by Henry Ling Limited at
The Dorset Press, Dorchester, DT1 1HD

Library of Congress Control Number: 2013950721

British Library Cataloguing in Publication data

A catalogue record for this book is available from
the British Library

ISBN 978-0-85702-230-1
ISBN 978-0-85702-231-8 (pbk)

Contents

About the authors

Celia Doyle started her professional career as a social worker in a local authority children's team but under the 1968 Seebohm Report reforms became 'generic'. Subsequently, she focussed on psychiatric social work, then for over eleven years was a specialist in child protection employed by the NSPCC. After a break for family commitments, she acquired qualifications in psychology recognised by the British Psychological Society and became an independent play worker. Subsequently, while working as a senior lecturer in university settings she undertook research into the emotional abuse of children, which culminated in a doctoral thesis. She has published extensively in the field of child protection. She continues to research and lecture in child protection particularly in early childhood studies at the University of Northampton.

Celia Doyle is a Research Associate in child welfare at the University of Northampton.

Charles D Timms originally qualified in biomedical sciences at Southampton University where he developed an interest in the influence of very early experiences on later health outcomes and the Barker hypothesis. He undertook research into foetal malnutrition, then continued his investigations into the impact of childhood nutrition on health in later life at Swansea University. He also gained insights into the nature and effect of head injury and brain lesions, including those associated with substance misuse, while working at St Andrew's Hospital in Northampton. He then turned his attention to the practical application of his studies and in order to qualify as a doctor, became a graduate-entry student studying medicine at St Georges, University of London.

Charles Timms is currently studying medicine at St George's Medical School, University of London.

Acknowledgements

First, we would like to thank all those colleagues who have inspired us, notably Professor Doreta Iwaniec, with her profound insights into the emotional abuse of children, and former mentors Margaret Oates, David N. Jones and Maddy Collinge. Other inspirational colleagues include Gill Handley, Eunice Lumsden, Sally Romain, Sukhwinder Singh, Prospera Tedam and staff at the University of Northampton.

PART 1
Understanding

Part 1 comprises four chapters. The first lays the foundation for a general appreciation of the nature of child neglect and emotional abuse. This is followed by an examination of practice points raised by a number of public inquiries and serious case reviews. Subsequently, there are two chapters which explore how neglect and emotional abuse might impact on children's development.

1

Definitions and the roots of oppression

This introductory chapter outlines some of the concepts and models which can assist in an understanding of neglect and emotional abuse.

Chapter overview

- Terminology
- Rationale
- Cosmological model of children's development
- Defining neglect and emotional abuse
- Roots of oppression and abuse
- Carer behaviour constituting neglect and emotional abuse

Terminology

In much of the literature, commentators use various alternatives to the term 'emotional abuse' and, as Navarre (1987) observed, 'in professional literature the terms "psychological abuse", "emotional abuse" and "mental cruelty" have been used interchangeably' (p. 45). Therefore, we include under the phrase 'emotional abuse' all terms such as 'emotional', 'psychological' or 'mental' combined with a word indicating some form of mistreatment such as 'abuse', 'maltreatment', 'cruelty' or 'neglect'.

We have attempted throughout to refer to individuals with respect and to use terminology which recognises the worth and value of people, whether children or adults. However, we appreciate that terms which are currently acceptable might change and acquire connotations which are denigrating or discriminatory. We also know that different interest groups have alternative claims to terminology. Hague et al. (2011,

p. 150), for example, assert that the term person 'with disabilities' is regarded as poor practice in the UK and, instead, the term 'disabled' person is used. Yet others prefer 'child/person with disabilities' because such phraseology emphasises the individual first and the disability or impairment second (e.g. Costantino, 2010). We also prefer 'with disability' rather than 'disabled person' because we believe that any apparent physical deficiency depends on environment and context. Therefore we use the term 'with disabilities' to refer to a state *in a particular environment or context* where aspects of the body have some functional limitation.

The word 'case' is frequently used throughout the book. Unlike the use of 'case' to describe a specific individual, it is employed as a synonym for 'instance'. It is a convenient generic word to encompass a situation and might refer to an organisation, a family system or the name of a child. We know that some people object to the word 'case' but trying to avoid it makes expressions far too unwieldy.

Clearly we cannot meet everyone's claim to the proper use of terms, nor can we anticipate the unknown. Therefore, we ask readers to substitute their preferred terms for any that do not fit with their philosophy or culture, or ones that become, at some point in the future, unacceptable.

Rationale

The first question we need to address is: Why write a book on child abuse and exclude physical and sexual abuse? Very many children suffer from all forms of abuse, and in still more instances there is physical assault or sexual exploitation committed against a background of neglect and emotional abuse. Our reply is, first, because physical and sexual abuse often dominate the general discourse on child protection, consequently, neglect and emotional abuse are all the more readily overlooked.

Furthermore, because the images of physical and sexual abuse are so powerful, it is difficult to read a book about general child abuse without the pictures of children like Victoria Climbié (Laming, 2003) seeping into our consciousness. Consequently, many of the key issues relating to physical abuse are inescapably addressed in general books on child abuse. Additionally, there are a plethora of works devoted explicitly to sexual abuse which only incidentally deal with neglect and emotional abuse.

An additional rationale for examining neglect and emotional abuse in detail is that these can be a precursor to physical and sexual abuse. For example, Peter Connelly, who was killed in 2007, began to be seriously physically abused after the boyfriend of Peter's mother became involved in the family. However, prior to this, his mother was described as 'an extraordinarily neglectful parent' (Jones, 2010, p. 59). Accurate, timely recognition of neglect and emotional abuse, followed by appropriate, supportive intervention, can prevent an escalation of mistreatment.

Families and institutions may reflect the dynamics of one of four types illustrated in Figure 1.1. These are not stringent categories and need to be viewed within the context of cultural mores. For example, a Victorian boarding-school, which might have been considered 'unexceptional' in late nineteenth-century Britain, would probably now be deemed rigid and abusively punitive by UK

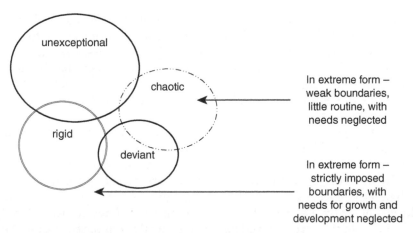

Figure 1.1   Dynamics of families, groups and institutions

Adapted from a model devised by Doyle and Oates (1980)

twenty-first-century standards. Neglect and emotional abuse often occur within settings which are chaotic, with weak boundaries or with rigid, inflexible, unresponsive ones. However, such settings can be easily penetrated by someone with unacceptably deviant attitudes and behaviour towards children, which can result in a particularly dangerous situation for all family members.

A difference between physical or sexual abuse and neglect or emotional abuse is that, theoretically, parents can completely avoid physically or sexually maltreating their children. In contrast, most parents will have to wrestle with whether they are being neglectful if, for example, they allow their children to stay home alone. Similarly, emotionally abusive behaviour can be an extreme form of necessary parental control. It is sometimes difficult to determine exactly when normal scolding becomes abusive denigration or when the imposition of a reasonable limit tips over into arbitrary control.

The next question requiring a response is: Can emotional abuse and neglect be justifiably linked into one book when they appear so distinct? Neglect raises the spectre of a physically unkempt, thin, frail child who is not given adequate food, warmth, clothing or hygiene. Emotional abuse, in contrast, produces the image of the physically cared for child, who is nevertheless humiliated, scapegoated, verbally abused and made to feel worthless.

However, what bridges the two forms of abuse is emotional neglect. A child cannot be physically neglected while being fully emotionally nurtured. In cases of dire poverty, children may be physically deprived but loving parents will try to provide when the opportunity arises whereas neglecting ones will make little attempt to provide care even when circumstances improve. When parents have the wherewithal to provide physical nurture but do not do so, there will inevitably be limited empathy and understanding of the child. Similarly, where there is emotional abuse, there will be emotional neglect. For example, constant denigration inevitably means giving insufficient praise and failing to value the child.

One key difference between neglect and emotional abuse is that neglect is nearly always the responsibility of carers. In instances of children neglected in foster homes, boarding schools, residential hospitals and children's homes, the staff are acting in *loco parentis*. Emotional abuse, in contrast, can be perpetrated by non-carers. Bullying in school by fellow pupils often takes the form of emotional cruelty. Racism or the taunting of children with disabilities by neighbours are similarly examples of emotional abuse.

We do not deny the importance of non-carer emotional abuse, that is mistreatment at the hands of bullies, neighbours and larger society, but it is not the main focus of this book. Children abused by people who are not carers or family members can usually turn for support to the people who are parenting them. It is acknowledged that, in practice, this is not always the case. There have been tragic instances of children bullied by their peers beyond endurance who have not wanted to burden their parents with their worries and have subsequently committed suicide. Although we recognise the importance of helping young people who are abused outside the family, the attention of this book is on those children for whom their home is neither a source of love and nurture nor a place of sanctuary and comfort.

Cosmological model of children's development

Underpinning the discourse in this book is our cosmological model of children's development. This is adapted from Bronfenbrenner's (1979) concept of an ecological model which positions the child in a series of nests which he terms 'systems'. In the innermost nest is the 'microsystem' comprising the person with his or her physical features and roles and immediate relationships. Surrounding this is the 'mesosystem', which is the interplay of the person and their key settings, such as nursery, school or even a social services department. Encircling this is the 'exosystem', broader organisations touching the child less directly. Finally, there is the 'macrosystem', which refers to wider cultural influences and the overarching ideologies of a society.

We prefer to adopt the idea of cosmos. This is derived from the Greek term κόσμος (*kosmos*), meaning 'order'. It proposes an ordered system as opposed to chaos. Wilber (1998) clarifies that the word does not just mean the physical universe; he adopts the word Kosmos to mean the entirety of being, 'the patterned nature or process of all domains of existence' (p. 64). Our model similarly can address the whole of a child's world. A child can only survive and develop confidently if the surrounding systems are reasonably ordered. As will be seen in the next chapter, when inquiries into cases of extreme abuse are examined, order had usually broken down and chaos ensued or an overly rigid system masked emotional turmoil and instability.

We have conceptualised the environments surrounding the child not as circular nests but as rectangles because there are four different elements of the environment and aspects of the child's development plus a fifth underpinning time dimension (see Figure 1.2). The rectangles have curved corners because one element of development

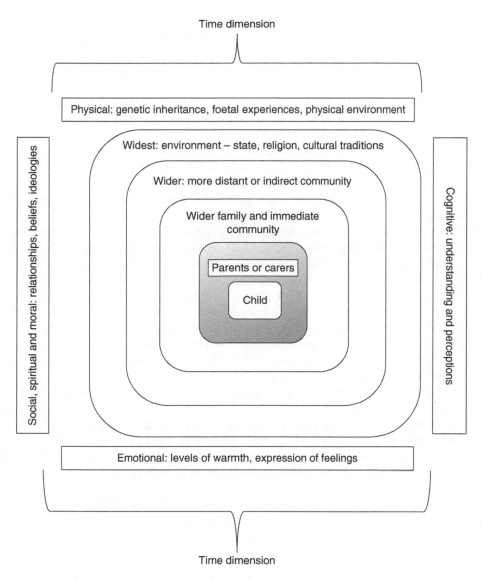

Figure 1.2 Cosmological model of child's development

merges into the next. Here we describe the five aspects, but not in order of importance, because each is equally important for a child's development:

(a) *Physical*: first, this is the child's physiological make-up and growth and the influence of genetic inheritance and foetal experiences. Next is the physical environment. Is it safe? Is it comfortable? Is there sufficient nutrition? Then there is the wider community and environment. Are there outdoor spaces for the children to play? Are the streets safe? Finally, there is the widest geography and physical environment. For example, children developing in Alaska are likely to have different life experiences compared to those brought up in hot, dry countries.

(b) *Cognitive*: for the child, this is the development of reasoning skills and cerebral acuity. More immediately in the environment, it is the education provided initially by family and carers and then through formal schooling. Finally, there is the value placed on education, skills and training by the local community and the state, and how learning and cognition is promoted in each particular cultural context.

(c) *Emotional*: both families and societies might value different types of emotional expression. Some families may be 'demonstrative', in which children are cuddled and told they are loved, whereas others are less so. The emotions engendered in the child and the reaction of both the immediate family and wider society will have an impact on the child's development.

(d) *Social, spiritual and moral*: this dimension encompasses relationships with other people and ways of behaving towards them. This includes standards of morality. Families, whether religious or not, have beliefs about human rights and how to relate to the wider world. Some families may be deeply influenced by religious beliefs whereas in others there is an absence of any spirituality. Tedam (2013) highlights the importance of spirituality in, by way of example, the lives of British Ghanaians. Singh (2013, p. 31) points out that the uncomfortable relationship social work has with religion has 'made it reluctant to embrace a more informed understanding of religious differences and their implications for practice'. Although religion may sometimes be absent, families, schools and wider society still provide guidance about how to relate to others.

(e) *Time*: this is the fifth dimension and is similar to Bronfenbrenner's (1994) 'chronosystem', which he described as the passage of time. This does not mean just the ageing of a person, but encompasses the changing environment as people progress through the life-course. Two people born at slightly different times will be influenced by different chronosystems. The idea of a time-dimension reflects the work of Elder (1998), with echoes of the 'life course theory' in terms of individual's differing experiences over time.

Defining neglect and emotional abuse 1: Concepts in the literature

Concepts of abuse are 'socially constructed'. This means that although victims have always suffered from abuse, at different times and in different societies there may be more, or less, recognition of the suffering. A clear example is of physical abuse: whereas the flogging of children in schools was seen not only as acceptable, but as necessary in the UK less than a century ago, now it would be seen to be abusive. There are similar changing concepts of neglect and emotional abuse which makes finding solid, unchanging, uncontroversial definitions difficult.

Although definitions of physical neglect have not been unduly contentious, it is difficult to measure what is meant by *adequate* food, clothing, shelter and supervision. It is also sometimes difficult to distinguish carers who abusively chose not to provide adequate resources from those who cannot do so, maybe due to poverty. The *Working Together* document (Department of Children, Schools and Families [DCSF], 2010, p. 39) explains that neglect 'is the persistent failure to meet a child's basic physical and/or psychological needs, likely to result in the serious impairment of the child's health or development'.

The above definition covers many children's needs, including 'Neglect may occur during pregnancy as a result of maternal substance abuse' (p. 39). Poor nutrition in pregnancy may be associated with poverty but can occur because a mother choses to eat too much sugar, fat and processed foods, which can be as damaging to the unborn child as substance abuse. This gives rise to the question of whether all women who knowingly disregard their health in pregnancy should be deemed neglectful and, if defined as such, what can be done.

The DCSF (2010, p. 38) definition of emotional abuse raises some questions, such as maintaining the maltreatment is 'such as to cause severe and persistent adverse effects on the child's emotional development'. This raises questions about whether behaviour such as humiliating someone is only abusive if it adversely effects their development. Demeaning, belittling or terrorising older people is mistreatment not because their future development is imperilled; rather, it is the damage to their immediate comfort and right to dignity that defines behaviour as abusive. The same should be true of children (Furnell, 1986).

The DCSF (2010) definition continues by giving examples of emotional abuse. However, account has to be taken of cultural expectations. In a UK village, children as young as six years may well be expected to call on friends in order to 'play out' unsupervised and a child prevented from doing this would be viewed as overprotected. However, on the streets of a large UK city, children 'playing out' unsupervised might well be viewed as neglected.

The above comments are not to criticise unduly the authors of *Working Together* (DCSF, 2010). Rather, it is to demonstrate how difficult it is to define emotional abuse with any precision.

Much of the literature of the 1980s and early 1990s was devoted to debates about appropriate definitions (Besharov, 1981; Egeland, 1991; McGee and Wolfe, 1991). However, one very useful definition was adapted from Hart et al. (1987) by Doyle (1998, p. 256):

> Emotional abuse of children consists of acts of omission and commission which are judged on the basis of a combination of community standards and professional expertise to be psychologically damaging. Such acts are committed by parent figures who are in a position of differential power that renders a child vulnerable. Such acts damage immediately or ultimately the behavioural, cognitive, affective or physiological functioning of the child.

The value of this definition is that it acknowledges that emotional abuse can be by both positive acts and failure to act. It recognises that abuse has to be judged by both the general environment and professional judgement. A child expected to undertake heavy household chores for long periods would not be abused if living

in a tough environment where it was necessary for survival for all the children to do so. However, if singled-out and burdened with such heavy chores where no other children either need or are expected to undertake such work, then emotional abuse is likely. Fundamental to abuse is a misuse of power and also that damage can be in the here-and-now. Although neglect and emotional abuse are chronic forms of maltreatment with cumulative effects, there can be serious specific incidents.

Illustration: Rhianna

Rhianna was the single mother of Jodi, age 10, Sean aged 6 and Swift age 5. Normally a caring mother, she had not come to the notice of any welfare agencies. Just before her 30th birthday she met Jack. He persuaded her to accompany him on a Caribbean cruise to celebrate her birthday. Rhianna felt that some winter sun would help her cope better with the children's demands. Her mother agreed to look after the children but just before the cruise her mother decided not to help out. Reluctant to abandon her holiday, she decided Jodi was old enough to look after Sean and Swift for ten days.

She left Jodi with instructions and some money. Jodi spent all the money in the first three days, the boiler broke down and in bitterly cold weather the children had no heating, hot water or food. After nearly a week, the neighbours eventually heard the two younger children crying and Jodi shouting, and they called the police.

This shows that neglect can be a 'one-off' with the devastating effect of the mother's prolonged absence on the children. The children were cold and starving, and if they had been left much longer the consequences could have been death from hypothermia. Furthermore, Jodi could be burdened by guilt because, although it was unrealistic to expect such a young child to cope in the circumstances, she may well have felt everything was her fault.

Defining neglect and emotional abuse 2: Harnessing Maslow's model

A model for understanding what constitutes neglect and emotional abuse can be derived from Maslow's (1987) hierarchy of needs model. This was originally developed for industry but can be adapted to developing children and how satisfactorily their parents, family and environment meet their needs. This is illustrated in Figure 1.3.

Whether the form of abuse is physical or emotional neglect or emotional abuse will depend on which needs are not being met by the child's carers. However, the

Potential for fulfilment

The meaning of 'fulfilment' depends on the cultural context and the child's own aspirations.

Child as agent: Central to meeting this need is a positive response to what fulfilment means to each child.

Failure to help a child have a sense of fulfilment constitutes primarily emotional abuse but emotional and physical neglect are also likely to contribute to this.

Esteem needs

A child's need for self-respect, feeling valued by significant others and an ability to respect others.

Child as agent: Self-esteem is subjective and therefore ultimately can only be defined by the child him or herself.

Failure to meet esteem needs constitutes emotional abuse or emotional neglect.

Belonging needs

Usually a sense of being a loved family member but includes a sense of community and a positive understanding by the child of her or his cultural heritage.

Child as agent: Account has to be taken of what children feel fulfils their belonging needs.

Failure to meet belonging needs constitutes emotional abuse or emotional neglect.

Safety and security needs

Includes basic physical safety such as protection from serious accidents as well as the fulfilment of attachment needs.

Child as agent: Safety can be objectively evaluated but feeling safe and secure is subjective. Therefore, account has to be taken of the child's views.

Failure to meet safety needs constitutes physical neglect.

Failure to meet security needs constitutes emotional neglect.

Physiological needs

Children will not survive without liquids, air, food, warmth, sleep and the ability to exercise muscles. This also includes basic stimuli needed for cognitive development.

Child as agent: Each child is an individual so that some children require different or additional physiological provision. While the obvious examples are children who have a chronic illness or disabling condition, this applies to all children.

Failure to adequately meet these needs constitutes physical neglect.

Love

Figure 1.3 Rungs of children's developmental needs

precise needs are individual to each child and, to determine this, communication with the young person in question needs to be undertaken.

There are other concepts which can assist practitioners who are trying to identify and define neglect and emotional abuse, including the power analysis described in the next section.

Defining neglect and emotional abuse 3: Power analysis

Read the two cases below and then decide whether the decision to define the situations as abusive should apply to: (i) both cases; (ii) just one of the cases, if so which one; or (iii) neither case.

CASE STUDY A

A 16-year-old girl, Vega, experienced a very chaotic home life because both her parents misused alcohol and drank heavily. They often had fights in which the house contents were largely destroyed. Vega tried to look after her three younger siblings, aged 7, 9 and 10, but wanted to escape her home. She had the opportunity of moving in with a nearby widower, Des, as nanny to his two young children, aged 2 and 3 years. Within a year they had married. Vega gave birth to a daughter, Leona. A few days after the birth, Des had a stroke and recovered slowly in hospital. Vega was now struggling financially because Des was a self-employed plumber and no work meant no income, and Vega had no idea of how to claim benefits. Des returned home but with a degree of disability, suffering from depression and in need of nursing. Meanwhile, Vega's parents threw their three children out and they moved in with Des and Vega. Vega became exhausted caring for six children, including her new baby, and a sick husband. She had few resources, help or support. When the health visitor paid a visit she found Leona was severely malnourished, grubby and under-stimulated. The other children, although rather grubby and very quiet, seemed well.

CASE STUDY B

A couple, Sam and Pat Aye, had a son Joe who, on moving to secondary school, started to hang around with a gang. One day he went off with them, played on a railway line and was killed by a train. The couple were grief-stricken. Three years later the couple had another son, Lee. Desperate to ensure that he did not suffer the same fate as Joe, they were over-protective and also very strict with him. He was never allowed out to play with other children in case they 'contaminated' him. They decided to educate him at home. He was not allowed to watch television, have a computer, listen to the radio or read newspapers. He had little exercise but was fed continually. He was eventually admitted to hospital in his mid-teens suffering from substantial obesity and Type 2 diabetes.

REFLECTION

Would you define Case A as one of neglect and/or emotional abuse or are the children simply 'in need'? If you believe it is a case of abuse, there must be a misuse of parental power or failure to use it for the benefit of the children, so who would you deem responsible, particularly for Leona? Where would you focus any intervention?

Would you define Case B as one of neglect and/or emotional abuse or are Lee's parents being understandably protective? Is there a misuse of parental power? Where would you focus any intervention?

Please note there is no absolute right or wrong answer and further information may make any judgements clearer. However, some points to consider include the possibility that empathy for the parents might lead to the conclusion that there is no emotional abuse in either case. However, coming to a definition of emotional abuse and neglect is not the same thing as making moral judgements about parents and carers. To decide on whether or not there is maltreatment, the power that the parents/carers hold and how they use it needs to be evaluated.

In Case A, both Des and Vega were disempowered by circumstances. Des's parental power had been severely diminished by his stroke. Vega was doing everything *'in her power'* to care for the children, but the demands were overwhelming, stripping her of the power to function. Intervention which did not address the circumstances which were disempowering her would have been ineffective.

In Case B, although there can be understanding and sympathy for Lee's parents, they nevertheless appear to be emotionally abusing him. They have prioritised their own wish to avoid the grief they had suffered when Joe died, over and above Lee's welfare. They have substantial parental powers but they have been using them negatively to prevent Lee from engaging in activities which would help, in terms of his cosmos, his physical, emotional, cognitive and social development. Ultimately, only the parents had the power to alter their approach to Lee. Although he might be helped directly to exercise and choose foods which would help him control his diabetes, he could only do so if his parents gave him a degree of freedom and choice.

The two cases illustrate how analysing power and the way it is used can help practitioners to define what is and is not abusive.

Forms of power

Power is not a single entity; rather, there are different forms of power. One commentator, Handy (1993), identified six forms: physical, position, resource, expert, personal and negative. These can be adapted to provide an understanding of neglect and emotional abuse:

Physical power: in cases of neglect, parents and carers often fail to use their physical power to cuddle and handle their children with affection and to keep their child safe from dangers inside and outside the home. In emotional abuse, physical power might be used, for example, to lock the child alone in a room for lengthy periods of time.

Position power: this is where parents or carers fail to use their position and the responsibility and respect that accrues to their position or use it to mistreat the child. This can include the power to alter the child's environment, perhaps to isolate the child. Another example is 'negating' abuse where parents deny the very existence of their child, with the parents using their position to ensure the child is not seen by concerned professionals.

Resource power: the resources here can be material or emotional ones. It is most evident in instances of neglect where the parents do not give their children basic care, nutrition, comfort or unconditional affection. The inadequate provision of resources is equally apparent in emotional abuse cases where affection, cherishing and praise are withheld.

Expert power: the parents do not need to be recognised 'experts' but compared to their young children, parents and carers have greater knowledge, understanding and insight. Where one child is singled out for neglect, parents often fail to use their evident caring skills to nurture that particular child. In emotional abuse, carers can use their understanding of a child's wants and needs to deliberately distress the child.

Personal power: young children are naturally attached to their parents and this power is misused, particularly in emotional abuse where children are made to feel that the abuse is their own fault and the parents are justified in inflicting distress on them. A variation is where one abusive parent figure uses their personal hold to disarm the formerly loving one.

Negative power: this is described as the power to subvert and stop things happening. It is best illustrated by those instances where a parent or carer who is already abusing a child uses complaints procedures or misinformation to ensure that professionals and protective agencies cannot investigate and reach out to help the child.

Roots of oppression and abuse

The cosmology of the child indicates that neglect and emotional abuse do not occur simply within the isolation of their family. The context and environment within which they live will make abuse less or more likely. Furthermore, the abuse of children is not completely separate from other oppressions and has much in common with wider forms of persecution and mistreatment. Oppression can be located in the macro environment, i.e. the state or beyond to a worldwide occurrence, or the micro environment, i.e. the residential or family home. Common to all forms of maltreatment are three essential factors, illustrated in Figure 1.4:

- abuse of power
- objectification of the victims
- presence of silent witnesses.

The abuse of power has been discussed above. Therefore the other two essential features, the objectification of victims and the place of silent witnesses, will now be examined.

Abuse of power:
Physical, position, resource, expert, personal, negative

failure to use above powers appropriately resulting in neglectful acts of omission
misuse of above powers, although only limited misuse of physical power,
resulting in emotionally abusive acts of commission

Objectification of victims
the children are not seen as full human beings with their own needs and rights

Silent witnesses
co-victims, denying, unaware or passive abusers

Figure 1.4   The roots of neglect and emotional abuse

Objectification of victims

For maltreatment to occur not only is power misused but the victims are objectified and witnesses silenced. Alongside oppressive discrimination there is a dehumanisation of the victims. Examining genocide in the Sudan, Hagan and Rymond-Richmond (2008) tracked how Janjaweed militias targeted black Africans and during attacks shouted dehumanising phrases like 'You donkey, you slave; we must get rid of you' (p. 882). The links between oppression, prejudice and dehumanisation is explored by Haslam and Loughnan (2012). They give societal examples of the objectification of oppressed groups such as 'Nazi portrayals of Jews as vermin' (p. 89). Another important point that they advance is that full human status is defined as a combination of positive human nature, such as interpersonal warmth, and human enculturation, which includes civility, morality and higher cognition. Under this definition, children who have yet to be encultured are readily denied full human status and objectified.

Leyens et al. (2000) discuss how anyone belonging to a group which is perceived as different from us is seen as less than human. Part of racism is 'seeing others as radically different from "us", and as such, lack typically human characteristics and are, therefore, considered infrahumans' (p. 187).

The objectification of abused children is sometimes subtle and normally loving parents might become abusive when they become so angry or stressed that they lose sight of their child's essential humanity. However, in other instances there is the persistent view of the child as 'it', an object or animal. In some instances the child no longer exists in the minds of the parents and such children, if too young to obtain alternative care, can suffer extreme neglect. In the next chapter, we will see examples of this and also how, in an emotionally abusive residential care regime, 'Pindown', the residential staff frequently denigrated the children; for example, a staff member referred to a resident as 'this little runt' (Levy and Kahan, 1991, p. 121).

Silent witnesses

Some abuse occurs in complete isolation, such as sexual exploitation where the perpetrator emphasises to the child that the abuse is their 'special secret'. However, it is rare for neglect and emotional abuse to be perpetrated in such secrecy and frequently other family members will be aware that something is amiss. There are, however, different reasons for witnesses to remain silent:

The co-abuser: the first reason for silence is that the apparent witness is either obtaining vicarious pleasure by seeing the child suffer or is motivated to mistreat the child but allows the more powerful family member to perpetrate most of the abuse.

The loyal protector: here the witness remains silent because he or she feels great loyalty towards the abusive carer or believes that to seek outside help would damage the family and the family reputation. There are also cases where workers in residential homes are aware of mistreatment but so admire the person instituting an abusive regime that they convince themselves that the system will ultimately benefit the children.

The co-victim: these are often other children in the family who are not directly abused themselves but are too frightened to disclose what is happening in the home. Other co-victims are adults in the home who feel terrified and trapped by the situation. A victimised parent may try to care for and protect the children but feels unable to seek outside help.

The immobilized witness: this tends to refer to extended family members, neighbours or even professionals who are aware that something is wrong but do not know what to do. They prevaricate, not knowing whether they might make the situation worse or unfairly condemn parents if they act. Various inquiry reports have described how professionals often become immobilised and, although they may engage in lots of activity, they do not make any impact on the core problem of the abuse of the children.

The unaware: these are people who may witness what is happening but do not realise the significance of events. They are able to find an 'innocent' explanation for abusive behaviour. Again, this can apply to professionals who receive complaints from worried neighbours or even see something amiss but dismiss the concerns.

Carer behaviour constituting neglect and emotional abuse

Fear inducing

This can take at least two major forms: terrorising, which is engendering traumatising fear in the child, and creating insecurity. An example of terrorising was a father who cut his wife's throat while a child was in bed being comforted by his mother. The child, though not touched, suffered severe post-traumatic stress. The other major form of fear is the creation of insecurity by leaving the children alone or with lots of strange, uncaring people. Adults can feel panic and insecurity if they do not know where they are or what is happening. Children who have even less control over their lives can similarly experience panic and mistrust.

Tormenting

This can be vindictive 'teasing' such as the mother who switched on taps in the house when a girl had a shower so that the water would suddenly become very cold. For the singled-out child there is the agony of seeing brothers and sisters given presents and parties at birthdays when the child is never given anything. Another form of tormenting a child is to threaten to kill their pet or destroy their favourite toys or possessions, and possibly carrying out the threats.

Rejecting

This can be active or inactive rejecting. An example of active rejection was the mother who constantly told her son that he was as useless as his father and would end up in prison just like his father did. Inactive rejection is emotional neglect and can be manifested by a total failure to show a child warmth or appreciation, with an absence of any non-verbal indications of affection, such as cuddling a young child.

Isolating

Again, this can take two forms. The first is preventing children from socialising with others. This is often true in physical neglect instances where other children avoid a neglected child because she smells. The other form of isolating is to deliberately lock children away on their own, as exemplified by the Pindown report (Levy and Kahan, 1991).

Degrading

There is overt verbal abuse and denigration, for example, when a girl disclosed sexual abuse by her brothers, her mother turned on her saying 'you dirty fucking cunt, you're a liar'. She continued to be verbally abusive to the girl and discussed her daughter's sexual abuse and personal affairs with the neighbours.

Corrupting

This includes involving children in crime. They may be forced to assist in burglaries or help adults to shop-lift. Other children are compelled to carry drugs, such as the 13-year-old who was made to pass drugs to relatives she visited in prison. Another example is the father who was violent to the mother and encouraged his sons to hit her as well.

Inappropriate roles

Children may be made the scapegoat for all their family's tensions and misfortunes. There are children who are used as weapons in family divorces and disputes. Some have to take on too much responsibility, such as the boy who took responsibility for protecting his siblings and mother against the mother's violent cohabitee. Other children are infantilised by the carers, who are over-protective and do not allow the child to grow towards independence.

Inappropriate treatment

This can include neglect where children who have a medical condition are not given appropriate treatment, such as the boy with a hearing disability who was not taken for any treatment by his parents, resulting in difficulties with learning and behavioural problems because he could not express himself. There is also the imposition of treatment a child does not want or need.

'Not existing' or negating abuse

As will be seen with several of the children in the next chapter, there is a complete denial of a child by carers. In 'not existing' abuse, there is a complete failure to meet the child's needs because the carers act as if the child does not exist. Reder et al. (1993) adopt the term 'not existing' abuse. However, this can cause confusion because it could mean the abuse rather than the child does not exist. Therefore, we have adopted the term 'negating' abuse to refer to this phenomenon.

Spotlight on research

Sidebotham et al. (2011) Fatal child maltreatment in England, 2005–2009.

The authors undertook a study of 276 serious case reviews of children whose abuse resulted in death or serious injury in England between April 2005 and March 2009. They found that although there were only four cases of death from organ failure, directly due to malnutrition, overall 'parental neglect was considered to be a contributory factor in at least 40% of the deaths, although data were often missing and the overall figure may be even higher' (p. 305).

They also noted that there 'were 41 apparent suicides in this cohort, with ages ranging from 8 to 17. Of those for whom information was available, 26 had died by hanging, 4 following overdoses, 1 by a stab wound and 1 by jumping from a height' (p. 304). These cases strongly suggest that emotional abuse, either as the sole form or as a component of other forms of abuse, can contribute to child deaths and serious injury.

Concluding this chapter and looking towards the next

Neglect and emotional abuse are as important as other forms of abuse, but because sex and violence are easier to recognise, they tend to be overlooked. They are also more difficult to define than sexual and physical abuse. In order to assess and intervene in these cases, especially where there is an absence of other forms of abuse, there has to be a holistic understanding of children in their cosmos, which means in their total environment with its five dimensions.

Returning to the study of Sidebotham et al. (2011) above, public inquiries and serious case reviews (SCR) are worse-case scenarios and undue concentration on these extreme cases can lead to overly prescriptive policies. Nevertheless, they can illustrate important points of practice. They are real cases and the events actually happened. The next chapter therefore examines a group of cases highlighting neglect and emotional abuse which were subject to public inquiries and SCRs.

Further resources

Horwath, J. (2013) *Child Neglect* (2nd edition). Basingstoke: Palgrave.

Iwaniec, D. (2006) *The Emotionally Abused and Neglected Child* (2nd edition). Chichester: John Wiley & Sons.

Rees, G., Stein, M., Hicks, L. and Gorin, S. (2011) *Adolescent Neglect*. London: Jessica Kingsley.

Stevenson, O. (2007) *Neglected Children and their Families* (2nd edition). Oxford: Blackwell Publishing.

Taylor, J. and Daniel, B. (eds) (2005) *Child Neglect*. London: Jessica Kingsley.

The NSPCC and CORE INFO provide helpful information: www.NSPCC.org.uk/inform. www.core-info.cardiff.ac.uk/reviews/emotional-neglect.

2

Lessons from inquiries

Over time, policy and practice have been influenced by landmark cases which are subject to popular debate, public inquiry and professional analysis. Many modern procedures in the UK can trace their origins back to the public inquiries following the death from abuse of children such as Maria Colwell (Field-Fisher, 1974). Other deaths, such as those of Victoria Climbié (Laming, 2003) and Peter Connelly (Laming, 2009), and, in Scotland, of Kennedy McFarlane (Hammond, 2001), have resulted in legislation and in major policy initiatives, as have reports into historic abuse in institutions in Ireland (Ryan, 2009). There have been a number of inquiries where the focus has been neglect and emotional abuse; it is to these that this chapter turns.

Chapter overview

- Public inquires and associated 'practice points'
- The Pindown regime
- Lessons from serious case reviews

There are good reasons for examining historic cases of neglect and emotional abuse. First, three highly regarded social work academics (Corby, Shemmings and Wilkins, 2012) note that much of child protection is very 'present-orientated' and comment that 'there is much that can be learned from an examination of the way in which our own and other societies have tackled the same sort of problems and concerns in the past' (p. 12). Although time has moved on, some of the practice dilemmas highlighted by past cases are still relevant to modern practitioners and are therefore worth revisiting.

Second, public inquiries are in the public domain and provide factually accurate case examples. Case illustrations, while based on reality, have to be heavily disguised to ensure confidentiality and are easy to dismiss as unreal. When public inquiry reports are used as the basis of case examples, readers know that the events described really happened and those who wish to do so can obtain the report and explore the case further.

The next section looks at seven public inquiries and, after a brief outline of the case prompting the inquiry, a 'practice point' relevant for current practitioners will be highlighted.

Case 1. Stephen Meurs

This is a case of death by neglect of a 15-month-old toddler (Norfolk County Council, 1975). One of the key issues is that at the time Stephen's mother was acting as a foster carer to other children.

On 4 July 1975 Stephen's mother, Sandra Meurs, pleaded guilty to his manslaughter. He had been found dead at his home in Kings Lynn. He was lying in his cot, which was described by the investigating police officer as indescribably filthy. The pathologist determined the cause of death to be malnutrition. Stephen was half the weight of an average child of his age. His chest, buttocks, stomach and thighs showed considerable excoriation.

Background circumstances

Stephen Meurs' paternal grandparents were affluent and originally from Holland, while his maternal family were white British and not prosperous. Stephen's father, Dennis, committed burglaries when he was 16 years old. The following year he moved in with Sandra (née Williams), married her and their first child, Elizabeth, was born on 10 February 1972. Stephen was born in December the following year, 1973.

Dennis Meurs engaged in further criminal activity and was therefore in prison when Stephen died. On 16 January 1974, four children of Sandra's friend, Carol Skinner, moved in with Sandra, with the agreement of social services, because of domestic violence in the Skinner household. The two younger children eventually went home, but the eldest two, aged 11 and 10 years, chose to stay with Sandra. Also in the household was a young homeless man, Walter Sharpless, who acted as an informal baby-sitter.

A pub landlady who visited the home on 9 February 1975 was shocked by Stephen's condition and reported her concerns. On 14 March, Stephen's paternal grandfather found him dirty, wet and covered with sores, and reported this to the social services. The same day the police also received an anonymous referral that the children were being left alone. A health visitor was asked to visit as a routine call and to deal with the matter 'very tactfully'. She consequently visited twice but Sandra refused point blank to let her see Stephen. On 9 April, Carol Skinner expressed concern about Stephen to the social worker because he had not been seen by her for some time. The social worker took no action and on 16 April Stephen died.

This is a case illustrating the *Cinderella syndrome*, which is where only one child in a family or setting is abused. Three children – Elizabeth and the two older Skinner children – were being seen fairly frequently and the inquiry report notes that the 'apparent good health of other children was enough to put others off the scent' (p. 12). It is also an instance of 'non-existing' or negating abuse, where a child appears to no longer exist to the parents. No one appears to have asked the children about the situation and, above all, few people tried to engage with Stephen.

Practice point

Avoiding 'silo practice': This case is an example of 'silo practice'; the social workers were visiting but their remit was the welfare of the Skinner children, so they believed that the baby in the household was not their responsibility. It therefore illustrates what can happen if practitioners focus on their allotted tasks and are unable to view situations holistically. Often workload and time-management pressures are such that practitioners would not cope if they strayed beyond their remit; they have to focus and maintain boundaries. Practitioners and students on placement therefore could do well to find out, before any home visits, what they need to do if they find that there are other children in a household. If the procedures indicate that they need to report concerns to another authority, then it is good practice to follow up any report to check that the matter has been dealt with appropriately.

Case 2. Lester Chapman

This is a case of death by misadventure of an 8-year-old boy, against a background of emotional abuse and neglect of the children in the family (Berkshire County Council, 1979). Lester suffered a catalogue of emotional and some physical abuse in a family where abuse and domestic violence were endemic. He ran away from home for the fourth time on 12 January 1978. His body was found in old sewage sludge where he had become trapped and he died of exposure.

Background circumstances

The children's cultural heritage, ethnicity or religion are not specified. Lester was the second eldest of four children in the household. At the time of his death, Wendy, his elder half-sister, was aged 9. His half-siblings, Shane and Marie, were 4¾ years and 2¾ years, respectively. As a child his mother, Linda, had run away from home and had been taken into care because she had a poor relationship with her father and was burdened by responsibility for her younger brother. When she was aged 16 she became pregnant with Wendy and married Lester Johnson, although he was not Wendy's father. Lester was born a year later.

Early in 1970, the NSPCC became involved due to allegations of neglect of Wendy and Lester. They were taken into care. Subsequently, Linda divorced Lester's father and married Leslie Chapman in July 1972. The children were returned to Linda, now Chapman. Lester's father made attempts to obtain custody of Lester and Wendy but did not manage to do so and seems to have faded from their lives. Shane was born in March 1973 and Marie in April 1975.

Throughout Lester's short life there were constant themes of the children being left alone. Both Mr and Mrs Chapman accused each other of using Lester as a scapegoat and there was mounting domestic violence, with Mr Chapman being bound over to keep the peace after causing grievous bodily harm (GBH) to Linda Chapman.

Practice point

Using diagrams for clarity: One of the key practice points arising from the case is that in emotional abuse cases there is no clear-cut issue with which to grapple and the child protection procedures do not serve practitioners well in such cases. Rarely are there specific events which trigger case conferences and the implementation of procedures. Here diagrams can help to highlight the emotional pressures on children. For example, the child can be placed in the centre and then adverse experiences impinging on the child's welfare added, as shown in Figure 2.1.

Figure 2.1   Forms of emotional abuse impinging on a child

Case 3. Malcolm Page

This was a case of substantial neglect of all four children in the family despite the children being subject to a Care Order (Denham, 1981). On 7 February, Malcolm Page, aged 13½ months, died in Basildon Hospital. The cause of death was hypothermia and malnutrition. The post mortem found in addition to malnourishment, an extensive nappy rash, gangrene of the toes and possibly the tip of the penis, and an abrasion to the jaw. One of his sisters, Suzanne, was also found to have burns on her legs from lying in urine. On 15 January 1980 the parents were found guilty of the neglect of Malcolm and Suzanne and sentenced to 12 months in prison.

Background circumstances

The family's cultural heritage, ethnicity or religion are not given. Malcolm's mother came from a family of eleven children. She left school at 15 and had a series of factory jobs until her marriage to Mr Page in January 1973, when she was seven months pregnant. Samantha was born in March 1973, followed by Simon in March 1975, Suzanne in January 1977 and Malcolm eleven months later.

Little is known of the background of Malcolm's father, Peter Page. However, he held the responsible job of stock controller and earned a reasonable wage but only gave his wife a third of this for the children and all household expenses. At the time of Malcolm's death the family were living in a three-bedroomed council terrace house.

The first major concern emerged on 7 March 1978 when the health visitor was 'horrified' by what she saw, which was squalid conditions with a carpet that was sticky and black with dirt, and there was also a foul smell. The children were grubby and Suzanne was saturated with urine. Mrs Page would not let the health visitor examine Malcolm. The health visitor referred the matter to the social services. The social worker visited on 16 March and agreed with the health visitor about the unacceptable conditions. The social worker visited again on 30 March with a home help organiser and it is interesting that the social worker felt there had been improvements in the condition of the living room whereas the home help organiser, on seeing the conditions for the first time, was shocked at how 'filthy' they were (p. 27).

At a fourth case conference, on 30 November 1978, the social worker, home help and health visitor appeared to feel that there had been improvements and there was general satisfaction with home conditions and the children's care. Just over two months later Malcolm was dead and the description by the investigating police, particularly of the children's bedrooms, was of truly unhygienic conditions, which was at odds with the reports of a satisfactory situation recorded by the practitioners regularly visiting the family.

Like Stephen Meurs, Malcolm was an example of negating abuse. The parents no longer recognised the existence of their child. Professionals who failed to insist on engaging with Stephen and Malcolm reinforced the parents' delusion that they no longer existed, thereby compounding the dangers to the children.

Practice point

Written contracts: The dominant theme of this case is the way in which practitioners lowered their expectations of the parents so that 'satisfactory' for the Page children would not have been satisfactory for most others. The practitioners who were regularly involved with the family stopped seeing and recording the precise details of the squalor around them. They were no longer shocked by what they saw and what was clearly unacceptable began to be accepted.

In addition, a pressure on the practitioners at the time was the prevalence of the view that social workers and other professionals were by definition 'middle class' and should therefore not be imposing their standards on 'working-class' families. By the 1980s this belief was transferred to ethnicity and race. In particular, it was deemed that white professionals should not impose their standards on black families. However, this leads to two unsatisfactory outcomes. First, its implications are a profoundly insulting generalised judgement on working-class or black families. The Pages, in their squalor and inadequate child care, were not representative of the 'working class'. Second, children, whatever the social class, colour or ethnicity of their parents, have basic rights to be protected from starvation, perpetually urine-soaked beds or harsh and unreasonable treatment.

In similar cases it is helpful to adopt a written contract with the parents detailing standards and expectations. A professional, who is uninvolved in the family, can usefully be co-opted to scrutinise the contract to ensure the expectations are appropriate. This can help to avoid mixed messages between practitioners and the parents. Any contract also needs to specify direct practitioner engagement with the children and it can be regularly monitored by practitioners' supervisors.

Case 4. Lucie Gates

This is an instance of death by misadventure but against a background of neglect of the children in the family (London Borough of Bexley, 1982). On 31 May 1979, three young children were left alone in the evening while their mother went to the local pub. During her absence an electric fire fell on Lucie, the youngest, aged 32 months, who died from extensive burns 19 days later.

Background circumstances

The family's cultural heritage, religion or ethnicity are not specified. Lucie's mother, Linda Gates, had one older sister and a twin sister, both of whom married and had no welfare intervention. Linda's four babies were described as 'accidents' and there was no known, actively involved, father for any of them. Linda's mother died when Linda was expecting her first baby and the child was adopted. Subsequently, Linda gave birth to 'William' on 12 March 1971 and 'Mary' on 15 June 1973.

Initially, Linda lived with her father. There were considerable concerns about neglect and minor injuries to the two children, so a health visitor, social worker and home help were involved in assisting her. The neglect continued when Linda moved into her own flat in February 1974. The family's first social worker appeared to have been preoccupied with developing a relationship with Linda at the expense of the children, and her positive reports are in contrast to those of the home help, who noted Linda punching the children and feeding them inadequately. At the time of Lucie's birth the case was handed over to a new social worker, although the first social worker continued to visit Linda informally for the following year. When the first social worker transferred the case to the second, there appeared to be no available case notes, so the new social worker had little idea of the seriousness of previous incidents.

There were continuing concerns about the behaviour and appearance of the children. At her two-year check, Lucie was described by a clinical medical officer as very under-stimulated. Yet, in contrast, many people who became involved with Linda, such as the family's social workers, spoke positively of her parenting and the children's appearance.

Practice point

Avoiding undue optimism: The Gates inquiry illustrates the damaging consequence of 'the rule of optimism', a concept coined by Dingwall et al. (1983). It can be defined as a desire 'to see the best in people, and have hope and optimism that their interventions can help a family function better, including for the child involved' (Littlechild, 2012, p. 6). This can result in harm to children being overlooked, particularly in neglect and emotional abuse cases where there are rarely reports of unequivocal incidents of abuse. Munro (2011, p. 35) wrote that some social workers 'are so focused on supporting parents that they are insufficiently challenging of problematic parenting'. In Norway, Christiansen and Anderssen (2010) observed that Child Welfare Service (CWS) workers felt:

> parents, despite all their problems, had personal resources and qualities. In retrospect, some of the CWS workers felt that emphasizing this had made them too optimistic and that they had lost track of the children and failed to make necessary decisions. (p. 36)

Practitioners can help themselves to avoid over-identifying with the parents by mentally role-playing the parts of the children. This is easier if close attention is paid to the children and they are engaged in communication with practitioners. Another strategy is to draw up a SLOT analysis of family functioning (see Chapter 10 for further details).

Case 5. Heidi Koseda

This is a case where one child appears to have been completely ignored by the parent figures (London Borough of Hillingdon, 1986). On 23 January, the body of Heidi Koseda, who was about 4 years old, was found in a bedroom in the family flat. She had died of starvation. On 25 September 1985 her mother's cohabitee, Nicholas Price, was found guilty of her murder and sentenced to life imprisonment. Her mother, Rosemary Koseda, was found guilty of manslaughter on the grounds of diminished responsibility. Heidi's half-siblings were made Wards of Court.

Background circumstances

The family's cultural heritage, ethnicity and religion are not specified. Heidi was born in 1980 to Rosemary and Henryk Koseda and her early life appears to have been happy. In October 1982, Henryk left and Nicholas Price moved in to the flat. The couple's son, James, was born in 1983, followed by their daughter, Lisa, in December 1984. The family had extended family support but, early in January 1984, Rosemary and Nicholas cut off contact with their extended families. Subsequently, the situation appears to have deteriorated and the police, health authority, social services department and the NSPCC were all involved in the family between September 1984 and January 1985.

Practice point

Confronting negating abuse: The report reveals how time and again Heidi was not seen by professionals even though there was involvement with her brother, James, who was observed on a number of occasions. Therefore, the key practice point in this case is that children do not only need to be seen, but also to be engaged in communication. As Ferguson (2010, p. 1110) writes, 'effective child protection has to involve not only professional mobility to reach the child, but ensuring that children move'. This will enable practitioners to assess them more fully.

Reder et al. (1993) viewed Heidi, along with Stephen Meurs and Malcolm Page, as examples of the victims of 'not-existing' abuse. By this, they meant that the parents shut the children away and ignored their existence. The term 'negating abuse' is preferred to avoid any confusion about the child rather than the abuse not existing. Negating abuse is particularly dangerous because often the children will give up and stop crying. This further reinforces the parental belief that the child does not exist. In Heidi's case, this was compounded by the actions of practitioners, such as an NSPCC officer who recorded that he had visited and seen the children looking well when he had neither visited nor seen the children. If there is some practitioner interaction with negated children, their parents have to accept that their child exists and the extremely dangerous negating abuse which can lead to death from starvation may be avoided.

Case 6. Paul

This is a case of substantial neglect over many years of a family of children (Bridge Child Care Consultancy Services, 1993). Paul died, aged 16 months, having been left for days in urine-soaked clothes and bedding. He had pneumonia and most of his body was covered with burns from lengthy contact with the acid in urine. He had septicaemia, with septic lesions on his toes and fingers. His father was convicted of manslaughter and cruelty by neglect of three of his other children. His mother was also convicted of manslaughter.

Background circumstances

The family's cultural heritage, ethnicity and religion are not specified. At the time of Paul's death the family were living in London in a large Victorian terrace council property which had been refurbished. Paul's mother and father were aged 36 and 44 respectively when he died, and were experienced parents. Paul had six older siblings living in the home, three sisters aged 13, 10 and 8 years and three brothers aged 6, 5 and 3 years.

Throughout the previous 15 years the children had, to a greater or lesser extent, suffered from neglect. One sister had been attacked, resulting in facial damage, by a pit-bull type of dog which appeared to have been in the household. There had also been concerns about the sexual abuse of the children, but these claims were never substantiated.

The report's authors provide some 129 pages of flow charts, with a series of columns noting the date, changes, other incidents, child development and sources of information. However, there is one further column 'What the child says and the impact of this', and what immediately strikes the reader is that this column is largely blank, despite the fact that the flow charts cover seven children over a period of 15 years. There seems to have been no attempt to engage the children by any of the social workers, yet the parents' voices and views are often prominent.

Despite the considerable distress expressed by the eldest girl about being bullied in school because she smelt, was 'filthy, had nits' (p. 124), when the social workers visited they recorded 'hygiene causes no medical problem for the children' (p. 127). There appears to have been no empathy and no thought given to the emotional impact on children of being singled out by their peers as dirty and smelly.

There is a marked contrast between the bland, unconcerned reports of social service and health visiting staff seeing the family regularly and practitioners or visitors who saw the children less regularly or the home for the first time. A person entering the family home to pick up a TV, a school nurse, members of the council Architects' Department visiting the home and a family acquaintance all expressed profound concern yet their anxieties were dismissed or ignored.

Practice point

Charting each child: There was considerable social work activity but this appeared to begin and end with providing financial and material help for the parents. There was slightly more attention paid to the children when a second allegation of sexual abuse was made, and again when one daughter was attacked by a dog. But there was no engagement with the children, no attempt to understand the emotional distress they were inevitably experiencing and no analysis of the increasing signs of neglect. This highlights that practitioners and their supervisors need to question the quality, and not just the quantity, of intervention.

Furthermore, some way of keeping track of professional engagement with each child, especially in large complex families, needs to be undertaken. The report shows how Paul seemed to have disappeared from the attention of any professionals in the months before his death. It is useful to have a separate chart for each child, recording within the context of other family events when the child was seen and communicated with. Large gaps in the chart can then be more readily identified.

Case 7. Khyra Ishaq

This is a case of extreme malnutrition, with food deprivation used as a punishment for all the children in the family. The situation was compounded by the fact that several of the children were withdrawn from school and home educated, so were not seen outside the family (Radford, 2010). On 17 May 2008 an ambulance crew, called by Khyra's mother, was unable to resuscitate 7-year-old Khyra, who was found on a mattress in an upstairs bedroom. The cause of death was bronchial pneumonia and septicaemia with focal bacterial meningitis. She was found to be severely malnourished and post mortem results suggested she had suffered from starvation for a considerable period, maybe up to nine months. There was also evidence that she had been caned on several different occasions in the 78-hour period before her death.

All but the eldest sibling were suffering from severe malnutrition, to the extent that they experienced 're-feeding syndrome' (see Chapter 11, p. 149) when treated and one sibling nearly died in hospital. On 12 March 2010 the mother and her partner were found guilty of the manslaughter of Khyra and of cruelty in relation to the other five children.

Background circumstances

The family is described in the inquiry as being 'of Black Caribbean, African and British heritage and all follow the Islamic faith' (p. 5). The marriage between Khyra's father and mother, Angela Gordon, was overshadowed by violence against both mother and children and ended between 2004 and 2006. Angela's new partner, Junaid Abu Hamza, joined the family in 2007. His own father had been imprisoned for punching to death Junaid's 5-year-old sister for not pulling the toilet chain. The father was a strict disciplinarian and Junaid exerted a similarly rigid and punitive system on Angela Gordon's children.

Monitoring the welfare of the children became more difficult because in January 2008 the mother withdrew Khyra and some of her siblings from school saying she would tutor them at home. In the UK, home education legislation, while facilitating high-quality education for some children, appears to ignore the wider welfare of the child and promote and prioritise the parents' wishes. It is worth quoting a statement in the report (Radford, 2010):

> The lack of any prescribed opportunities for children to formally express their views or to actively participate within the assessment or decision making process of home education, or to have any independent access to external processes, represents a direct contradiction to the aspiration of safeguarding and human rights legislation and guidance. (p. 8)

Practice point

Challenging aggression: A key feature of the case is the way social workers retreated in the face of parental complaints. In December 2007, the mother was aggressive and criticised the school, threatening to go to the press. Undaunted, the head teacher made a referral to social services due to mounting concerns about the children appearing to be exceptionally hungry. Social services refused to follow up the referral. When an Education Social Worker attempted to visit, Angela Gordon threatened her with a breach of European law and another referral was made to social services. When subsequently two social workers visited on 21 February 2008, the mother immediately registered a complaint of harassment. Consequently, social services took no further action and by April 2008 had agreed to close the case.

Sometimes intervention by authorities is inappropriate and parental complaints are justified. However, alarm bells should ring when the grounds for complaints or legal action appear to have no basis and are diffuse, as in the case of Angela Gordon, who marshalled a variety of legal threats to dilute intervention. In these cases, practitioners need to keep careful contemporaneous records. Because such parental behaviour can suggest substantial risks to the children, which the parents are attempting to hide, practitioners need to insist on discussions with senior managers and should have access to legal consultation. Farmer and Lutman (2012) noted how their study of child neglect suggested that practitioners needed high levels of skill to engage uncooperative parents and cope with belligerence and antagonism. Threats of violence can distort intervention and assessment, as Baynes and Holland (2012) warn:

> Caution is advised about increasing the participation of violent men in child protection meetings without further research into the impact that this has on the others present. It may be necessary to think creatively about enabling these men's engagement with the process in a manner that does not endanger other family members or workers. (p. 64)

For practitioners and students on placement, it is worth exploring what support from their agency they can expect *before* they meet with parental aggression and threats so that they know in advance what to do, rather than having to find this out when suffering from the shock and fear of threats.

The Pindown Regime

The public inquiry reports above focused on abuse within the family. However, there have been a number of reports of institutions, usually examining physical and sexual abuse (e.g. Kirkwood, 1993; Ryan, 2009). One public inquiry (Levy and Kahan, 1991) explored emotional abuse in local authority institutions. The value of examining this 'Pindown' inquiry is because it illustrates how professionals can abuse power and it also focuses largely on the emotional abuse of adolescents, whereas most of the inquiries outlined above involved younger children.

The Pindown Inquiry report (Levy and Kahan, 1991) is about children traumatised by emotional neglect and emotional abuse. It is not about one or two miscreant carers, but rather it highlights a sustained and systematic regime instituted by senior social workers in four children's residential homes in Staffordshire. At least 132 children were subjected to Pindown. On 13 October 1989 the High Court granted an injunction banning the use of Pindown in any form whatsoever for children in the care of local authorities.

Pindown involved keeping children aged between 9 and 17 years locked in solitary confinement for up to 84 days. While in confinement, children did nothing or meaningless tasks, such as writing out a telephone directory, and had no exercise or recreation. Generally, the rule was 'strictly isolated no contact at all' (p. 121) and this often meant not attending school. There was also complete withdrawal of privileges, which might at first sight seem an acceptable method of discipline; acceptable, that is, until it is realised that 'privileges' included medication, food, drink and education. They were allowed no personal possessions. There are reports of clothing, bedclothes and mattresses being removed so that children had to wear underwear or pyjamas with no footwear and could not lie down. There were substantial dangers to the children. One child placed in Pindown, Jane, was so unhappy she took an overdose and had to be hospitalised, while a confinement room could not be used as an ordinary bedroom because the floor was unsafe and there was no fire escape.

What emerges from the inquiry report are the openly negative attitudes towards the children on the part of many of the staff. The children were sworn at and denigrated. For example, at a review meeting a child was told 'you are fucking useless' (p. 120). Generally, at these review meetings all the negative instances and behaviour of the children were highlighted with little mention being made of any positive aspects.

The fact that social workers instituted and operated this system, which was based on an 'ill-digested understanding of behavioural psychology' (p. 167), demonstrates the need for child-centred training. Social workers require education geared towards skills in empathising with young people's perspectives and in understanding their emotional development.

Serious Case Reviews

More recently in the UK, public inquiries have been largely superseded by 'Serious Case Reviews' (SCR). Each year several cases involve neglect and emotional abuse. These can range from a 2-year-old, neglected, inadequately supervised child who drowned in a garden pond (Bristol Safeguarding Board, 2011), a 7-year-old child with a disability where neglect contributed to death due to infection (Flintshire LSCB, 2012) to a 16-year-old girl who died of an overdose after years of emotional abuse and neglect (Newcastle Safeguarding Children Board, 2011).

One notable serious case review, SRC [CE001: 2000–2009], was produced by Brabbs (2011). The children, adopted by a two doctors whose socio-economic status was high, were emotionally abused over a period of many years.

SRC [CE001: 2000–2009]

On 18 October 2010, research scientist Dr Newcombe-Buley, aged 45, pleaded guilty to 14 offences of child cruelty and was sentenced to four years in prison. Her husband, also a research scientist and company director, Dr Newcombe, aged 43, pleaded guilty to three offences and received a two-year suspended prison sentence.

The three children adopted by the couple were Child B, a boy born 1996, Child C, a girl born 1997, and Child D, a boy born 1999. The children were therefore approximately 14, 13 and 11 years old at the time of their adoptive parents' conviction. Neither of the adoptive parents appeared to have had an extended family and no grandparents, aunts, uncles or other relatives are mentioned in the report.

The children were siblings whose birth parents misused substances amid domestic violence and mental health problems. In November 1999, the Stoke-on-Trent Adoption Panel matched the three children with the Newcombes. Adoption Orders were made in June 2001. Although the summary report does not specify the ethnicity, culture or religion of the children, it appears that they may not have shared the ethnic origins of their adoptive parents.

The abuse took place over nine years, was directed against all three children and included an absence of warmth and affection, extreme denigration and verbal abuse, inadequate food, attempted suffocation, dousing in freezing water and physical assault. Abuse had been disclosed by Child B on numerous occasions and Child C once, but their accounts were largely ignored by various social workers. When Child B ended up in hospital having been assaulted by another unrelated child, a social worker again refused to believe his allegations, but the Consultant Paediatrician would not discharge him and at last he was helped to disclose in full.

Practice point

The main feature of the case is the need to listen to the concerns of lay people. Social workers and the police repeatedly dismissed the children's allegations whereas lay people believed the children's accounts and passed their concerns to the authorities on at least five occasions. A stranger, for example, helped Child B after he sustained injuries when he jumped from a window to escape abuse and ensured he went to hospital, where he was kept in for assessment, but the social workers involved arranged for Child B to be returned home without speaking to him. A man who found Child B sleeping rough, believed his account of being abused and told the police, but Child B was returned home. Child C told a friend about the abuse and the friend's mother recorded the information and made a referral to Social Care, but the investigating social worker took the matter no further.

The police and social workers demonstrated no understanding that fear may make children retract information and the Stockholm syndrome may lead children to deny that abuse is occurring, as happened with Child C and Child D. The outstanding feature of this case is the courage of Child B. Concerned for his siblings, he tried disclosing time and time again, despite the fact that he probably suffered retribution each time he was not believed and returned home.

The issues discussed in this chapter tend to reflect the findings of an Ofsted (2011) report whose authors examined 67 serious case reviews to see what lessons for practitioners could be learned. They highlighted five major issues which, somewhat dishearteningly, are similar to the points raised by the public inquiries in this chapter. Their five points are:

1. The child was not seen frequently enough by the professionals involved, or was not asked about their views and feelings.
2. Agencies did not listen to adults who tried to speak on behalf of the child and who had important information to contribute.
3. Parents and carers prevented professionals from seeing and listening to the child.
4. Practitioners focused too much on the needs of the parents, especially vulnerable parents, and overlooked the implications for the child.
5. Agencies did not interpret their findings well enough to protect the child.

Look back over the summaries of the inquiry reports and the serious case reviews and identify which of the five points above could apply to each case.

REFLECTION

Concluding this chapter and looking towards the next

Of value to practitioners, managers and students are the analyses of the serious case reviews undertaken by leading investigators such as Brandon et al. (2012). They noted that neglect was a background factor in 60 per cent of serious case reviews for children of all ages. While they were able to report on improvements for children subject to a child protection plan and for younger children, they nevertheless remarked on the inadequacy of training, stating:

> An understanding of normal development in childhood is an essential component of child protection practice. Overall, there is a dearth of child development teaching on professional courses for those who will be working with children. Where children have communication impairments the onus is on the professional, not the child, to find ways of communicating. (p. 2)

This is also reflected in research by Leeson (2010) and Handley and Doyle (2012), who found that social work qualifying courses rarely provide adequate training in important areas of child protection, in communicating with children and in understanding the impact of abuse on a child. Similarly, in her detailed review of child protection issues, Munro (2011) wrote:

> Degree courses are not consistent in content, quality and outcomes – for child protection, there are crucial things missing in some courses, such as detailed learning on child development. (p. 97)

The next two chapters therefore explore aspects of child development and the impact, first, on children's physical and physiological growth, and, secondly, on the children's psychosocial and cognitive development.

Further resources

Beesley, P. (2011) *Ten Top Tips for Identifying Neglect*. London: BAAF.

Brandon, M., Bailey, S., Belderson, P. and Larsson, B. (2013) *Neglect and Serious Case Reviews*. Norwich: University of East Anglia/NSPCC.

Davies, C. and Ward, H. (2012) *Safeguarding Children across Services*. London: Jessica Kingsley.

Ferguson, H. (2011) *Child Protection Practice*. Basingstoke: Palgrave Macmillan.

Unwin, P. and Hogg, R. (2012) *Effective Social Work with Children and Families*. London: Sage.

Vincent, S. and Petch, A. (2012) *Audit and Analysis of Significant Case Reviews*. Edinburgh: Scottish Government.

3

Child development: physical and physiological factors

In line with the child's cosmos and our adaption of Maslow's model, described in Chapter 1, we explore the impact of neglect and emotional abuse on children's physical and physiological development (although the various conditions can only be briefly outlined).

Chapter overview

- Physical and physiological determinants of development
- The developing brain
- Physiological consequences of chronic stress
- The impact of parental substance misuse
- Nutritional issues
- Physical safety
- Hygiene

The purpose of this chapter is not to describe children's basic physical development – this is helpfully covered in works such as those by Meggitt (2006) and Sheridan et al. (2008). Instead, this chapter examines the impact of neglect and emotional abuse on their physical and physiological development.

Physical and physiological determinants of development

There are a number of factors which contribute to the growth and development of humans. These are:

(a) *the intra-uterine environment*: this can include malnutrition caused by the mother's inadequate diet or by conditions such as oligohydramnios, which is a decrease in the amount of amniotic fluid surrounding the foetus and can adversely affect foetal growth and cause kidney abnormalities. There are other processes, such as twin-to-twin transfusion syndrome where, in the case of some monozygotic twins, the blood supply is diverted from one twin to the other, resulting in one child becoming anaemic with subsequent poor neurodevelopment.

(b) *hormones*: growth failure in children who are small for gestational age when born and then subsequently fail to show catch-up growth is linked to abnormal growth hormones, insulin-like growth factors and insulin levels (Chatelain et al., 2007).

(c) *disease*: a range of diseases can adversely affect children's growth and development. Severe dental caries can damage growth because children with poor teeth often eat a restricted diet because of the pain of eating (Sheiham, 2006). Coeliac disease, a gluten intolerance, if undiagnosed, can lead to diarrhoea, malabsorption of food and poor growth, as can children with chronic intestinal inflammation which is a feature of Crohn's disease (Heuschkel et al., 2008; Walters et al., 2007).

(d) *genetic factors such as growth genes, and genetically based syndromes*: an example of a condition caused by a range of genetic defects is the Beckwith-Wiedmann syndrome (BWS). Features include macrosomia, which is greater weight and length growth for dates, a large tongue, ear pits and creases, neonatal hypoglycaemia (low blood sugar just after birth) and exomphalos or omphalocele, in which the abdominal wall fails to close during foetal development. However, when examining children with either large or small growth, knowledge of the family background is helpful because stature can be inherited.

(e) *accident and misadventure*: babies are relatively well protected in the womb if the mother has an accident. However, there can be developmental misadventures which mean that babies can be born without being fully developed and the cause is often unknown. Examples include babies born with cleft lips and palates, or with a condition (similar in appearance to exomphalos) called gastroschisis, where the abdominal wall fails to close, typically to the right of the umbilical cord; the baby is born with the intestines outside the body. Cerebral palsy is a condition caused by an injury to the child's brain before, during, or shortly after birth.

(e) *early post-natal and subsequent nutrition and care of the child*: much of this chapter will examine the impact of deficient nutrition, love and attention in the early years and throughout childhood and adolescence.

Although there may be discrete reasons for a lack of development, sometimes there may be combinations of factors. This means that children with disabilities caused by genetic conditions or disease might also be subject to neglect and emotional abuse. In such instances, any impaired growth is likely to be due to a combination of factors. However, children with disabilities are particularly vulnerable because of 'diagnostic overshadowing'. This is where poor development is readily attributed to a child's disease or disability, while poor care is overlooked.

The developing brain

A brief summary of how the brain works is helpful here. Important in our discussion are cells in the brain called neurons. These have a tail-like area called the 'axon', a main circular body containing the nucleus, and branch-like structures around the edge called 'dendrites'. To function, the neurons in the brain need to connect or 'communicate' with each other. They do so by a tiny electrical charge which leaps a gap, called the synapse, between the axon, which sends the communication, and the dendrites of another neuron, which receives the communication. This leaping is facilitated by a chemical transmitter. As the electrical impulse is activated, the transmitter is triggered. It bridges the gap and sets off a further electrical charge and thence a chain reaction in a particular area of the brain. This is a complex process because there are very many neurotransmitters and, during the electrical-chemical chain reaction, any one neuron might be bombarded by 'communications' from many thousands of other neurons.

The brain of the growing individual starts to develop in the womb and continues to do so throughout the lifespan. However, there is a substantial acceleration of development in infancy and early childhood. When babies are born they have about 100 billion neurons and a basic brain architecture, which is established largely in the first two months post-fertilisation. However, as shown in Figure 3.1, the neurons only have tentative connections. They are weak and unformed, and therefore children need stimulation and consistent experiences to develop firm connections between neurons and synapses. The developing brain is 'activity-dependent', meaning that the electrical activity in every circuit – sensory, motor, emotional or cognitive – shapes the way that circuit is constructed.

An image of the development of the brain and increasing excitation of neural circuits can be imagined as a grassy mountain range on which several families decide to settle. There are no real paths therefore the new inhabitants start to find their way to their neighbours, picking out routes. Several of the routes will be used regularly and they become firm tracks which last for years. Other tracks may be used for a while but they will prove less popular and eventually these rarely used tracks will fade away.

The adolescent brain

There is evidence of substantial changes in brain architecture during adolescence and these can explain some of the apparent anomalies in the behaviour of young

Illustration of the neurones and densities of connections of the synapses in the brain.

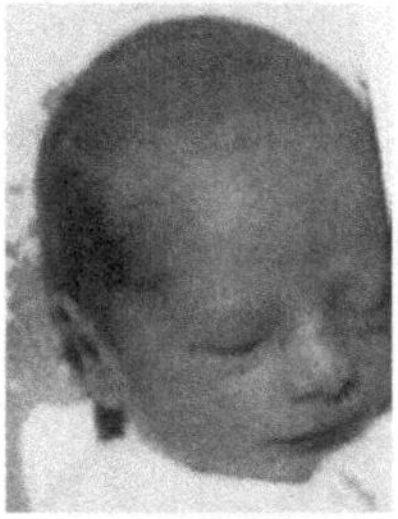

At birth the connections between the neurons are weak or still to be formed. Brain development is activity-dependent, therefore babies need new experiences to ensure the cells are activated.

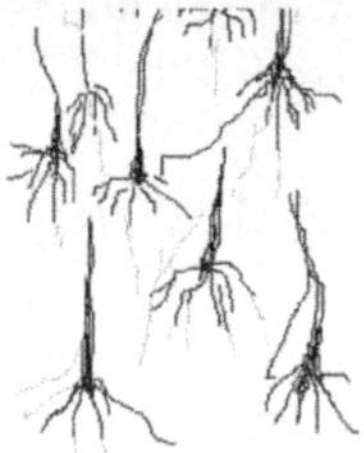

At about 3 years old there are many connections between synapses because children, given appropriate affection, stimulation and activity, are learning rapidly and the brain is busy absorbing new ideas and experiences.

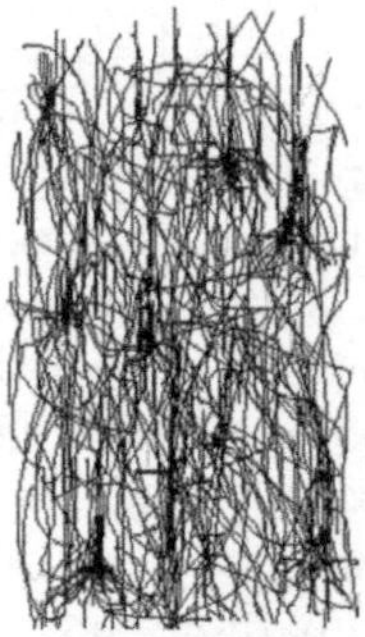

At 7 years old there are fewer neural circuits because of the process of pruning, whereby unused circuits are eliminated and children's neural processing is streamlined. Nevertheless, children are still learning rapidly and are bombarded with new experiences.

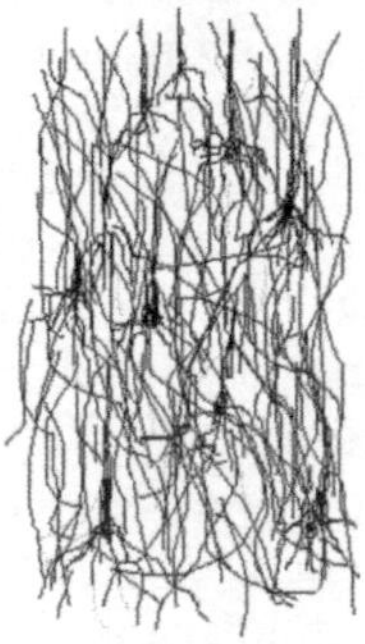

By 16 years the neural circuits have been further pruned, allowing the remaining circuits to work more quickly and efficiently.

Figure 3.1 The connections between the neurons in the developing brain

people in their teenage years (Morgan, 2007). Around the age of 10 there is an increase in 'neurogenesis' or the production of neurons, especially those located in the parts of the brain most associated with cognitive skills, such as reasoning, logical deduction and decision-making. This continues for two or more years.

Additionally, in early adolescence there is a reduction in the 'grey matter'. The cerebrum is the largest and most developed part of our brain and its outer layer, the cerebral cortex, is composed of several thousand neurons. The matter here, comprising neurons and other cells called glia, is darker in colour than the nerve tissue containing more nerve fibres and myelin, called 'white matter'. Myelin is a protein-based material that forms a sheath insulating the axons of certain neurons. Sturman and Moghaddam (2011, p. 1706) suggest the reduction in grey matter 'may be related to a massive pruning of synapses observed during this period'. There is an increase in white matter associated with myelination during which the axons are made stronger. Returning to the mountainside analogy, it is as though during childhood lots of different ways of reaching the neighbours are tried and eventually those that are dead-ends or convoluted to follow are disbanded. Then having decided which routes are best for travelling between neighbours, the paths are built up so that they are well-delineated and can be used more quickly and efficiently.

At the same time, there are changes in the body's biochemistry. In adolescence, for example, there are alterations in levels of dopamine. This is a neurotransmitter that is associated with excitement. McCutcheon and Marinelli (2009) found that in adolescent rats the dopamine levels were raised and then, having peaked, decreased. This suggests that levels might be high in early adolescence, which makes risk-taking enjoyable, but as levels decrease young people need to engage in greater levels of risk-taking to obtain the same level of excitement. With adulthood come more opportunities for legitimate ways of taking risks, such as jobs with an element of responsibility or danger like tree-surgery or fire-fighting.

The impact of neglect and emotional abuse on brain architecture and functioning

The brain is a dynamic neural system and has the ability to adapt and change in response to inputs such as novel experiences or injuries; the term employed to describe this is 'plasticity'. Therefore, any discussion of the impact of adverse experiences needs to be prefaced with a statement of caution because our understanding of the plasticity of the brain, especially earlier in life, is still evolving (Anderson et al., 2012; Kolb and Teskey, 2012; Stiles, 2012).

To illustrate the essential nature of early life experiences, Fox et al. (2010, p. 29) explain that a 'square house cannot be built on a round foundation'. A neglected child will have insufficient stimulation and therefore fewer connections between the neurons. This is likely to lead to learning disabilities which in the more extreme cases, particularly when the neglect starts early and is prolonged, will not show a marked improvement however good the child's care at an older age. De Bellis (2005, p. 160) explains that 'neglect interferes with the effective development of prefrontal cortical regions and, thus, executive functions. This process can … result in inattention, inability to focus, and poor academic achievement in neglected children.'

One outcome of neglect in early life is that the under-stimulation of the brain and lack of connections between the neurons can lead to passivity and an inability of the child to process and tolerate intense negative or positive experiences. Gray (2012), in her work on adoption, illustrates how adoptive parents sometimes despair of the incapacity of their originally neglected children to enjoy experiences like birthday parties. Some children react by trying to avoid the celebrations whereas others become uncontrolled, such as 'Celeste', described by Gray, who on being given birthday cakes began shouting, running around wildly and hitting out at her adoptive family. Early neglected children might also later show a disengagement, when they seem to experience life 'in the third person rather than the first person' (Gray, 2012, p. 81). Associated with this is a loss of the sense of self so that they have difficulty representing their own needs and might be more vulnerable to exploitation by others. Their lack of a sense of self can also lead to an inability to reflect on their behaviour, and take responsibility for it.

Children who are subjected to confusion, shouting, violence and insecurity, in contrast, will have lots of connections but these are likely to be equally confused and negative. Masten et al. (2008) found that children who had been maltreated recognised emotions, and especially fear, significantly faster than those who had not been abused. This might seem to be an advantage, but if children are concentrating their efforts on guarding against adults who are violent or abusive, they are not making connections in other areas, such as warm emotional expression or learning to concentrate.

Parental verbal abuse is an area of particular interest. A study by Choi et al. (2009) used diffusion tensor imaging (DTI) to analyse white matter, comparing 16 healthy young adults who had experienced parental verbal abuse (but no other maltreatment) with 16 controls who had not been abused. It was found that white matter, like the fornix cerebri, in the brain of the verbally abused group, when compared to the controls, showed differences in terms of aberrant crossing patterns and changes in the diameter of the axons and the degree of myelination. Subsequent research by Tomoda et al. (2011) showed that parental verbal abuse, again in the absence of other forms of maltreatment, appeared to lead to alterations in the region of the brain that plays a crucial role in processing of language and speech.

Physiological consequences of chronic stress

Before discussing the impact of stress, we need again to exercise a degree of caution because of our developing and changing understanding of the plasticity of stress response mechanisms (Korosi and Baram, 2010). Nevertheless, many children living in emotionally abusive environments are subject to long periods of stress. This may be caused by aspects of abuse, such as verbal threats, witnessing domestic violence or the insecurity of being left with strange caregivers for long periods.

Stress can adversely influence the brain architecture (McCrory et al., 2011). As De Bellis (2005) explains, this is because in the developing brain, elevated levels of chemicals associated with stress reactions may 'lead to adverse brain development through the mechanisms of accelerated loss (or metabolism) of neurons' (p. 158). Stress can result in the production of more prefrontal, cortical dopamine than is needed, thereby impairing prefrontal cortical function 'causing inattention, hyper-vigilance, problems in learning new material, psychotic symptoms, and paranoia in developing children' (De Bellis, 2005, p. 155).

When a child is subject to stress, adrenaline is released by the adrenal glands to prepare the body for a flight or fight response. The result of this is increased heart rate, blood pressure, and faster breathing to acquire more oxygen for the body. At the same time the kidneys secrete glucose to give the body energy for combat or to run away. Blood containing glucose and oxygen is redirected to the brain and major muscle groups.

Additionally, there are three hormone systems, the adrenocorticotropic, vaso-pressin and thyroxine, which are responsible for the physiological response to stress. When children experience stress, the anterior pituitary releases ACTH (adrenocortocotropic hormone). This results in the secretion of corticosteroids, including cortisol and aldosterone. The role of cortisol is to increase blood sugar, decrease bone formation and aid fat, protein and carbohydrate metabolism to help the person fight or flee during a short period of stress. However, children who have been neglected and maltreated show raised levels of cortisol even in adulthood (Watts-English et al., 2006). Prolonged, high cortisol levels can damage the body because cortisol helps convert proteins to energy. Therefore, if it continues to do so over long periods, it will impair the proteins in the muscles. It can also lead to weight gain, disruption of insulin production resulting in diabetes, and eventually it can weaken the immune system.

Another area of concern, particularly associated with domestic abuse where a pregnant mother may be threatened and emotionally abused, is the effect on her growing baby. During pregnancy a women's experience of fear and stress can impact on the developing foetus with long-term consequences. For example, increases in the corticotropin-releasing hormone stimulate the discharge of ACTH, which is transported to the foetus through the placenta. Stress might depress the developing foetal immune system. Furthermore, the placental arteries might be constricted, thereby reducing the flow of blood, with its supply of essential nutri-ents and oxygen, to the foetus (Weinstock, 2008). Maternal stress is associated with babies who are born earlier and small for their dates, factors related to a greater risk of impaired cognitive and social development (Talge et al., 2007). Furthermore, many mothers subject to domestic violence may be struggling to look after themselves and have inadequate nutrition. Consequently, there is a strong possibility that their babies will have cognitive, social and behavioural develop-mental difficulties (Monk et al., 2013).

The impact of parental substance misuse

'Teratogen' is the term for any materials or processes that interfere with the normal development of the foetus, causing congenital abnormalities. Two familiar teratogens external to the mother are X-ray irradiation and German measles. In terms of harmful substances which are ingested, thalidomide is one of the best known examples.

There is no abuse or negligence on the part of mothers in the overwhelming number of cases of children born with congenital abnormalities, and any concept of 'blame' is therefore unhelpful. Mothers might also face unenviable choices between risks to their child of untreated conditions such as epilepsy or depression and the risks posed by the medication which could alleviate these (Oberlander et al., 2008). There can also be abnormalities caused by paternal factors and damage to the sperm.

Only women who have been pregnant can begin to understand the nature of the experience. Therefore, arguably, it is inappropriate to condemn women who continue to ingest harmful substances despite knowing that they will adversely affect their unborn child. Nevertheless, women have a right to the findings of research and health education about the effects on the foetus of avoidable teratogens so that they can make informed decisions.

A negative attitude towards an unborn child can, although by no means always, indicate negativity towards the child once born. Furthermore, women who are unable to refrain from taking excess alcohol or harmful substances during pregnancy may well be struggling to cope with stresses in their life. As will be seen below, many substances adversely affect their baby, making caring for the children more challenging. Consequently, stresses on the parents will increase and have the effect of impairing their ability to nurture their children. Therefore, substance dependency and use can lead to a downward spiral resulting in neglect, emotional abuse and harm to the children. Some of the most common substances are outlined below.

Benzodiazepines: these are anxiolytics and hypnotics used as tranquilizers or to induce sleep; familiar ones are diazepam and temazepam. Benzodiazepines are addictive and therefore, if prescribed, the medical staff doing so have a responsibility to minimise any pharmacologic dependency (Denis et al., 2006; O'Brien, 2005). They have some side-effects which can impair parenting, such as inducing cognitive deficits in the carers which can persist after withdrawal. They can compound the difficulties for people who are misusing other drugs and substances (Verbanck, 2009). The main area of concern, however, is benzodiazepine ingestion in pregnancy and its effect on foetal development. There is limited evidence of major impairment (Enato et al., 2011). However, Uzun et al. (2010, p. 92) conclude that there is a 'higher risk of oral cleft, the floppy infant syndrome, or marked neonatal withdrawal symptoms'.

Cocaine: cocaine can damage the unborn child because it disrupts the flow of blood through the placenta. It crosses the placental barrier easily and is recycled in the amniotic fluid. Consequently, there are increased risks not only of spontaneous abortions, but also of congenital abnormalities. There is probably an adverse effect on foetal brain growth due to a decrease in the diameter of the blood vessels within the skull (intracranial vasoconstriction). There are likely to be a catalogue of problems to other organs and an adverse impact on birth weight. However, many people who use cocaine also misuse a number of other substances and therefore it is difficult to identify precisely which adverse pregnancy outcomes are due specifically to cocaine (Cain et al., 2013).

Opiates: these are not directly associated with congenital defects. However, fluctuating opiate levels can lead to the death of the foetus *in utero* (Logan et al., 2013). Opiate use is also associated with later impaired retention of learning and memory deficits (Sithisarn et al., 2013). Mothers addicted to opiates may not be eating well and therefore their babies may suffer from foetal malnutrition and low birth weight. Also, if opiates are injected without care to ensure needles are sterile, there is the risk of blood-borne viruses such as hepatitis C and HIV. One notable feature of opiate use is the 'neonatal abstinence syndrome' (NAS), the withdrawal symptoms experienced by babies after birth when they are no longer receiving the opiates through the placenta. There is dysregulation in the functioning of the baby's central, autonomic and gastrointestinal systems. This can result in various signs, such as a high-pitched cry, sleeping and feeding problems, tremors, convulsions, sweating, vomiting and diarrhoea (Logan et al., 2013; Napolitano et al., 2013).

Tobacco and nicotine: there are a number of constituents of tobacco that can adversely affect the developing foetus, including carbon monoxide, cotinine and nicotine. There is increasing evidence that these can lead to many adverse effects on the developing baby. Nicotine can cross the placenta, accumulating in the amniotic fluid and it is genotoxic so can cause genetic mutations. It can adversely affect lung development in the foetus, resulting in impaired lung function and susceptibility to respiratory diseases (Maritz and Mutemwa, 2012). There is now considerable evidence that smoking can result in intrauterine foetal growth retardation, leading to small-for-dates babies (Hamad et al., 2012). Conversely, maternal smoking can also cause future obesity and metabolic syndrome in some babies (Ino, 2010).

Alcohol and foetal alcohol syndrome: there is increasing evidence that heavy consumption of alcohol in pregnancy can damage the developing foetus. For example, there is an increase in demand for folic acid during pregnancy because it is important for DNA synthesis and cell propagation. Heavy and chronic exposure to alcohol adversely affects the transport of folic acid to the foetus (Hutson et al., 2012). Binge drinking is also implicated in various foetal developmental problems or alcohol-related birth defects (ARBD). These can include cardiac abnormalities, renal agenesis and hypoplasia, i.e. an absence or underdevelopment of the kidneys and neural tube defects. Additionally, there may be other irregularities, such as the exposure of the spinal column or protrusion of brain tissue through a skull defect (Jones et al., 2013). These conditions can, however, arise through congenital abnormalities not associated with the mother's lifestyle.

Foetal alcohol syndrome (FAS) was first identified by Jones and Smith (1973). Generally, the term 'foetal alcohol spectrum disorders (FASD)' is used to describe the range of adverse outcomes due to pre-natal exposure to alcohol. There is a pattern of features which seem to cluster together, including distinctive facial and head anomalies and slower, less efficient mental processing (Burden et al., 2009).

Burd et al. (2010) note that in instances where children are diagnosed with FASD there is a high correlation between alcohol misuse and cigarette smoking. This might be because mothers who drink a lot of alcohol also smoke heavily. Alternatively, it might be that cigarette smoking effects the foetus adversely and the combination results in a more marked FASD condition. Although the main focus of the discourse on FASD is on alcohol crossing the placenta during pregnancy, there is evidence that a father's alcohol consumption may affect the sperm and therefore transmit effects to the foetus.

There are continuing effects, especially in terms of neglect and emotional abuse on children and family life after the children are born. Melhuish (2011, p. 211), for example, warns about 'the relationship between parents and their substance of choice and how this relationship takes precedence over their relationships with their children'. There is a further exploration of some of the emotional burdens carried by children whose parents abuse substances in later chapters, especially Chapter 7.

Nutritional issues

Foetal and neonatal malnutrition

The importance of the maternal diet and the effects of poor maternal nutrition are becoming increasingly understood. Specific dietary advice is given to those wanting to become pregnant and during pregnancy. For example, the Department of Health (2011) recommend taking folic acid supplements before conception and during the first 12 weeks of pregnancy in order to prevent neural tube defects such as spina bifida. Also, advice is given to avoid food and supplements containing vitamin A due its derivative, retinoic acid, being a teratogen, meaning it can interfere with the developing foetus and cause birth defects.

Research into calorie and protein deficient maternal nutrition during pregnancy, resulting in low birth weight, stems from an investigation of a famine known as the Dutch Hunger Winter Cohort Study (Stein et al., 1975). It is based on a period during the Second World War during which the German government withdrew food provisions to areas in the west of Holland. As a result, the population within these areas suffered serious malnutrition. Birth records from this period indicate a preponderance of low birth weights. The subjects from this cohort have been monitored in order to gather information on the effect of low calorie maternal nutrition. The results have shown increased levels of a plethora of diseases, including cardiovascular disease, type II diabetes, high blood pressure, pre-eclampsia, kidney disease, schizophrenia and breast cancer in those born in this period. Barker (1997) studied UK birth records and his findings correlated with those of the Dutch Hunger Winter Cohort Study. The research is also supported in studies involving rats (Delghingaro-Augusto et al., 2004; Kwong et al., 2000).

This has led to the Barker or 'foetal origins' hypothesis, in which it is proposed that the foetus up- or down-regulates certain genes in order to protect against an altered internal environment, i.e. poor nutrition. If these altered environments are prolonged, the modifications persist throughout life, leading to the increased risk of the diseases itemised above. A WHO report (Mendis et al., 2011) further confirms this hypothesis, explaining that when mothers are malnourished the foetus prioritises 'brain growth at the expense of other tissues such as the abdominal organs' (p. 46).

Further to this, it has been shown that rapid overfeeding of low birth-weight babies can further increase the effect of these genetic modifications, because the baby is programmed to deal with restricted nutrition and therefore overfeeding can accentuate the risk of these diseases (Singhal et al., 2004).

Abuse-induced anorexia nervosa

There may not be an abuse background in all cases of anorexia nervosa. It is a complicated condition and there is evidence that there is often an interplay between a person's personality, their immediate environment and wider cultural influences, such as the emphasis on dieting and the societal promotion of attractiveness linked to thinness. There are caring parents who suffer bewilderment and agony because of their much loved child's refusal to eat adequately. One professional dilemma is to distinguish between those families in which there is unconditional love and support and those in which there are emotionally abusive pressures and psychological games which lead the child or young person to exert control in the only way they can, by regulating their food intake and taking command of their body shape.

Illustration: Reuben

The physical stature of Reuben's family was quite small, but by the time he was 13 years old he weighed barely 26 kilograms. He had some learning disabilities and was therefore in a special school. He was the product of an incestuous relationship and lived with his mother and his father, who was also his grandfather. Their other babies had all died early; consequently, they were over-protective of Reuben. As he grew older, he was so stifled by this over-protection that he determined to control his own body. He was found to be hiding or throwing food away. When the school nurse tried to give him nutrition and calorie-rich drinks, he was able to detect this and refused to take them. For years, paediatricians assumed that his low weight was genetic, but eventually the school nurse demonstrated that Reuben's weight increased when he went into respite care and decreased when he returned home. Reuben was placed with skilled, long-term foster carers, more regular feeding patterns were established, he no longer refused food and his weight increased.

Overeating and emotional obesity

Maternal obesity and maternal over-nutrition has been shown to have many adverse effects. As well as being a risk factor for maternal problems such as pre-eclampsia, gestational diabetes and hypertension, maternal obesity and over-nutrition is linked to adverse offspring health outcomes, such as obesity, type II diabetes and birth defects (Blomberg and Källén, 2009; Howie et al., 2009; Ovesen et al., 2011; Stothard et al., 2009). Research has shown that rats that are fed a high fat diet gave birth to offspring with hypertension (Khan et al., 2003). The mechanisms for over-nutrition have not been fully established, but developing theories suggest there is a genetic modification in the satiety system. The offspring therefore have an increased appetite, leading to the problems witnessed (Freeman, 2010; Grattan, 2008). Environmental confounding factors such as post-natal overfeeding and inherited eating habits may also play a part in these findings.

Alexander et al. (2009) question how far obesity is a child protection issue and comment: 'although many factors contribute to the development of childhood obesity at a societal level, parental responsibility is also an essential element in the prevention and treatment of obesity in children' (p. 137). Knutson et al. (2010), in America, examined 571 children aged between 3 and 9 years. Of these, 16.3 per cent were obese and a further 14.9 per cent were at risk of obesity. The findings demonstrated that neglect was significantly associated with measures of obesity in younger children, aged 5 years and younger, although less so with the older age group.

Non-organic failure-to-thrive

Failure-to-thrive (FTT) is a term used to indicate a child's faltering growth and development. Some children are naturally small and most FTT is due to an underlying disease or medical condition, i.e. it is 'organic'. The division between organic and non-organic FTT is open to debate because there may be factors, such as a baby's weak suck, a low appetite with no obvious cause or weaning difficulties, which are linked to factors on the borderline between the physiological and the psychological. Some children simply appear not to like the texture of solid food but have reached an age and developmental level when they need more than milk. Also, even if the faltering weight appears to be non-organic, there may not be abuse. In some of the poorest families, food can become inadequate because of lack of money. More frequently, a child may start to reject food. Then the parents' response, despite their good intentions, may make matters worse. Understandable parental anxiety, in particular, can lead to an increase in problems. In most cases, the advice and guidance of a health visitor, nutrition specialist or psychologist will resolve the difficulties.

In order to diagnose non-organic failure-to-thrive a number of factors have to be ruled out:

(a) Feeding difficulties: this is often seen in children born with a gap in the lip, palate or both, called a 'cleft'. Many of these babies have difficulty sucking and require special teats and bottles to assist in swallowing milk. Although corrective surgery is effective, this is not available until the infant is aged about 2–3 months, with further surgery usually performed between 4 and 12 months.

(b) Vomiting or regurgitation.

(c) Diarrhoea: possibly indicating coeliac disease or cystic fibrosis.
(d) Inflammation/infection: severe infections compromise growth and might be indicative of HIV or immunodeficiency.
(e) Genes and genetic syndromes, including inherited metabolic disorders.

Blood tests can rule out a number of diseases and conditions which can impact on growth, including renal, metabolic, liver, thyroid and coeliac diseases, inflammation, iron or protein deficiency and Turner's syndrome. Urine analysis can exclude urinary tract infections and acynotic heart disease.

When examining failure-to-thrive, practitioners are likely to need information about: the family background; family hereditary conditions; circumstances surrounding maternal health and the birth of the baby; and the baby's early progress and medical history. They will also observe the baby to see how far there is: (i) chronic malnutrition, indicated by stunting and low weight and height for age and often a proportionally small head; or (ii) acute malnutrition, indicated by wasting, a low weight for both the child's height and age, with a lack of tissue on skeleton and often a sad expression.

One of the key features of non-organic failure-to-thrive is not only that medical conditions indicating malabsorption of food are ruled out, but also that the child puts on weight given normal care by hospital staff or substitute carers and then loses weight when returned to the parents.

Growth charts are used to plot the development of children. Weight, length (for babies), height and head circumference can be plotted. The charts have a series of curved lines, or centiles, which indicate the typical growth rate of the child population. The third centile for weight means that out of every 100 children, the weight of three will fall below the line and 97 will be above it. Normally, a few days after birth children can be plotted on one set of lines or centiles and, if all is well, their

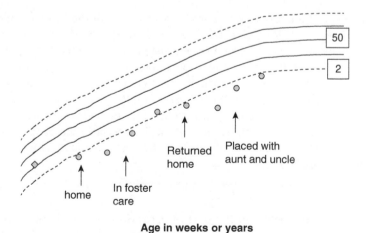

Figure 3.2 Child's growth chart demonstrating weight plots crossing centiles suggestive of non-organic failure-to-thrive

height, weight and head circumference will follow along the centile, whereas crossing lines might indicate a problem. There are different charts depending on the age and gender of the child, and specialist ones for children with genetic conditions such as Down's syndrome. Confounding factors have to be excluded. For example, when weighing babies, the same scales should be used each time because some scales are less accurate than others. For additional examples of weight faltering, see Wright (2005, pp. 182–3) and Iwaniec (2006, p. 133).

Physical safety

Throughout childhood, most parents worry about their children's safety and as babies start to become more mobile, especially when they start to toddle, the dangers posed by the average home seem legion. Medicines and chemicals have to be transferred to high, preferably lockable, cupboards; electric sockets need to be covered; stair gates installed; knives, scissors and sharp tools hidden. The list goes on, and despite the precautions inevitably accidents happen. Children with the most assiduous carers can suffer from preventable mishaps. This can be due to a momentary lapse of attention, lack of knowledge on the part of the carer or a child who is unusually adept at circumventing safety precautions. Identifying when accidents are understandable misfortunes and when a symptom of neglect and abuse can be difficult. One factor to consider is how far parents have ignored basic safety advice. The case of Dora serves as an example.

Illustration: Dora

It was winter time and Dora, aged 2 years, toddled around the living room drinking juice from a baby bottle. When she did not want to carry her bottle, the parents habitually put it on the mantelpiece over an open coal fire with no guard. The parents had repeatedly been asked by the health visitor to cover the fire with a guard, which she had provided. She also warned the parents not to put the bottle on the mantelpiece because Dora would stretch across the fire to reach it. The parents took no notice of this advice and, inevitably, one evening Dora fell into the fire and was badly burned. This was deemed to be a case of abuse through neglect because the dangers had been repeatedly pointed out to the parents and they had been provided with safety equipment which they had not used.

There is sometimes the belief on the part of practitioners that there is no concern if any injuries can be attributed to accidents. This appeared to be the view of the social workers in the Lucie Gates case described in Chapter 2. Yet if a flow chart of all the injuries and admissions to hospital from causes such as avoidable accidents and overdoses of the mother's medication had been collated, the continual, avoidable suffering of the children would have become apparent. One or two injuries are inevitable, and, arguably, minor injuries in the course of rumbustious play are probably to be welcomed as evidence of the absence of over-protection. However, continued, substantial accidental injuries caused by poor supervision are a cause for concern. Parents who are unwilling to take safety advice, putting their own pride or comfort before that of their child, are simply not 'good enough'. They fail to meet their children's physiological and safety needs, which is the first requirement of any carer when they have the wherewithal to do so. They will also ultimately fail to meet their child's esteem needs because a child's sense of self-worth will be low when they realise that parental considerations take priority over their own safety.

Munchausen syndrome by proxy/Fabricated or induced illness

Muchausen syndrome by proxy is also known by a number of other terms, such as 'fabricated or induced illness by carers' (Department for Children, Schools and Families, 2008, 2010; Lazenbatte, 2013), 'paediatric condition falsification' (Kucuker et al., 2010), 'factitious disorder by proxy' (Frye and Feldman, 2012), or 'malingering by proxy' (Stutts et al., 2003). These terms all refer to parents and carers who need to attract the attention of medical providers and use their children to acquire this attention through declaring their children to be ill and, in some cases, using drugs or other substances to create symptoms of disease.

The impact on the children is that they suffer some physical discomfort and danger, but there is inevitably the confusion and disruption of repeated attempts at diagnosis and some treatment regimes. There is also the stress caused by the regime imposed by the parent to make a healthy child appear ill. The issue of inappropriate treatment is further explored in Chapter 7.

Hygiene

Conditions like head lice or nits, threadworm and even scabies can readily be caught by children whatever their living conditions and personal hygiene. Parents are assured that head lice prefer clean hair. However, the difference between neglected and well-cared for children is that caring parents will make appropriate and usually successful efforts to get rid of the condition. Neglected children tend to have the conditions for longer periods, with the parents making few attempts to eradicate them. The consequences of untreated disorders can lead to complications. For example, children with untreated head lice may scratch their heads frequently, resulting in abrasions in the skin of the scalp and increased risk of scalp infections. In rare cases, the child may develop typhus, a dangerous condition which is transmitted through the bite of the louse.

Similarly, illnesses such as gastroenteritis and pulmonary infections can be suffered by any child. However, recurrent bouts can indicate that children are living with inadequate food hygiene or are contracting repeated infections because of stress-induced suppression of the immune system due to a lack of care.

There is also the general picture of the neglected child who smells and looks dirty. For such children, there might well be dangers of infection but, with reference to the child's cosmos, there are also important social aspects. Paul's eldest sister (see Chapter 2) clearly suffered rejection and personal degradation in school because of her poor hygiene. Even professionals might find getting close to and relating to such children difficult. Ferguson (2005, p. 782) commented on 'the impact of contamination fears where workers distance themselves from marginalised and diseased children, like Victoria [Climbié], who had scabies'.

Concluding this chapter and looking towards the next

This chapter has summarised some of the impacts that physical neglect, in particular, has on children's development. This can start before birth, and parents who may be eating inadequately, drinking too much alcohol and misusing substances because they are already suffering stress, may give birth to children who require greater medical and physical care than most, which can only add to their stresses. The prospects for their children are bleak without some assistance. The next chapter looks at the impact of neglect and emotional abuse on children's social, emotional and cognitive development.

Further resources

Meggitt, C. (2006) *Child Development: An Illustrated Guide* (2nd edition). Oxford: Heinemann Educational.

Sheridan, M., Sharma, A. and Cockerill, H. (2008) *From Birth to Five Years: Children's Developmental Progress* (3rd edition). New York: Routledge.

Information about developmental neuroscience can be obtained from: www.annafreud.org/index.php.

Information on the impact of early malnutrition can be obtained from: www.dutchfamine.nl/index_files/study.htm.

Details of child growth charts and how they should be used can be accessed at: www.rcpch.ac.uk/growthcharts.

4

Child development: psychosocial factors

This chapter summarises what is known or hypothesised about psychosocial human development in our earlier years. It explores, within each major framework, the potential impact of neglect and emotional abuse. The various theories can be only briefly described, therefore at the end of each section there will be guidance to additional detailed information about the theories.

Chapter overview

- Psychodynamic theories
- Socio-emotional development
- Behavioural concepts
- Cognitive approaches

The purpose of this chapter is not to describe children's basic psychosocial development, but instead it examines the implications of neglect and emotional abuse in relation to key psychosocial developmental theories.

Psychodynamic theories

Sigmund Freud's concepts gave momentum to the idea that childhood was more than just a rather troublesome stage that had to be 'got through' until the child was strong enough to contribute to the family and society.

Until the later nineteenth century, European infant mortality was high. For example, in mid-eighteenth-century London, in both wealthy and poorer families, two-thirds of children died before the age of 5 years. Therefore, parents' main concerns would be for a child to survive physically into adulthood. However, child mortality then declined, so that by the 1850s the rate had reduced to less than a third of children dying before their fifth birthday (Razzel and Spence, 2007).

Subsequently, as concerns about physical survival diminished, there was more motivation to examine the psychological importance of childhood. This coincided with a quest throughout Europe to find out 'how things work', hence the rapid progression and expansion in recent times of theories which give insights into human socio-emotional and cognitive growth.

Freud's psychodynamic theory

Freud was born in Friberg, Moravia, in 1856. He worked primarily in Vienna but, in 1937, to escape the Nazi threat, he moved to England, dying in London in 1939. He was working on his theories well into his seventies, so it is difficult to capture his intricate, sometimes revised and complicated concepts in a few short paragraphs. However, it is important to give at least a basic outline because his ideas have been so influential, resulting in an explicit acknowledgment of the importance of emotional nurture and sensitivity towards children in the early years.

Underpinning all Freud's other concepts is the idea that human consciousness has three levels:

- the conscious mind of which we are aware;
- a powerful unconscious which can influence our thoughts and behaviour but is rarely under our control; and between these
- the preconscious or subconscious which requires some effort to access but is more readily reached than the unconscious mind.

The realisation that the unconscious is not just a passive repository for memories but an active component of the mind was one of Freud's key contributions and is encapsulated in the term 'psychodynamic' theory.

A second key element of Freud's ideas is that humans change qualitatively during childhood and youth. An individual's personality and ability to function during adulthood is sculpted during childhood. Even given optimal care and circumstances, all children will experience some conflict centred round a particular domain within each stage. These domains are:

- Oral: early infancy up to one year;
- Anal: what is now defined as the 'toddler' years, 1–3 years;
- Phallic : mid-childhood, 4–6 years;
- A latent period: 7–12 years;
- Genital: adolescence, 13–18 years.

Another important idea developed by Freud is that an individual's persona comprises three components: the id, ego and superego. A baby is born with drives, impulses and needs which are collectively termed the 'id'. As the central nature of the individual, the 'ego', emerges, these impulses are controlled by the 'superego', a type of conscience.

The impact of neglect and emotional abuse

If at any stage, the developing child experiences distress, especially emotional abuse and neglect by carers, there can be negative repercussions in adult life. For example, according to Freud's hypothesis, babies who are inadequately fed are likely to grow up with an unconscious hunger for oral satisfaction, possibly over-eating, having an addiction to alcohol or cigarettes, or an insatiable emotional hunger. Toddlers who are shamed during toilet training, or who live in an 'out of control' environment, are likely to repress, i.e. push into the subconscious, the feelings of shame or turbulence. This might lead them to develop obsessions about hygiene and cleanliness or start over-controlling others using force and aggression to assert their will.

In terms of the three aspects of the emerging persona, emotional abuse and neglect can lead to a malfunctioning 'superego', which can be either too rigid or too weak. Tensions between the superego and the id lead to emotions, experiences and memories being repressed, thrust deep into the unconscious, only to emerge as 'ego defences'. Some of these defences can usefully protect the individual against intolerable emotional challenges, but others can result in negative outcomes. An example of the latter is someone who is made to feel profoundly guilty about same-sex desires during the genital stage. The person might so forcefully repress their feelings that they turn their self-loathing into a fierce hatred of homosexuality.

There are many criticisms of Freud's concepts, notably that he developed confused and confusing theories of children's sexual development because he could not accept the disclosure of sexual abuse revealed by many of his patients, dismissing their accounts as 'fantasy'. Yet despite criticisms, Freud's ideas have influenced subsequent figures – post-Freudians, such as Adler and Jung, who developed or refined his ideas. Meanwhile, others, including Melanie Klein and Freud's own daughter, Anna, drew on psychodynamic theory to increase our understanding of young children.

Erikson's 'lifespan' perspective

Among the most influential post-Freudians is Erik Erikson (1995). His major contribution was to provide a model for human development throughout the lifespan. Borrowing from a soliloquy – 'the seven ages of man' by Shakespeare's character Jaques from *As You Like It* – he outlined his 'Eight Stages of Man'. 'Man', incidentally, is a significant term because some critics argue that Erikson's ideas related mostly to male development. He posited that at each stage children experience internal conflicts and if they are not supported to establish predominantly positive foundations, emotions and perspectives at each stage, then their personalities can be damaged. The eight stages are:

1. Trust versus vs mistrust
2. Autonomy vs shame and doubt
3. Initiative vs guilt
4. Industry vs inferiority
5. Identity vs role confusion
6. Intimacy vs isolation
7. Generativity vs stagnation
8. Ego integrity vs despair

Secure children who can trust and rely on their carers and environment will be able to explore the world, develop control and then use their initiative to learn about themselves, others and their environment. Satisfying this stage, they will work with industry to acquire competence and skills which will in turn lay the foundations for an assured view of their identity. They will then move into adulthood able to form close relationships, be productive, be ready to nurture the next generation and, ultimately, reach the latest stages of life with acceptance and contentment.

The impact of neglect and emotional abuse

Despite criticisms of Erikson, practitioners will recognise that children who are neglected or abused in their earliest years often have difficulty trusting both themselves and others. If neglect or emotional maltreatment continues, then feelings of shame, guilt and inferiority predominate. This is usually expressed as a low self-esteem or sometimes a compensatory, over-high self-esteem.

Another aspect of Erikson's theory which has resonance for practitioners is the issue of identity, with which many adolescents appear to struggle. During adolescence the young person's appearance (and, for boys, voice) change markedly. It is therefore hardly surprising if they keep pondering 'Who am I?' In the case of emotionally abused children, the issue of identity can be particularly complex and they may well be forced to adopt a predominantly negative identity, especially if they experience other stigma, such as prejudice against a disability or skin colour.

Illustration: Leila

The evening before Leila's birth in Tripoli, her father, Hani, who worked as a builder, fell and died. Leila was born with *spina bifida* (myelomeningocele). Given efficient hospital treatment at birth and with only her lower spine affected, Leila has been able to walk with difficulty. To add to her problems, Leila's grieving extended family rejected her.

Consequently, her mother, who had a brother living in London, came to England to join him and his family. Throughout her childhood, Leila's mother constantly asked her 'why didn't you die instead of Hani?' Her uncle was kind, but her aunt and cousins bullied her. Despite her disability, she attended mainstream school and there the bullying continued in the form of racism and mocking her physical condition. As a younger child this had made her unhappy, but she coped by living from day-to-day and enjoying what she could.

As an adolescent, however, she began to reflect on her identity. She concluded she was ugly, unfeminine and a burden to her family. Her future seemed bleak, believing as she did that she would not be able to find a job, live independently, form friendships, get married or have children. She also felt her mother wanted her dead. She started cutting her arms and attempted to hang herself. She survived and, with the help of her uncle, the medical team, a social worker and, ultimately, a dedicated sixth-form college, she emerged into adulthood with a more positive identity.

Further information

Erikson, E.H. (1995) *Children and Society*. London: Vintage.

Jacobs, M. (2003) *Sigmund Freud* (2nd edition). London: Sage.

Storr, A. (2001) *Freud: A Very Short Introduction*. Oxford: Oxford University Press.

Socio-emotional development

This section starts with attachment theory, especially the work of John Bowlby, who combined his understanding of psychodynamics with ideas gleaned from biology, especially the study of newly born animals. This is followed by a summary of the development of the expression and awareness of emotions.

Attachment theories

Bowlby (1951), working in the context of post-Second World War concerns about 'juvenile delinquency', noted that many distressed adolescents had been brought up in institutions or had poor early relationships. He therefore argued that it was important for mothers to care continually and sensitively for their babies. He largely ignored the role of other family members or carers. This suited the politics of the time because after the war, the jobs taken over in wartime by women were required for returning soldiers. Therefore, a theory that suggested that women needed to care for their children at home and on a full-time basis suited the political agenda.

The notion that children can only develop emotionally and socially with secure relationships with one mother-figure was challenged by Rutter (1972), while Bowlby (1988) himself acknowledged that attachment to fathers can also be an important factor in children's development. Meanwhile, since the 1980s, pioneering researchers such as Judy Dunn have also highlighted the importance of sibling relationships. As Dunn (1983, p. 787) remarked, 'regarding mother and child as a dyad isolated from the other relationships within the family is extremely misleading'. It seems that for optimal development children need consistent, secure, loving care but this can be with a group of reliable carers and family members, not just a 24-hour mother.

Bowlby (with Ainsworth, 1965) formulated the idea that children who are positively attached to their carers developed an equally positive 'internal working model' that the world was to be trusted and they are lovable. Current understanding of brain architecture demonstrates the evidence of connections within the brain which will, in effect, give children a working model of relationships. However, the human brain, and particularly the early developing brain, is dynamic and changing (Karmiloff-Smith, 2010), and therefore it is not possible to take a snapshot of a child at a particular age and predict their future development.

To give Bowlby's ideas 'scientific' credibility, Mary Ainsworth created the 'Strange Situation Procedure (SSP)', a laboratory experiment in which a child between about 10 and 24 months old is placed initially with his or her mother and then with a stranger. Then, twice, the mother leaves the room for a while. Many children become distressed when the mother leaves, but rush to her for comfort when she returns. These children are deemed to be 'securely attached'. Those who do not do so are said to be insecurely attached and show either 'avoidant attachment' or 'ambivalent attachment'. The hypothesis is that insecurely attached children have continuing problems with relationships throughout the lifespan. However, there are criticisms of the SSP, not least the unethical nature of a procedure which deliberately causes distress to young children. Rutter et al. (2009, p. 531) disputed whether SSP should be used 'to clinically assess parent–child relationships'. They outlined more ethical and arguably more effective assessments of attachment. Another major issue is the experiment's cultural insensitivity because in some non-Anglo/American cultures children show high rates of insecure attachment. Yet it is hard to evidence that these cultures produce equally high rates of adults who are unable to form satisfactory relationships.

The impact of neglect and emotional abuse

There is evidence that genetic factors will influence attachment and the impact carer behaviour has on individual children (Bakermans-Kranenburg and van IJzendoorn, 2007). Nevertheless, there is a consensus that young children need to feel secure with dependable, loving carers. A child left all day and night with unresponsive and uncaring parents is likely to have emotional developmental problems, as are children passed around like a parcel to inconsistent, relatively unsympathetic carers.

Cody

Just before his seventh birthday, Cody was taken into care because he had been left with one of his mother's friends while she had gone on holiday to Blackpool. There she had been arrested for a severe violent assault against a shop-keeper and drugs offences. Cody was known to the authorities and had had so many changes of home and carers that it was difficult to track them. Since birth he had been left with assorted friends, neighbours, and often his maternal grandmother.

His foster carers, who had cared for many children, were concerned because he was so unresponsive. He had a fixed smile but neither laughed nor cried. He seemed wary and afraid. He rarely spoke and did not appear to want to be touched. Care proceedings were deemed essential and a Guardian *ad litem* was appointed by the family court. She was an independent social worker whose remit was to represent his interests in the legal proceedings. She wanted to ascertain his feelings and wishes and so started by asking him to draw his family. Cody drew nothing for a while and then scribbled figures all over the paper. Asked to name them, he gave a random list of people, animals and toys. When asked to draw himself in the 'family' he turned the paper over and drew himself alone on the other side.

Growth of emotional recognition and expression

As explained in the previous chapter, infants are not born with a fully developed brain. During their first year, most babies respond to emotions in others. For example, they may well respond to distress shown by their parents by becoming distressed or frightened themselves. Neonates who are shown one expression of emotion for a while will show increased interest when a new emotion is introduced (Papalia and Milton, 2003).

During their second year, infants start to use the emotions shown by trusted others, especially parents, as cues to their own behaviour. So they may be confident handling a new object if their parent looks happy and encouraging. At this age they will also begin to try to comfort others in distress. Initially, they may offer something that comforts them, such as giving an upset parent their own dummy. In these earlier years, while children feel a range of emotions, they are only able to identify basic ones such as happy, sad and angry (Kopp, 2011).

As children reach the ages of 3–5 years, they begin to develop the ability to add more emotional words to their vocabulary, such as 'surprise' and 'scared'. Earlier, they may have categorised all strong negative displays as 'angry', but now they make distinctions, perhaps separating 'disgusted' from 'angry' (Papalia and Milton, 2003).

From about the age of 6 years onwards, children extend their recognition and ability to describe an ever wider range of emotions. Additionally, they begin to show proficiency in hiding emotions. Therefore, to be polite, a child may say they love a present that really disappoints them. Also, most children are able to put themselves in the positions of others (Harris, 1989). This is illustrated in the Sally-Ann test where a child is shown doll (A) who has a marble. Doll A puts the marble in a basket and leaves. Another doll (B) takes the marble out of the basket and puts it in a box. When Doll A returns, the child is asked where Doll A will look for the marble. Most children over about 4 years old will correctly say that Doll A will look in the basket. Although knowing the marble is in the box, they understand that Doll A's perspective is different.

One important point made by Widen and Russell (2008) is that children need to develop cognitively in broad terms in order to begin to 'learn' about and understand their own and others' emotions. Therefore, anything that limits cognitive growth is likely to restrict these emotional capabilities. For example, people with learning disabilities such as Down's syndrome, although usually sociable, show some emotional limitations (Jahromi et al., 2008). Additionally, children with an autistic spectrum disorder may face greater challenges than most. As the word 'spectrum' suggests, the condition cannot be described in absolute terms – each person is an individual and skills such as speech and language can vary from child to child. However, Kanner (1943) first described the features of 'autistic disturbance' in 11 children. He believed they were born with the condition rather than it being caused by parental difficulties. He identified four main features: (1) difficulties forming relationships; (2) an absence of spontaneous richly imaginative play; (3) an obsessive insistence on routines; and (4) substantial communication difficulties. It seems that connections in the brain concerned with relationships with other people do not follow the usual progression, leaving the person struggling to make sense of the world of communication and emotions, which they experience as a confusing and possibly frightening one. Children on the autistic spectrum appear to have difficulty with understanding the perspectives of others and do not do well in the Sally-Ann test (Baron-Cohen et al., 1985).

The implications of neglect and emotional abuse

One effect of abuse is that children may well supress negative emotions. If a parent is rejecting, contemptuous, mocking or aggressive when children show fear or distress, they may supress and bury their emotions in order not to attract the rejection, belittlement or anger. Roth and Assor (2010, p. 474) showed that key emotional skills – 'sadness recognition, awareness of sadness, and empathy' – failed to develop when children were made to repress sadness and other negative emotions. The possibility that relationship problems or even serious pathologies will develop in the place of empathy is an outcome for some children who have early experiences of emotional abuse and neglect.

In terms of children with autistic spectrum disorders, we have fortunately moved on from the hypothesis that such conditions are caused by 'refrigerator mothers', ones who are cold and detached (see Langan, 2011). Many mothers and fathers of children with an autistic spectrum disorders are dedicated and loving (Rocque, 2010). Nevertheless, inevitably, as with any group of parents, there will be some who are abusive. The distress caused by uncaring neglect or emotional assaults to children who already have difficulty understanding and interpreting the motivations of other people, is substantial.

Further information

Bowlby, J. with Ainsworth, M. (1965) *Child Care and the Growth of Love* (2nd edition). Harmondsworth: Pelican.

Harris, P.L. (1989) *Children and Emotion*. Malden, MA: Routledge.

Rutter, M., Kreppner, J. and Sonuga-Barke, E. (2009) Emanuel Miller Lecture: Attachment insecurity, disinhibited attachment, and attachment disorders. *Journal of Child Psychology and Psychiatry* 50(5): 529–543.

Behavioural concepts

It has been said that while psychodynamic theory was based on studies of neurotic people, behaviourism was based on observations of neurotic rats. Nevertheless, despite many limitations of behavioural theories, the proliferation of star charts on families' kitchen walls and the smiles and congratulations lavished on a 4-year-old whenever he manages to eat some green vegetables owes their existence largely to behavioural theorists.

Behaviourism

Behaviourism traces its roots to the work of Pavlov, who (to explain simply) found that dogs salivated at the sight of food. A bell was rung whenever food was presented to the dogs and eventually the dogs would salivate to the sound of the bell even if the food was absent. Behaviour can be changed by repeated exposure to a stimulus. Some behaviours can also be extinguished by the absence of reinforcing stimuli.

The impact of neglect and emotional abuse

Among the problems for neglected and emotionally abused children are inconsistent messages. Rather than having consistent patterns of approval or disapproval through which they learn appropriate conduct, the same behaviour might be rewarded, punished or ignored depending not on the correctness or otherwise of their behaviour but on the mood or whim of the adults around them.

Illustration: Karen, Kyle, Kirin and Kate

Their school had long been concerned about the four siblings, aged 7, 6, 5 and 4 years, who were thin, rarely washed, with lustreless hair, and frequent small dispersed bruises. Their behaviour in school was erratic. They were uncontrolled and disruptive for most of the time, but would become very quiet and rigid if teachers showed any irritation. They were also known locally to steal, especially from other children and shops. One day the children's bruises were more severe than usual and they had clear belt marks. An investigation was undertaken and although there was concern about the physical abuse, professionals were equally concerned about the parents' attitude to discipline. The parents took no notice of stealing, bullying and bad behaviour if they were in a contented mood. However, they would lash out indiscriminately at all four children when they were in a bad temper. The children were not learning to distinguish good from bad behaviour, but rather to respond to adults' good or bad moods.

While behaviourism has some messages for child development, humans are far more complex than other animals because we have a brain which allows us to contemplate, reflect and solve problems. Additionally, we have an anatomy that allows elaborate communication through language. Chomsky (1959), for example, found that language development is innate and not just a pure, behavioural stimulus–response mechanism. For example, at about 4 or 5 years old children start to use rules of grammar that come from within them: they recognise the construction of adding '-ed' to a verb for the past tense such as 'she skipped away'. This means they will say, for example, 'she goed upstairs' rather than 'she went upstairs'.

Social learning or social cognitive theory

Another challenge to the pure behaviourist model of development was presented by behaviourists who nevertheless realised that, unlike rats, humans have an ability to make sense of a complex world and act not just on the basis of physical stimuli–response conditioning, but also on what they observe and how they interpret their experiences.

One of the leading proponents of this was Bandura (1977), who showed in experiments that children who observed adults behaving aggressively towards large 'Bobo' dolls subsequently behaved more aggressively towards toys compared to children who had not observed the aggression. As Bandura (1999, p. 23) explained, the 'human mind is generative, creative, proactive and self-reflective not just reactive'. He also argued that social learning theory can explain human behaviour across a range of cultures and in collectivist as well as in individualistic societies. Bandura (2012) later explained that rather than his initial term 'social learning theory', he preferred 'social cognitive theory' because his ideas described how people motivate and regulate their behaviour rather than just how they acquire knowledge and competencies.

The impact of neglect and emotional abuse

One important form of emotional abuse is the exposure of children to aggression and cruelty between adults, particularly between parents, namely intimate partner or domestic violence. Another particularly vulnerable emotionally abused group are children who are in families where they are not directly attacked, but daily witness the abuse of siblings; where the focus has tended to be on 'Cinderella', with little sympathy being shown towards the 'ugly sisters'. Yet, what is learnt by witnessing violence and abuse against others in the same household is likely to be extremely negative.

The introduction of a cognitive element to behavioural theory has given rise to cognitive behavioural therapy, an effective intervention for many conditions involving maladaptive thinking. For example, it is deemed a 'useful treatment for anxiety disorders in children and adolescents' (James et al., 2013, p. 27).

Further information

Bandura, A. (1977) *Social Learning Theory*. Englewood Cliffs, NJ: Prentice-Hall.

O'Donohue, W.T. and Ferguson, K.E. (2001) *The Psychology of B.F. Skinner*. Thousand Oaks, CA: Sage.

Cognitive approaches

The importance of the work of social cognitive theorists is the acknowledgement that as human individuals grow, they are not mere input-output robots, and nor can they be simply programmed like computers. The mind is complex and children have an internal life, processing information and making sense of their world. Piaget contributed further to these ideas with a particular emphasis on thought-processes and children's capacity to learn.

Piaget

It is difficult to summarise Piaget's work, partly because he lived a long, active life and refined his ideas over time. However, a key feature of his theory is that children's minds are not simply miniature adult ones; they change qualitatively during childhood and consequently children have to be ready, in a biological as well as emotional way, to develop new skills.

He identified four key developmental stages:

- Sensory-motor: from birth to about 2 years
- Pre-operational: 3 to 7 years
- Concrete operations: 7 to 11 years
- Formal operations: 12 years to adulthood.

Children need new stimuli, and at different ages and stages they will make different sense of the various experiences. For a baby, the family's pet hamster will simply no longer exist from moment to moment as the hamster comes in and out of the baby's sight or touch. Therefore the hamster's death will have little meaning. For a child of about 8 years, their pet's death may be distressing but also puzzling. The child might grasp the concrete differences between life and death which they can sense, such as death being not moving and not breathing. In adolescence, the young person may have a more sophisticated understanding and does not need to see the dead hamster to appreciate that it has died, it can no longer function, it will naturally decay and its death is permanent.

According to Piaget's work, children have 'schemas', i.e. sets of ideas linked to actions. They then experience something that challenges their schemas. They may repeat actions to test if the challenge is a real one, rather like a scientist testing a hypothesis. Therefore, infants repeatedly throwing toys out of their pram are not deliberately teasing their long-suffering carer, who has to keep picking them up, but rather they are testing and re-testing what happens when objects disappear. Older children may be able to discuss with others or think through these challenges to their current schema. These encounters make children uncomfortable and they seek to regain comfort or 'equilibrium'. They therefore make the effort to 'accommodate' the new experiences by creating a new schema.

A key idea of Piaget is the idea of being ready. Readiness is a combination of brain development and exposure to experiences. Piaget believed that for most children exposed to particular ranges of experiences, these two coincided at certain ages so that there tended to be identifiable stages of cognitive development.

One other important concept was that of egocentricity, which is evident in children up to about 7 years old. This means not that children are 'morally selfish' in the everyday use of the term, but that they naturally view the world from their own perspective; after all, they have no other. This means that, for example, if a parent becomes ill, children will assume it relates to something they have done.

There have been criticisms of Piaget's theories. For example, Piaget saw the stages in holistic terms, so that the child moving from one stage to the next does so with all their cognitive abilities. This was challenged by ideas about 'domains'. It has been recognised that, for example, some children may develop linguistic or social relationship skills rapidly but mathematic abilities more slowly. Therefore, moving from one stage to the next is far more complicated, diverse and specific to each individual child.

Another major criticism is that Piaget underestimated children and, as Donaldson (1978) and other psychologists found, when children understand the context, they can function with greater ability. Furthermore, Piaget did not make allowance for children's language development and their relationships with adults. For example, they might interpret the word 'more' as meaning 'looking different' rather than the adult interpretation of 'more' as a greater number, mass or volume. Nevertheless, many of Piaget's insights into children's needs for opportunities to learn and gain new experiences are important messages.

The implications of neglect and emotional abuse

Piaget's theory was developed from his interest in why children make mistakes which older children do not, such as not realising that a ball of clay can be fashioned into a ball or a worm but remain the same volume. It is a natural and important feature of childhood that mistakes are made and children feel able to experiment or articulate their 'theories'. An emotionally abused child who is mocked and condemned for being 'stupid', 'careless' or 'clumsy', will be inhibited from experimenting with objects and ideas, and therefore their cognitive development is likely to be delayed.

Children who are well cared for will handle and observe different shapes and materials, thereby developing manual dexterity and understanding of the material world in terms of cognitive learning. A neglected child left in a cot all day has little opportunity to play and experiment, and so has little to challenge his or her initial schema. Such children will not readily move through the cognitive developmental stages. A neglected child, left with little stimulation and encouragement, will develop neither age-appropriate thinking nor motor skills.

Vygotsky and sociocultural theory

Despite the value of Piaget's ideas, one major criticism is that he viewed the child as an individual 'little scientist' but did not really look at children in their environments or culture. Vygotsky's (1978) work addresses this. He argued that children are surrounded by other children and adults, and therefore cognitive development is a collaborative process.

One key idea is that children reach a stage where they have the potential to achieve tasks or understanding but have difficulty filling that potential on their own. This has been translated into English as reaching the 'zone of proximal development'. It is important for children to have the assistance and guidance of adults or older children in order to help them cross this zone.

Vygotsky did not manage to extend his theories because, unlike Freud, Bowlby and Piaget, he did not have a long career. Born in 1896, he was brought up in Russia and died in 1934. Much of his work was not translated from Russian until the 1960s.

However, others have added his to ideas. For example, Wood et al. (1976, p. 90) coined the word 'scaffolding' to describe the support given by adults who exert just sufficient control to enable the child to complete tasks and move through zones.

The impact of neglect and emotional abuse

The importance of sociocultural theory is that it makes central the role of other people in helping children learn and achieve. For example, the neglected or rejected child left to watch television all day will not develop age-appropriate cognitive skills. They may absorb some information, but without interaction geared to support them, they cannot move properly forwards when they reach a zone of proximal development.

Further information

Daniels, H., Cole, M. and Wertsch, J.V. (eds) (2007) *Cambridge Companion to Vygotsky*. Cambridge: Cambridge University Press.

Muller, U., Carpendale, J.I.M. and Smith, L. (eds) (2009) *Cambridge Companion to Piaget*. Cambridge: Cambridge University Press.

Concluding this chapter and looking towards the next

This chapter and the previous one outlined the impact of neglect and emotional abuse on aspects of children's development. The next chapter turns to fear and the need, during assessments, to recognise its impact on children who are neglected and emotionally abused.

Further resources

Beckett, C. and Taylor, H. (2010) *Human Growth and Development* (2nd edition). London: Sage.
Lindon, J. (2010) *Understanding Child Development* (2nd edition). London: Hodder Education.
Miller, P.H. (2010) *Theories of Developmental Psychology* (5th edition). New York: Worth Publishers.
O'Hagan, K. (2006) *Identifying Emotional and Psychological Abuse*. Maidenhead: Open University Press.

PART 2
Assessment

Part 2 comprises four chapters. The first three highlight factors which can contribute to the complexity of the assessment process, namely fear, the presence of siblings, and inappropriate roles for children. The fourth looks specifically at assessment processes.

5

The fear factor

When undertaking assessments, account has to be taken of the nature and impact of fear on children generated by neglect and emotional abuse.

Chapter overview

- Fear in neglect and emotional abuse
- Insecurity and damaged attachments
- Abandonment and 'negating' abuse
- Fear and criminality: a modern 'Oliver Twist'
- Terrorising threats
- Witnessing the abuse of others and domestic violence
- Over-protection
- Spirit possession
- Consequences of fear:

  o Post-traumatic stress
  o Attachment and the hostage/Stockholm syndrome

Fear in neglect and emotional abuse

Fear is sometimes the natural outcome of neglectful care which damages attachments and creates insecurity. However, sometimes fearfulness is purposefully engendered, especially in those instances of emotional abuse where children are controlled by being made afraid. Consequently, the children may become fearful in every aspect of their cosmos. They experience fear:

- of their carers because of constant threats;
- for others, such as worrying about their parent in cases of domestic violence or for siblings who are maltreated;
- of the 'outside world'.

Insecurity and damaged attachments

If we think back to the model of children's developmental rungs, the newborn infant requires nourishment, drink, warmth and other physiological necessities. However, very rapidly there is the need for safety and security. Swaddling babies is an ancient tradition in many cultures and although less necessary when there are easily washed clothes and disposable nappies, wrapping a baby carefully but securely can often be calming. As the infant develops relationships, the secure blanket gives way to secure relationships.

Attachment theory suggests that in order to develop and explore the wider world, children need a secure base, otherwise they will become anxious and fearful. While Bowlby (1951; Bowlby with Ainsworth, 1965) initially suggested that creating this security was entirely the role of the child's mother, Rutter (1972) clarified that this secure base could be provided by a small constant group of caring figures which could include a child's father. Leaving a child with lots of different carers who are strangers to the young child is a form of emotional abuse and neglect. But if a mother is unavailable, other familiar carers can provide security. The important concept is that of the consistency of care.

Illustration: Harry

Shortly after Harry's birth his mother, Lynn, suffered from post-natal depression. She had little affection for her new baby and a sense of overwhelming tiredness. She felt guilty about her inability to cope. Harry's father, Jon, realised that his wife was not coping. His widowed father lived near to Jon's workplace. Each weekday Jon dropped Harry off to be cared for by his grandfather. Both men helped with Harry's care at the weekends. Lynn slowly recovered from her depression and became attached to her son. Shared care between the parents and Harry's grandfather continued throughout his childhood and, despite the emotional absence of his mother in the first years of his life, Harry seemed to develop without problems of insecurity and showed no signs of attachment difficulties.

There are a number of theories about the developmental consequences of poor attachments. One of the most prominent, although controversial, theories of different types of attachment was first proposed by Mary Ainsworth (described in the previous chapter). It became a template for the ability to function in later life (Howe, 2011). We now appreciate that there is probably a physiological basis for Bowlby's theory of attachment, although more recent research about brain plasticity means that we can be less certain about the enduring effects of Ainsworth's categories of secure versus insecure early attachment (Kolb et al., 2011; Kolb and Teskey, 2012; Maurer and Hensch, 2012; Vida et al., 2012).

Abandonment and 'negating' abuse

Leaving alone

One dilemma for modern parents is to determine when it is appropriate to leave children alone at home. What age should they be before they can come home after school to an empty house, be left on their own overnight or babysit younger children? The answer is 'it depends' on the children's cosmos, i.e. their own maturity and wishes, their immediate environment and cultural norms. There are different judgements for children living in a close-knit, established community where neighbours automatically keep an eye on all the children compared to one where families live in isolation and everyone keeps 'themselves to themselves'. As discussed below, over-protecting children and giving them insufficient opportunities to exercise independence can also be emotionally abusive and can impair development.

There are, nevertheless, obvious cases of neglect of the child's welfare on the part of parents and these tend to be symptomatic of an underlying emotionally abusive relationship. Lucie Gates (see Chapter 2) died when an electric fire fell on her while her mother was out, leaving her and her young siblings alone. This might appear an unfortunate accident. However, the public inquiry demonstrated that this was the finale to a catalogue of abuse and neglect. As the paper by Ruiz-Casares et al. (2012) below illustrates, being left alone inappropriately can create substantial fear in children.

Spotlight on research

Ruiz-Casares et al. (2012) 'I hold on to my teddy bear really tight': children's experiences when they are home alone.

Based in Canada and encompassing 364 young people (both English and French speaking), the research team conducted an online survey. This was through the auspices of a telephone helpline for children, 'Kids Help Phone-Jeunesse J'ecouté'. The researchers found that a third of the survey participants were left home alone before the age of 11 years and a twelfth before the age of 8 years. A third of the respondents were left for over 10 hours, including one in six who were under 12 years of age.

Many of the older children enjoyed being on their own because it gave them peace and they felt safe. One young person, whose mother had mental health issues, said 'I would rather be home alone than getting the crap beat out of me'.

(Continued)

(Continued)

Many others, particularly the younger children and those left overnight, became psychologically distressed. A 17-year-old wrote: 'I worry that I will be murdered. *I have always been afraid of this.*' Another girl stated: 'I spent half the day in the bathroom with a baseball bat.' Some were so afraid that they could not sleep. A number were worried about their own behaviour: 'I'm scared [that] I will overdose on something and no one will be there.' Others, especially those left for over 20 hours, said it confirmed that their parents did not care about them.

Negating abuse

Stephen Meaurs, Malcolm Page, Heidi Koseda and Paul (see Chapter 2) shared characteristics described by Reder et al. (1993), in their classic work, as suffering from 'not existing' or, as we prefer, 'negating' abuse. Their existence seems to have been negated by their parents. The children were left or locked away in part of the house and ignored. They were given no food, drink, warmth or care and succumbed to a slow, lingering death.

Reder et al. (1993) describe the double bind in which children who are suffering from negating abuse are placed. The parents do not want the burden of meeting the children's physical and emotional needs. If the child makes more demands, the greater the attempts of the parents to ignore them will be. However, if the child becomes quiet and makes no demands, they will be left to starve. Meanwhile professionals can inadvertently collude with the parents against the children. The reports on Malcolm Page and Paul reveal that, while visitors to the homes were shocked by the conditions and concerned for the children, the lead practitioners focused on the parents' needs, totally overlooking the condition of the children. This reinforces the denial of the child's existence. Meanwhile, in the cases of Heidi Koseda and Stephen Meurs, the practitioners did not insist on seeing the children. The health visitor who was expected to check Stephen's health simply accepted the mother's refusal to let her see Stephen, thereby feeding his mother's denial of his physical needs. The parents' fantasy that Heidi did not exist was compounded by the NSPCC inspector, who recorded his own fantasy that he had visited and seen a healthy Heidi at a time when she was probably already dead.

Practitioners need to identify how many children belong to the household and ensure that they are able to relate to each one. Babies can be picked up and if they seem light or unresponsive a health visitor can be alerted. Checks can be made of schools for school-age children, although, as the Khyra Ishaq case demonstrated, some home-educated children are less easy to access. Simply accepting the situation and deciding that nothing can be done is to reinforce the parents' views that the child does not exist. Often talking to the parents, explaining the importance of seeing the child, offering assistance and support, can lead to the development of trust. Ultimately, if the refusal to allow the child to be seen is persistent, aggressive and adamant, then this should be viewed as a potentially dangerous, high-risk child protection situation.

Fear and criminality: a modern 'Oliver Twist'

In 1999, a 17-year-old boy was driven by his father to a school in the Netherlands. The boy fired a gun 10 times, shooting and wounding four students and a teacher. He was aiming at another boy who had dated his 15-year-old sister. The important point of this case is that, in the subsequent court proceedings, the father was held to be responsible for the boy's crime because the 'power of the father most certainly resulted in the fact that the boy felt compelled or obliged to commit the crime' (Le Sage and De Ruyter, 2008, p. 800).

This section looks at the emotional pressures, fears and insecurity created by carers who force or entice their children into criminal activities. We acknowledge that there are instances where such behaviour can be seen as justified or at least unavoidable. For example, parents in an oppressive regime might find it difficult to encourage their children to obey laws that they consider unjust and immoral. Alternatively, parents may be so disempowered by poverty that they have to encourage their children to steal in order to survive. Other parents may have been born into a criminal network and have little hope of keeping their children away from their associates' felonious activities. Nevertheless, there are carers who, to meet their own needs for gratification and without giving any thought to their children's welfare, draw them into criminal activities.

The classic fictional account of a child forced into crime by carers is of Oliver Twist, Dickens' Victorian orphan, who was threatened with death if he did not commit a burglary. He was forced to climb through a small window of a house to open the door to the adult burglars (Dickens, 1837/2012). 'Dickens drew directly from life' (James, 1999, p.115) and the characters in Oliver Twist were based on his observations of the reality around him. Nowadays children are used in a similar way and are caught between two substantial fears: carer threats, including the fear of losing affection, and the forces of the law.

Another source of insight into the dilemmas facing young people is portrayed in West Side Story, a musical which depicts gang membership and culminates in the death of a young person. Many gangs are non-delinquent friendship groups for young people. Nevertheless, there are some street gangs where the members risk being involved in serious crime and place their lives in jeopardy (Madan et al., 2011). Children join dangerous groups due to a complex interplay of factors in multiple domains, but their families can push or pull them towards criminal gangs (Sharp et al., 2006; Wood and Alleyne, 2010). Emotionally abusive or neglectful carers can push children towards gangs which represent a surrogate family (Rubble and Turner, 2000; Sharkey et al., 2011). However, family attachments are not always absent and children may be pulled towards gangs to which other, older family members belong (Alleyne and Wood, 2012; Eitle et al., 2004; Hammond, 2008).

Finally, there are the neglected and emotionally abused children who are drawn into criminal activities to meet their own needs. Neglected children may start rummaging in bins or stealing other children's packed lunches and then target shops or burgle homes to acquire life's necessities. Similarly, emotionally abused children may steal gifts to try to buy affection or to comfort themselves.

Terrorising threats

Children can be directly intimidated and terrorised but, in other instances, there is fear felt for someone or something else, such as a pet which is threatened. Children may be held hostage and threatened in domestic disputes in order to force a parent to comply with another adult's wishes. Alternatively, the abusive parent enjoys wielding physical power not by direct assault but by threatening it. Another source of terror is where a parent loses control due to substance misuse or mental health problems.

Illustrations

Janice

Janice recalled being terrified of her father, who was rarely physically violent but was a threatening presence. She recalled weekend afternoons when, as a child, she had to sit with her six siblings and both parents in complete silence while the parents watched television. Her father had a large knife and if any child stirred he would point with the blade towards the child with a threatening, jabbing movement.

Roland

Roland's parents were wealthy. His mother had a substantial problem with alcohol and drugs. Roland's father also drank heavily but rarely seemed to be adversely affected by alcohol. Roland, their only child, was frightened and insecure because of his mother's volatility and mood swings. She would alternate between excessive displays of affection, shouting and swearing at him, and ignoring him. One day, when Roland was aged 6 years, the family were on holiday and his mother, who had been drinking, suddenly grabbed him and for no apparent reason dangled him over the hotel balcony, four floors up, and threatened to drop him. His father eventually managed to persuade his wife to bring him back inside. Roland was left terrified and traumatised by the episode.

Witnessing the abuse of others and domestic violence

Our contention is that children who are exposed to the abuse of others, despite experiencing no direct maltreatment, are themselves emotionally abused. The term 'domestic abuse' has been deliberately chosen because alternative phrases, such as 'intimate partner abuse', while accurately describing what is meant, exclude the impact of the maltreatment on any children in the situation. Domestic violence, which can be physical, sexual or emotional, is a short-hand way of encapsulating the violence and abuse that occurs, predominantly behind closed doors in domestic settings, which is not directly or predominantly targeted towards the children but still harms them. It can also embrace abuse between adults in the home who are not partners, such as between a parent and a grandparent who lives with the family. In some families, all vulnerable members are subjected to abuse, but in others, the children are not the main targets of any mistreatment and it is these child witnesses that are the focus of this section.

There is considerable debate in the literature about whether domestic abuse is always about an adult male being physically and/or emotionally violent towards an adult female. Authors like Dutton (2012, p. 99) question this assumption, stating that 'women beat their husbands more frequently than husbands beat their wives'. This is challenged somewhat by an NSPCC population survey of 6,196 respondents (Radford et al., 2011), which found that in 93.8 per cent of cases it was the male that had beaten the other parent. Nevertheless, violence and hostility can occur between any combination of adults. This was illustrated by the death of English playwright, Joe Orton (1933–1967), who was beaten to death with a hammer by his male partner, Kenneth Halliwell (Lahr, 2002). Same-sex partnerships are no insurance against domestic violence.

Parents subject to domestic abuse might have difficulty 'escaping' or protecting their children from being aware of what is happening (Yamawaki et al., 2012). A few of the reasons are itemised below:

- The threat to life is substantial and the victims are told if they try to escape they will be tracked down and killed.
- Partners may stay because they are trapped by psychological dynamics, e.g. 'Stockholm syndrome'. This is described below and is an adaptive psychological process which enables us to cope with a threat from which we believe we cannot escape. It creates or strengthens the bond of dependency and affection from the victim towards the oppressor. This may be a particular issue for men who may have the resources and physical strength to retaliate or leave but find themselves emotionally trapped.
- There may be practical issues, such as having nowhere to go.
- There are sometimes strong cultural pressures to stay with an abusing partner.
- Another group of partners who may be particularly isolated, vulnerable and cannot easily leave their home are those with disabilities (Hague et al., 2011).
- Cultural and societal pressures on men abused by women might include a conviction that men should not show any violence to women and therefore physical retaliation and restraint, even if the man is stronger, are impossible. Additionally, there are cultural norms that men are meant to be tough and resilient, so male victims may feel humiliated and embarrassed, and unable to disclose their victimisation (Nowinski and Bowden, 2012).

- People who have had to overcome criticism and prejudice to form their partnership subsequently find it all the more difficult to disclose abuse within the relationship (Bartholomew et al., 2008).

Carers may resent official intervention and any label of 'child abuse' because they argue that the children are not the direct focus of any physical or emotional violence. However, the evidence that children suffer significant harm when in a household in which domestic violence occurs is now overwhelming (Levendosky et al., 2013). The impact of the adult hostilities on any children in the family is largely negative. First, they may live in dread of being physically caught in the cross-fire of any violence. They may also fear that they are the cause of the emotional explosions, shouting or fighting between the adults. They will be concerned that a much loved parent might come to harm. When they witness their parent being beaten, they may perpetually fear that it will be their turn next. Finally, children living with domestic violence and abuse may experience divided loyalties, loving both parents but rejecting their behaviour towards each other.

For some children there is the additional burden of secrecy. Iwaniec (2006) explains that in some cultures and minority ethnic families there are cultural obstacles to intervention. She explains that 'pressure to uphold family honour (*izzat*) and fear of bringing shame (*sharam*) are additional barriers to dealing with family violence' (p. 55).

An added concern is for those children who are also the translators for their parents, as the case of Krystyna exemplifies.

Illustration: Krystyna

Krystyna's family were from Eastern Europe and had come to live in Scotland. Her father was a builder and there appeared to be plenty of well-paid jobs in Scotland. Her father had a limited command of English, but her mother had none. Krystyna, aged 12, had learnt some English in school. She had a younger brother aged 5 years. There had always been violence from Krystyna's father towards her mother, although it was never directed towards the children, with whom he was jovial and patient. The violence towards the mother increased after about a year in Scotland as a recession meant there were few building jobs and the parents' dream of a new life faded.

Krystyna's mother could no longer cope with the violence but felt that because she could not speak English she would have to ask her daughter to get help for her and act as translator with the authorities. In preparation for this, she started to give her daughter full details of everything negative that the father had done to her, including sexual cruelty. Krystyna became profoundly depressed and suicidal because of her divided loyalties and what she was learning about her father, who she loved deeply.

Anderson and Bang (2012) explain that victims of domestic violence can often suffer depression and mental health problems. Where the violence is between two parents, neither parent might be able to nurture the child. The authors explain: 'during childhood, participants may have perceived that they had no adult capable of protecting them, thus increasing a sense of fear, despair and helplessness that may have continued into adulthood' (p. 62).

The impact of domestic violence on the unborn child

There is mounting evidence that domestic violence aimed at pregnant women has a deleterious effect on their unborn child. Flach et al. (2011, p. 1388) explain that 'domestic violence during pregnancy was also associated with behavioural problems in the child at 42 months'. Aizer (2011, p. 535) comments that 'severe violence in pregnancy reduces birth weight by 163 grams, with a larger effect if the violence occurs earlier in the pregnancy. These effects are similar to the estimated impact of smoking during pregnancy on birth weight.'

Over-protection

Parents who protect their children with great vigilance are rarely viewed as abusive. Yet consider the following case example.

Horace

Horace lived with his mother, aunt and grandmother in a small, relatively isolated cottage. Each day he was driven to school in a nearby village by his mother but stayed in the car until it was time for registration. At break times he had to stand by the school railings with his mother and grandmother who would arrive and wait for him. At midday his mother collected him to take him home for lunch. Again, after school he would be driven straight home by his mother, had tea and went straight to bed. At the weekends he appeared to stay inside his house and never played with other children. In school, he was not allowed to eat or drink anything in case he choked. His mother would not permit him to have swimming or physical education lessons in case he injured himself. This continued throughout his primary school years and appeared not to change as he moved to secondary school.

CASE STUDY

REFLECTION

Identify the physical and emotional neglect that Horace is experiencing. Identify the emotional stresses that Horace might be suffering. In what way might Horace be living in fear?

COMMENT

Unsurprisingly, Horace was physically unfit because he had no exercise. He had few social skills because he could not relate naturally to his peers. He was not developing any safety or 'streetwise' skills, such as learning to cross roads. Above all, his relatives had inculcated a sense of dread in him about the outside world. They convinced him that anything outside the home was dangerous, leaving him not only perpetually afraid of imagined dangers, but also trapped in a pernicious bond with his three female relatives.

Spirit possession

For some children, a particularly terrifying form of emotional abuse is to be condemned as a witch or spirit-possessed. This can lead to physical abuse and neglect. In the case of Khyra Ishaq and her siblings, her step-father believed they were possessed by 'Djinn spirits' and starved the children in the belief it would rid them of the evil. Although physical assault is often used, withdrawal of food is viewed as a way of weakening the evil spirits (Akilapa and Simkiss, 2012).

Six children living in the UK between 2000 and 2010 are known to have died as a result of beliefs in spirit possession and witchcraft (Obadina, 2012). In Ghana, Adinkrah (2011) reported a catalogue of abuse directed towards 'child witches', including three children who were held in dungeons and deprived of social contact. Meanwhile, in the USA, some religious groups view adopted children as particularly susceptible to spirit possession, and examples of abused 'spirit-possessed' children include toddler Javon Thompson, who was starved to death by a religious cult in 2008 (Mercer, 2012).

Children of any age can be accused of witchcraft or spirit possession. Some, however, are more vulnerable than others, including those with disabilities especially epilepsy and autism (Stobart, 2009). In the UK, trafficked children and ones placed in private fostering are at particular risk (Pearce, 2012). Some apparently advantaged children, such as girls who are very good academically, are sometimes more likely to be seen as 'witches' (Adinkrah, 2011).

There is terror for the children so accused. Even if they avoid the worst forms of maltreatment, they are often isolated and humiliated within their families and communities. Children may themselves come to believe they are witches and some girls can grow up believing that their babies will also be possessed by spirits. Recalling the cosmos of the child, the spiritual/social dimension is as important as all others when making assessments. Tedam (2013) argues that children should be safe wherever they are, including places of worship, and highlights the importance of assessing families' contact with faith organisations.

Consequences of fear

When a person becomes fearful and detects a threat, the sympathetic nervous system (SNS) prepares the body to cope with emergencies. In humans, this powerful physiological cascade can be activated by emotional and physical threats. The body responds with a coordinated response of the metabolic, immune, autonomic and neuroendocrine systems. This is designed to help the person fight the threat or flee from it. Energy is mobilised so that blood pressure is increased and the blood is diverted from other functions to the skeletal muscles (Lupien et al., 2009; Thompson et al., 2012). If people are repeatedly exposed to stress but there is no obvious flight or fight possible, then long-term damage to the cardiovascular system can develop.

One very interesting aspect of stress outlined by Ulrich-Lai and Herman (2009) is that positive stimuli, especially if new and not self-administered, cause a physiological response which is very similar to the stress response. Episodes of delight/elation and fear/terror appear to produce much the same biological reaction. This is an area still ripe for research but might suggest why some children who have been subjected to episodes of terror seem to seek exciting and elating experiences in adolescence and beyond. Another point raised by Ulrich-Lai and Herman (2009) is that longstanding engagement in rewarding behaviours, such as eating appetizing food, reduces stress, while experiences which give pleasure have anti-stress effects. This again suggests a physiological as well as a psychological reason for activities such as over-eating for comfort or over-spending on unnecessary goods, both of which can be indicators of distress in children and young people.

Post-traumatic stress

Post-traumatic stress has now become a well recognised consequence of harrowing experiences. There tends to be three aspects to post-traumatic stress: the intrusiveness of memories of the events; attempts to avoid any recall of what happened; and basic physiological responses.

Intrusive memories can interrupt life at any time through flashbacks, which involve not just a visual memory but can also encompass all the senses. Flashbacks occur during the day, but victims may also have nightmares when asleep. Traumatised children sometimes engage in repetitive play which has its foundations in the upsetting events.

In an effort to escape intrusive memories, victims might avoid any reference to the events. This can include forgetting what has happened or refusing to talk about experiences. Other reactions can include a lack of interest in any activities, complete emotional disengagement from life and estrangement from others. Younger children may lose skills they have gained, such as language acquisition.

Finally there are the physiological reactions, such as those identified by NICE (2005, p. 7): 'PTSD sufferers also experience symptoms of hyperarousal, including hypervigilance for threat, exaggerated startle responses, irritability and difficulty concentrating, and sleep problems.'

Research is showing that brain regions, especially the hypothalamic–pituitary–adrenal axis, the amygdala, the hippocampus, and prefrontal cortex, are affected by post-traumatic stress. Wilson et al. (2011) warn of the possibility that mistreated children might be misdiagnosed with ADHD due to the overlap in the presentation of neuropsychological symptoms.

As with other forms of stress, there are long-term effects of post-traumatic stress disorder. One interesting study by Burns et al. (2010) showed a link specifically between emotional abuse in childhood, post-traumatic stress and difficulty regulating emotions. Emotional dysregulation applies to the inability to be aware of a range of emotions, respond emotionally appropriately and inhibit impulsive responses when these would be harmful or inappropriate. Burns and colleagues (2010) conclude: 'results indicated that a history of emotional abuse is a more powerful predictor of emotion dysregulation in a large sample of female undergraduates than childhood sexual or physical abuse' (p. 812).

Finally, not everyone who is traumatised suffers post-traumatic stress. A substantial number of hormones, neuropeptides and neurotransmitters are activated when a response to stress is activated. There will be differences between individual responses based on each person's own interaction of these physiological processes, which helps to explain why some people are more resilient to stress than others.

Attachment and the hostage/Stockholm syndrome

Fillmore (1981) and Doyle (1985) first introduced and explored the idea that abused children entrapped in abusive situations experienced psychological accommodation similar to that suffered by hostages, kidnap victims and concentration camp prisoners – a phenomenon termed the 'Stockholm syndrome'.

An understanding of the nature of the Stockholm or hostage syndrome is absolutely essential for practitioners. Time and again investigators have dismissed allegations because the child appears to be 'attached' to carers and seems not to be fearful in the presence of the alleged abuser. Practitioners have too often accepted superficial evidence that all is well when children defend their abusive carers and hide any mistreatment, without examining circumstances in more depth.

Lester Chapman (see Chapter 2) repeatedly ran away from home. It would seem logical that young children would be prompted to run away from abuse, be happy to be removed from their abusers or at least show fear towards those who maltreatment them. However, paradoxically many children cling to their abusers, steadfastly refuse removal from home and, rather than showing fear of the people maltreating them, defend them, show increased attachment and protect them.

However, children are not the only sections of the population to appear to become attached to abusers. People who are imprisoned, physically or emotionally, and then maltreated by hijackers, hostage-takers, kidnappers, political regimes and even abusive partners can become devoted to those harming them.

This phenomenon was recognised and named during the 1970s. Prior to this, psychoanalysts noted that children sometimes appeared to welcome abusive behaviour or copied it, often inflicting harm on other children, and suggested that people identify with their aggressor as a way of defending themselves against anxiety (see Frankel, 2002).

After the Holocaust of the 1939–45 war, there was a questioning of why some German concentration camp prisoners appeared to take on the values of the camp guards. However, it was the momentum of hijacks and kidnapping for both criminal and political motivations during the 1970s and 1980s that led to a clearer understanding of the hostage or Stockholm syndrome (Kuleshnyk, 1984; Strentz, 1980). The name of the syndrome emerged following observations of the attachments that formed between three bank staff in Stockholm, who were held hostage, and their captors.

In some families, not all children will be emotionally entrapped. So, in the case of Lester Chapman, while he ran away, his sister Wendy made no complaint. Another dimension is in domestic violence cases where one parent becomes entrapped by the other abusive one (Levendosky and Graham-Bermann, 2000). Here, the child may not develop the syndrome, can clearly see what is happening and becomes angry with both parents, one for being abusive and the other for appearing to accept mistreatment, with neither parent appearing to care about the child.

Although the Stockholm syndrome is often described in stages, these will be experienced differently by each individual. While there is a progress through different emotions, some people may become stuck at one stage and never experience subsequent ones. Other people will move back and forwards between the stages and yet others may barely experience some, seeming to skip a stage and experience few of the feelings associated with the missed stage (Doyle, 1997b).

The usual pattern is to respond first to some form of threat or verbal attack with shock. If the threat is great, the child may freeze. This is called 'frozen fright'. This initial shock often gives way to denial. The child may not believe that the parent meant what they were saying, that the threat was a joke. Or they may simply have a feeling of unreality, a disassociation between what is happening and themselves.

After this comes fear and, physiologically, this will be accompanied by the stress response. The children's powerlessness in the face of the abusers leads to anger and fear being directed towards some other 'safe' person. This is why child protection practitioners can encounter as much resentment from the children as from their abusers. The children may behave angrily at school or engage in acts of minor vandalism against their neighbours. Alternatively, they will show a flight response and become quiet and withdrawn. They will become fearful of the outside world and turn their anger against themselves.

As the fight/flight response does not lead to any escape from the abuse, the children look to their abusers for rescue. They will start to feel that if they can be good enough, useful enough, then their parents might value them or at least stop abusing them. They will therefore become very compliant, wanting to please and trying to see their abusers in the best light. Natasha Kampusch (2010), who was kidnapped as a child, explains:

> The kidnapper ... trapped me in a mixture of dependence and gratitude. You don't bite the hand that feeds you. For me there was only one hand that could save me from starvation. It was the hand of the very same man who was systematically starving me. In this way, small rations of food seemed to me like generous gifts. (p. 174)

Children start to make excuses for their parents' behaviour: 'I must irritate them so much, they are really very patient'; 'Mum/Dad can't help it, s/he is so tired'. They look for and remember any signs of goodness, any slight sign that the parents might care for them. So they attempt to dismiss the abuse and focus on any small acts of kindness. If the parents want them to put on a display of affection, they will do so to please the parent.

As even these strategies fail, the children will begin to feel depression and despair. As they absorb the messages, overt or implied, from their abusers that they are useless, incompetent and of no value, they assume that they are so worthless that no one would want to assist them. There is no point disclosing, complaining or running away because they will not be believed or helped. Their only hope is to keep their head down and avoid attention. As they focus on parental kindness and manage to compartmentalise distressing incidents, they believe that their parents are doing them no harm and they have no complaint. They may even start to adopt their abusers' values. This can lead them to form relationships as adults, with partners who also mistreat them. They might also concur with their parents' view that it is appropriate for children to be neglected or emotionally abused, and then they become the next generation of abusive parents. Interestingly, Lieberman et al. (2011, p. 405), researching abused mothers who did not abuse their children, found that those who could give 'coherent narratives of their lives and were forthright in discussing their childhood abuse' were far less likely to be abusive compared to those who gave disjointed, confused and idealised versions of their childhood.

Concluding this chapter and looking towards the next

This chapter looked at particular forms of neglect and emotional abuse associated with fear and terror in children. The next two chapters explore other specific manifestations of these abuses. Chapter 6 looks at the place of the child in his or her family and considers those children who are 'singled out' for abuse. There is also a continuation of the theme of the negative emotional impact on individuals who witness abuse, and so the indirect emotional abuse of siblings who have to witness the maltreatment of their brothers or sisters is explored.

Further resources

La Fontaine, J. (ed.) (2013) *The Devil's Children*. Farnham: Ashgate.
Stanley, N. (2011) *Children Experiencing Domestic Violence: A Research Review*. Dartington: Research in Practice.

Books for children who have suffered from trauma include:

Homes, M.M. (2000) *A Terrible Thing Happened*. Washington, DC: American Psychological Association.
Sunderland, M. (2003) *Teenie Weenie in a Too Big World: A Story for Fearful Children*. Milton Keynes: Speechmark Publishing.

6

Siblings and the Cinderella syndrome

This chapter looks at children and that part of their cosmos which is their immediate family. It explores the issue of children who are 'singled out' for abuse. This is important in relation to assessment because their maltreatment can be masked by the evident good care of their siblings. It also examines the emotional abuse of 'favoured siblings', whose needs might be overlooked during assessments.

> ## Chapter overview
> - Definition of 'sibling'
> - The Cinderella (or Culhwch) syndrome
> - Why children are 'singled out' for abuse
> - The emotional abuse of 'non-abused' siblings

Definition of sibling

The classic definition of a sibling is a brother or sister born of the same mother and father; this can include children who live apart and have little contact. However, here the focus is on any children in the family cared for by the same parents, and so can include half- or step-brothers and sisters as well as foster siblings. In the case of Stephen Meurs (see Chapter 2), there were foster children in the family and their presence probably had an impact on the care that Stephen received. Had all four children been regarded as a sibling group, the social workers might have found it easier to recognise their responsibility towards Stephen as well as to the two foster children.

The Cinderella (or Culhwch) syndrome

The Cinderella syndrome does not refer solely to situations where birth-children are favoured above and beyond a step-child, but to any situation where specific children in the family are abused and rejected while the rest of the children are cared for adequately.

Interestingly, the rejection of one child in this way appears to cut across cultures because there are versions of the Cinderella story throughout the world. There is a magical traditional West African folktale about Chinye (see Onyefulu and Safarewicz, 1994). Chinye's mother died and her father took a new wife who had a daughter, Adanma. Chinye was treated as the family drudge and had to collect water for the family. With the help of a flamingo and a mysterious old woman, Chinye collected small gourds full of jewels. When Adanma went to collect her own gourds she greedily chose the large ones which were full of wasps that chased Adanma and the step-mother away.

Most of the other international versions have a step-mother with one or two daughters. However, in an English version of Cinderella, a child called Tattercoats does not live in a step-family but with her grandfather, who rejects her because his beloved daughter died giving birth to her (see Greaves and Chamberlain, 1990). Another variation, the Egyptian Cinderella, is one of the earliest versions of the story. Rhodopis is a Greek slave to a master in Egypt. Because she looks very different from the other servants, she is bullied by them. Her master gives her slippers and when the Pharaoh holds a party the other servants force Rhodopis to stay away, but a heron picks up one of her slippers and drops it in the lap of the Pharaoh. He determines to find the owner of the slipper and marry her, which he eventually does (see Climo and Heller, 1989).

Although traditionally Cinderella is female, there are male versions of the tale, such as the Welsh story of Culhwch, who was born in a pig pen and whose mother died shortly after his birth. His father married again and Culhwch's new step-mother had a daughter, whom she was determined he would marry. When he refused she put a curse on him that he could only marry a giant's daughter (Berresford Ellis, 2002). Additionally, there is the Irish tale of Billy Beg, a king's son who was deeply attached to his pet bull. Billy's mother died and the new step-mother hated Billy and, to torture him, tried to kill the bull. The bull eventually killed the step-mother and after being given magical powers by the bull, Billy rescued a princess from a dragon and married her (Green and Root, 1997).

Why children are 'singled out' for abuse

The various fairy tales encompass many of the reasons why children are singled out for abuse, including, as in the story of Rhodopis, a child who looks different from the rest of the family. There is substantial evidence that step-parents pose risks of abuse to children (Turner et al., 2007), although many step-parents give their step-children truly excellent and devoted care. A point of interest in the Cinderella syndrome is why the remaining birth-parents fail to protect their own children. Again, the folktales give us some indications of the disempowering and depressing effects of losing a beloved partner to death or divorce. As in the Tattercoats story, death can cause disabling grief. Furthermore, a feature of several Cinderella stories is the manipulation of the birth-parent by a step-parent. This can happen in real life, as the case of Miranda illustrates.

Miranda

The relationship between Miranda's parents broke down when she was 5 years old. Her father, Mike, was a long-distance lorry driver, with his job taking him away for weeks at a time, so custody was awarded to her mother.

Four years later her mother, Heather, met Hugh, a wealthy businessman who was himself divorced but saw his three children every weekend. Hugh used his power and influence to persuade Heather that Miranda had learning disabilities and food allergies. Slowly but inexorably, Hugh created a wedge between mother and daughter. Heather began to believe her child had health and learning difficulties. Miranda's diet was increasingly restricted and when Hugh's children came for the weekend, they had delicious food while Miranda had to eat plain food such as rice cakes because of her supposed food allergies. She was generally ignored and neglected, and she received few birthday or Christmas presents, whereas Hugh's children were loaded with gifts. When she was 11 years old, Miranda was sent to a boarding school which the parents rarely visited. The school realised that she had no food allergies and she began to tell the staff about her abusive home life.

The school contacted social services, whereupon Hugh said he would not have her home again or pay her school fees. Meanwhile, the social services made attempts to find Miranda's father, who was coincidentally trying to find her. With a new wife and baby, Mike had settled into a job involving local rather than long-distance driving. Miranda was reunited with her father, her new step-mother proved a generous and caring woman, and Miranda enjoyed having a baby brother.

Cases that can be more difficult to understand are those families where one child is neglected and emotionally abused by both birth parents. In some instances, the reason is because it is assumed that the adults are birth-parents when in fact one of them is a step-parent. Doyle (2012) described the case of Lloyd, who was the middle child of three siblings. Although to all the neighbours and community the children appeared to be full siblings, Lloyd had been conceived while his father was away. Lloyd was rejected by his parents because he was a reminder of his mother's infidelity. Nevertheless, during our direct work, we have encountered children who at first sight appear indistinguishable from their siblings and yet they are still rejected, as the case of Darren illustrates.

CASE STUDY

Darren

Darren was the fourth son of parents who had experienced no problems with their first three children and were committed to their family. The father, Mr Bee, was a builder who often worked on projects away from home. Mrs Bee became pregnant with her fourth child just as her mother was diagnosed with cancer. During the pregnancy the cancer worsened and Mrs Bee's mother died the day that Darren was born. Both parents had been longing for a daughter and were bitterly disappointed to have another son. Shortly after Darren's birth there was a serious fire in the family home and the eldest son nearly lost his life. Mrs Bee was struggling to cope with all these adversities. The family were rehoused and seemed more settled. Then Mrs Bee became pregnant again, but this time she gave birth to a daughter. Darren's three brothers and his sister developed satisfactorily and, like their parents, were tall and well built. Darren remained very small.

Social services were alerted by Darren's school, where staff had become increasingly worried about him. Darren wore inadequate, scruffy clothes, seemed ravenously hungry, stole food from other children and hoarded it in his bag, queued up for two school dinners, and was withdrawn with poor speech. His brothers and sister, in contrast, were well dressed, well built, boisterous and outgoing. Darren was also reported to the social services by worried neighbours who found Darren rummaging through their dustbins.

When a social worker visited she found the family sitting around the television and fire in the living room. Darren, however, was sitting on his own in a cold, dimly lit corner of the room. The parents complained about his behaviour, saying he was always stealing food and would ruin his clothes. They maintained that Darren caused all the family problems and was sullen and sulking. When the social worker asked to see his bedroom, she found that in the four-bedroomed house, the largest room, shared by the three eldest boys, was clean, with bright decorations and toys. The parents had a well-decorated room and a third bright, toy-filled room was for their daughter. Darren's room, the smallest one, had dingy, peeling wallpaper, a small bed with a plastic mattress and a dirty sleeping bag on top. There were no toys or decorations and no bulb in the light fitting.

REFLECTION

Can you list the reasons why Mrs Bee may have had difficulties relating to Darren? What about Mr Bee's situation. How might he feel about Darren? Can you think how Darren's brothers and sister reacted to Darren's treatment? How might Darren be feeling about what was happening to him, given that he appeared to have been given less love and care than his siblings since birth.

Parents who are grieving the loss of someone significant to them can have more difficulty bonding with a new baby and Mrs Bee was very close to her mother. In addition, there was the disappointment that Darren was not a girl. Then, when Mrs Bee did have opportunities to bond with him, she was further traumatised by the house fire and then became pregnant again.

The cultural context in which Mr Bee lived was that men provided materially for the family but women were responsible for child care. This, and the fact that his job took him away from home, meant that he did not look closely at the quality of his wife's child care. He worried that Darren's small stature and behaviour meant that he had a disability, but again, culturally, that was something that he could not talk about and he kept his anxieties to himself.

The children would have been fearful that their parents' love was conditional. They knew that the parents did not give unconditional love because they could see that it was not given to their brother. At the same time, influenced by Mrs Bee, they would have viewed Darren as difficult and 'different'. Interestingly, when Darren was received into care, after six months his parents asked for his return. The brothers were openly hostile to this because it meant that the three of them would have to share a room again.

Darren had little concept that he was lovable although he had received some affection from his father and one of his brothers. This assumption that everything was his fault and no one would love him meant that he showed clear signs of the Stockholm syndrome. He adored his mother and always wanted to give her presents, was desperate to go home when he was taken into care, and never complained about his treatment at home.

Another situation which is more difficult to appreciate is where foster carers neglect and abuse the foster children while favouring their own children. Having obtained a care order, social workers had some difficulty finding a foster home for Darren. Nevertheless, the first long-term foster carers were delighted to have Darren because they had two daughters and the mother could not give birth to more children. They desperately wanted a son and Darren was an enchanting-looking boy. However, after nine months social workers found he was being neglected again. His developmental delay, a consequence of his rejection since infancy, was such that the foster carers realised he would never be the son they dreamed of and they rejected him.

The emotional abuse of 'non-abused' siblings

Iwaniec (2006) explains that severely neglected and emotionally abused children and their non-abused siblings are often physically distant. The siblings do not play with the target child, who in turn might become mute. Sometimes the siblings can become aggressive. This gives the appearance that the siblings are co-abusers with the parents.

The 'non-abused' children are in fact being emotionally abused. First, they are likely to be living in fear, although this will be deeply repressed. They see what is happening to their sibling and wonder if they could suddenly be rejected by their parents. They worry that they will do something to lose their parents' favour. Their insecurity, although heavily masked, is likely to be profound. Lloyd, in Doyle (2012), describes being rejected by both parents while his brothers were unquestionably favoured. After considerable suffering and adversity, Lloyd managed to make a good life for himself but his brothers 'have fared less well. They are unable to find jobs and have become involved with drugs. While Lloyd is very optimistic about his own future, he is left wondering about the effect of abuse on siblings witnessing abuse rather than being directly abused themselves' (p. 211).

Siblings may try to protect themselves by identifying with the abusive parents and they might appear to lack empathy with the maltreated child (Hollingsworth et al., 2008). Sometimes when, in a large family, a small group of the children are singled out for abuse, one or two manage to ingratiate themselves with the abuser, who is happy to take advantage of the opportunity to divide and rule. Adeline Yen Mah and her siblings were emotionally abused and neglected by their step-mother, Niang, who favoured her own children. To escape mistreatment, their eldest sister started to ally herself with her step-mother, as Mah (2002, p. 65) describes:

'Why is *she* being so favoured?' Big Brother asked. ...

'She has allegiance to Niang written all over her face', Second Brother added. 'She makes me sick'. ...

'She has obviously defected' Third Brother related. 'The way she struts around?'

This alliance with abusing parents might protect some children in the short term, but it can leave them isolated and carrying a burden of guilt, possibly for the rest of their lives.

Alternatively, the favoured children might empathise with their abused sibling. But then they are likely to feel powerless to help and can suffer guilt for not having done something to assist, even though in reality this would have been difficult. Confronting their parents will only antagonise them, as will any overt attempt to defend their sibling. They can, however, manage some level of protection, especially if they can provide support when their parents are not present, as illustrated by the case of Sylvia and Muriel which is described in greater detail in Chapter 9. Muriel was rejected by both of her parents because they wanted a boy and she was not a prepossessing child. Packed off to boarding school at the age of 4 years, she was protected and loved by her elder sister, Sylvia, who was at the same school.

Spotlight on research

Gass et al. (2007) Are sibling relationships protective? A longitudinal study.

This study comprised 192 families with a variety of familial structures, from single-parent ones to complex, reconstituted step-families. All had at least two children, with

(Continued)

(Continued)

the older one being over 7 years old. The measures were a self-report of family stress, the quality of sibling relationships, the mother–child relationship and the level of the children's disturbance. Account was also taken of each family's socio-economic status and the gender mix of the children.

The results suggest that affectionate sibling relationships protect children from the impact of stressful life events. This finding was the same regardless of the quality of the child–mother relationship, the age gap between the siblings and the gender composition of the sibling group.

When one child is singled out for abuse it is important to assess the family dynamics. There are instances when one child is scapegoated. This child may be presented as difficult, but basically he or she is a symptom of the problems in the family. If these issues are not resolved and the child simply removed, another child then becomes the family scapegoat. However, when the abuse is severe and there are specific reasons why a particular child is rejected, removal can have benefits all round.

Illustration: Gareth

Andrea and Stan had three children, June aged 5, Gareth aged 3 and baby Brin. Stan was step-father to June and Gareth and the father of Brin. While June and Brin were evidently thriving, Gareth was small and not well developed. One day when Stan was at work, Andrea was heard by neighbours screaming and threatening to kill Gareth. When social workers arrived she asked for him to be taken away or she would kill him. He was received into care.

The social worker undertook a careful assessment and found out that June's father had been a married man who was nevertheless affectionate towards Andrea. But Gareth was the result of a rape. Andrea had been deeply ashamed and traumatised and had told no one; not even Stan knew. In discussion with Andrea and Stan, it was agreed that Gareth would be placed for adoption. The parents received some further counselling and therapeutic work was provided for the three children. The family settled, June and Brin developed well and the family needed no further intervention. Gareth was adopted by a couple who were experienced parents and he also made good progress.

Had Andrea's problems been less deep-seated it might have been possible to help her overcome her feelings of shame and trauma and eventually bond with Gareth. However, sometimes what the child represents cannot be altered and a vicious rape is often one such circumstance. Therefore, the removal of the child may be inevitable.

Concluding this chapter and looking towards the next

This chapter has looked at why some children are singled out for abuse. These can be some of the most difficult cases to recognise because the family has every appearance of being unexceptional (see Figure 1.1, p. 5). When questions are asked about the parenting, the good care of non-abused siblings means that any issues such as behavioural distress or failure-to-thrive in one child are attributed to the child being temperamentally difficult or to his/her genetic inheritance.

Children may be singled out because they have the role of family scapegoat, which is needed by the family for whatever reason. So if the child is removed, another child will become the scapegoat. The next chapter looks at the various roles, including family scapegoat, with which neglected and emotionally abused children are burdened.

Further resources

Caspi, J. (ed.) (2011) *Sibling Development*. New York: Springer.
Sanders, R. (2004) *Sibling Relationships*. Basingstoke: Palgrave Macmillan.
Silverstein, D.N. and Livingston-Smith, S. (eds) (2009) *Siblings in Adoption and Foster Care*. Westport, CT: Praeger.

7

Inappropriate roles for children

In the previous chapter mention was made of the child as a witness and a scape-goat. This chapter explores additional ways in which children can be burdened with inappropriate roles.

Chapter overview

- The child as a weapon and the Medea syndrome
- The scapegoated child
- Age-inappropriate roles
- Inappropriate medical intervention and 'sick person' roles

Glaser (2011, p. 873) points out that some 'caregivers are not able to distinguish the psychological boundary between the child and themselves. They are therefore capable of using the child for the fulfilment of their own need.' The case of 'Paul' (see Chapter 2) illustrates parents who use their children to obtain material benefits from the authorities. As Srivastava et al. (2005, p. 132) observe, 'practical support provided to families for the benefit of the children may even be exploited by carers to further their own individual interests'. This chapter looks at the ways children are used to satisfy parental desires to the detriment of the children. The roles covered in this chapter are by no means exhaustive. The literature contains more roles, such as the 'mascot', who is the family joker and deflects attention away from the family difficulties (Fischer et al., 2005). Furthermore, practitioners may be able to identify inappropriate roles for children not covered in the litera-ture. For example, we have experienced the 'chairperson', often an elder sibling, who amid family bickering and the consequential chaos manages to coordinate family communication and delegates tasks so that the family functions reasonably well. In this chapter, then, we cover some of the most commonly encountered roles, which demonstrate the burdens that this form of maltreatment – largely of emotional abuse – imposes on children.

The child as a weapon and the Medea syndrome

Many parents who divorce or separate do so in a manner that ensures their children's welfare is paramount. Although the children may experience some emotional distress, they are not abused by their parents. There are instances, however, when the parents not only neglect their children's well-being during divorce, but use the children to damage their estranged partner. Minty (2005, p. 68) comments that sometimes there is 'the deliberate use of the child as a missile'. This section looks at how parents might behave abusively towards their children to attack others, such as estranged partners or 'the authorities'.

The Medea syndrome

Medea, according to ancient Greek mythology, helped Jason, of Argonaut fame, to obtain the Golden Fleece. She then left her family and married him. The couple had two sons, Mermeros and Pheres. In Euripides' play, Jason then leaves Medea for Glauce, the daughter of Creon, the king of Corinth, but assures Medea he will support her and she can be his mistress after his new marriage. Medea is, to put it mildly, furious. She kills Creon and Glauce. However, this does not satisfy her anger. To take further revenge on Jason, she kills her two sons, who are also his children.

To provide balance, it is perhaps worth mentioning that fathers in Greek mythology were also sometimes prompted to kill or sacrifice their children. Zeus killed his own son, Phaeton, and Tantalus, in an attempt to please the gods, killed his son, Pelops, and served him up in a stew for them. Agamemnon also sacrificed his daughter, Iphigenia, to placate the goddess Artemis.

Returning to Euripides' play, Medea uses her children as a weapon against her husband and rejoices in her husband's distress at the loss of his sons. In contemporary society there are examples of parents who kill their children in an act of revenge against a former spouse, often in the context of an acrimonious divorce. Such instances are rare but there are plenty of other cases where parents, while not killing their children, use them as pawns in their partnership, particularly when the relationship sours. Furthermore, sometimes extended families become involved so that the children can be passed around like parcels and used to send acrimonious messages to estranged factions of the family.

On occasions, one parent primes a child to claim that the other parent is abusive. This leads to false allegations, usually of sexual or physical abuse. A skilled investigator can find out if a young child has been primed because what they say and how they 'show' what happened will not be consistent. They may also give a different account when in the presence of the priming parent than when that parent is absent. What can be more difficult is where an older child is persuaded that the other parent is totally at fault and a false allegation of wrongdoing would serve them right. Where the child and priming parent are united in their anger and wish to hurt the other parent, then accounts can be more believable.

Minty (2005) also highlights another invidious form of emotional abuse that can occur during an acrimonious divorce, which is to make a treat for the child conditional on the estranged parents' behaviour. For example, 'You won't go to the party if your mother doesn't agree to …', 'You can't expect me to let you do that while your father is behaving so unreasonably'. The parent is trying to make the child angry with the estranged partner by withholding treats while blaming that parent for the child's loss.

The use of a child as a weapon is not just confined to acrimonious divorces and separations. Sometimes they are used to hurt other members of families. For example, grandparents may be prevented from having access to their grandchildren because the parents resent the grandparents. This may well deny the children a valuable source of support and can distress the children if they have already formed a close relationship with their grandparents.

Anti-authority attack weapons

A further example of the child as a weapon is the use of children to attack 'the authorities'. One strategy is for the parents to incite their children to attack helping professionals or be so disruptive that assessment and intervention becomes very difficult. Another strategy is encompassed by the case study of Bonnie and her children.

CASE STUDY

Bonnie

Bonnie had spent much of her childhood in care. By the time she was 20 she had three children under the age of 5 by two different men. Neither of the fathers had shown any interest in their children. Bonnie had no relatives or close friends to support her. She had had periods of help from the social services, although it tended to be short-term intervention when she was in crisis. She was going through another period of difficulty, having had her handbag stolen, along with her money and phone, problems with neighbours and with a new boyfriend. She was drinking heavily and not eating well. With her phone stolen, she walked to the social services offices, dumped her children in reception and said that she would kill them if they were not taken into care.

REFLECTION

From the account, do you think that this might be a case of neglect or emotional abuse? Give reasons for your answer. What, if any, might be the risks to the children? What extra information would be needed to make a more certain decision about what is happening? How might you approach intervening with Bonnie and her children?

COMMENT

Otherwise caring parents can experience so many pressures that they can genuinely no longer cope. If they are not helped they may threaten to kill their children or themselves. Their behaviour is a desperate cry for help and, if given appropriate assistance, their ability to provide good care will be restored.

There are others, however, who regularly make threats against their children, often in front of them, in order to manipulate support systems: 'If you don't agree to my request, I'll kill the bugger and it'll be your fault.' Such threats and actions, which are used simply to attack 'the authorities', are profoundly distressing for the children. They will feel bewildered and insecure, and if they have sufficient command of language they will be terrified if they overhear any threats to kill. Therefore, this behaviour by parents constitutes emotional abuse and possible abandonment.

Assessment needs to distinguish between parents who can be helped to overcome their desperation and provide good care for their children and those who are generally abusive and habitually use their child as a weapon.

The scapegoated child

In the last chapter we explored the idea of the singled-out child. Sometimes, as illustrated by the cases of Darren or Gareth in the previous chapter, there are reasons why one child is rejected. When Darren and Gareth were removed, their families settled and functioned reasonably well. But in other families where there are difficult and distorted relationships, one child can become a scapegoat, who is blamed as the cause of the family problems, and if that child is removed, then another sibling can become the new scapegoat. Again, careful assessment is needed to distinguish between the child who has been singled out because of what that child represents and the child who has been 'singled out' as the general family scapegoat because there will be a different outcome depending on the reason for the singling-out.

When parents have mental health problems or misuse substances, there is no inevitability that their children will be neglected or emotionally abused because many cope well or at least provide 'good enough' parenting. However, sometimes the family only appears to function because the children are burdened with inappropriate roles. In some studies of families with parents who misuse alcohol, the children are seen to take on different roles, such as: hero, mascot, lost child and scapegoat (Fischer et al., 2005; Wegscheider-Cruse, 1989). The 'hero' is driven to succeed and achieve accolades to demonstrate that the family is unaffected by the drinking. The 'mascot' distracts everyone from the family distress by being cute and funny. The 'lost child' is withdrawn, quiet and generally overlooked. However, Wampler et al. (2009) argue that the role that is most damaging to the child is that of 'scapegoat'. They explain that where a parent is misusing alcohol, the rest of the family controls their anger but the scapegoat is the one who does not do so, and therefore shows overtly disturbing and often anti-social behaviour. While the family and agencies pay attention to the scapegoat, the adult drinking problems are ignored. Although some doubts have been expressed about the practical usefulness of these categories of role (Vernig, 2011), the 'scapegoat' is apparent in many instances where the adults in the family have major problems, especially where the family has a veneer of respectability.

Although the troublesome child is often the scapegoat, the role is sometimes thrust on to children who have few evident behavioural problems, but, in whatever way they behave, they are deemed a problem. If they become quiet and withdrawn, they are viewed as sulking and keeping themselves aloof from the family. If they try to behave like their siblings, their minor peccadillos are exaggerated while those of their brothers and sisters are overlooked. If they are outgoing, then they are accused of showing off and being too demanding. The family needs a scapegoat to distract attention away from the adults' issues and therefore, if the scapegoated child is removed, another will take on the mantle of 'fall guy'.

Age-inappropriate roles

The usual age-inappropriate roles are either a young child having to act as a parent, burdened by too much responsibility for the family, or, alternatively, a child not being allowed to grow-up towards independence.

Little parent

'Parentification' is a term to describe the process whereby parental roles and responsibilities are abdicated by parents and carried out by children and adolescents. (Hooper et al., 2012, p. 165)

As mentioned, some substance misusing parents prove to be loving carers. However, having said that, it is important not to move to a position of denying the harm that some substance misusing parents inflict. This is illustrated in the case of Boyd.

Illustration: Boyd

After an acrimonious divorce between his parents when Boyd was aged 8 years, he saw little of his father. He and his two younger sisters, then aged 2 and 3 years, lived with his mother, who started drinking heavily. By the time he was 11 years old, Boyd had to shop, prepare the family's meals, wake his sisters, give them breakfast and take them to school. His mother was often sick and he would clear up the mess. He also had to listen patiently to his mother, who constantly complained about all her difficulties.

His mother was spending much of the family income on drink, so by the time he was 14 years old, Boyd had a newspaper round, helped to wash up in a local pub and offered to clean cars to earn enough money for himself and his sisters. He became very isolated because he was too tired to concentrate in school and he missed a lot of schooling because he had to stay home and cope with the housework. Neither he nor his sisters could bring friends home because they never knew whether the house would have signs of their mother's vomit or excrement, or, if inebriated, her behaviour would be aggressive and unreasonable. One evening he snapped and he started hitting his mother, whereupon neighbours called the police.

When evaluating if a child is being emotionally abused by having to undertake a caring role, the key words are '*too much*' responsibility. Some responsibility is beneficial and helps children to develop independence. Some young carers report that they feel privileged to be able to help their families. It is also difficult to determine what 'too much' is because temperamentally children seem to enjoy different levels of responsibility.

Even when their caring role is onerous, young carers may not be emotionally abused because the parents are doing *all in their power* to relieve their children of caring burdens but a lack of welfare provision means that they have to rely on their children. Arguably, in these cases the children are suffering harm but it is the state that is guilty of emotional maltreatment, not the parents, because of inadequate social support.

However, neglect and emotional abuse is present when the parents inflict unreasonably burdensome caring roles on their children. This is the case when parents are offered services but they refuse them because they feel more comfortable using their children. Alternatively, they may demand more of their children than necessary and use their care needs to exert control over their offspring, abusing their parental power. The difference between abusive and non-abusive parents who rely on their children's care is usually only determined after a careful assessment.

The everlasting infant

Over-protection is a form of emotional abuse when it restricts children's development. There is evidence that over-protection tends to result in young people either rebelling and placing themselves at more risk, or simply acquiescing and becoming anxious, underachieving and failing to assess risks adequately (Ungar, 2009). There-fore, ironically, over-protection can lead to increased risks to young people.

The motivation of parents of over-protected children varies considerably. Sometimes over-protection can be readily understood. For example, deciding how much freedom to give children at what age is a dilemma for most parents and many are guided by other parents in the area. If most parents in a community allow chil-dren to walk to school at the age of 10, then it is relatively easy for a parent to decide to do the same. However, some parents, particularly those caring for children with relatively rare medical conditions, do not have these easily accessible guidelines. These parents have to take special regard of safety issues as their child is growing up, but they cannot easily discuss their decisions with parents who are in the same situ-ation. Wiegerink et al. (2006), for example, found that young people with cerebral palsy can experience social isolation because of the double disadvantage of parents who are over-protective and barriers outside the home, such as transport and nega-tive social attitudes. Similarly, Atkin and Ahmad (2001, p. 622) studied young people with sickle cell disease and found 'infantilisation was experienced by most of the respondents'. These young people faced a combination of parental over-protection and societal racism and discrimination.

There can also be cultural issues leading to a sense of infantilisation and conflicts between the generations. Mujtaba and Furnham (2001) found that there was an association between British Asian schoolgirls, conflict with parents, eating disorders and parental over-protection. Despite the negative impact of the over-protection, most of the girls acknowledged that it was a sign of parental affection.

What is more clearly emotionally abusive is where the parents infantilise their chil-dren by maintaining rigidity and authority. Children can be forced to remain depend-ent and are denied everyday choices which their peers are increasingly allowed to make, such as what to wear, how to organise their spare time and what music to listen to. Some parents are overly intrusive and controlling, and deny their children any sense of self-esteem or fulfilment. Sometimes the infantilisation is apparent because they wear clothes of a style that is far too young for them, or they are not allowed modern technology such as a mobile phone, even in adolescence, or they have no social life.

Inappropriate medical intervention and 'sick person' roles

In some instances, children are designated the 'sick' role and inappropriate therapies are forced on them. Arguably, Candace Newmaker, whose case is discussed in Chap-ter 9 (Mercer et al., 2003) appeared to be an insecure, bewildered child requiring unconditional love. She was labelled with any number of 'illnesses', for which she was given an overwhelming cocktail of medicines. Ultimately, it was a form of therapy that killed her.

Inappropriate therapeutic and medical intervention can include neglect of suitable treatment when this is clearly needed. Children with chronic illnesses or disabilities can be particularly vulnerable. In relation to children requiring enteral feeding, i.e. nutrition through a tube, Kennedy and Wonnacott (2005) provide vivid examples of abuse. This includes not giving enough food to ensure the child remains light enough to carry, or not allowing gastrostomy feeding because parents view it as 'abnormal', despite the fact that the child is starving. One group who are especially susceptible to this form of emotional maltreatment are those with hearing impairments. An example of the neglect of a child's physical requirements leading to complex layers of emotional abuse was summarised by Gardner (2008, p. 47):

> A child's deaf needs were completely ignored by the family. The young person grew up feeling his family/relatives did not want to talk to him or love him. Because of his deafness, his family restrained him from going out or seeing friends and undermined his skills. He had no friends or social life. He was growing up completely frustrated and feeling he lacked any identity and was unwanted.

Conversely, the term 'medical child abuse' describes medical intervention instigated by caregivers which is unnecessary, is emotionally stressful and may cause physical and psychological harm to the child. A particular feature of this form of mistreatment is that the abuse is delivered, although not instigated, largely by medical staff and as part of the medical system because of misinformation provided by the caregivers. Sometimes the motivation is a desire for material gain. For example, in the UK in November 2012, a mother was imprisoned for nearly four years after she had made her son, from the age of 6 to 9 years, pretend he had cancer. She claimed he had autoimmune lymphoproliferative syndrome (ALPS) and then lymphoma. She shaved his hair and eyebrows and forced him to stay in a wheelchair. She claimed £85,899.44 in benefits and was given a car big enough to cater for the wheelchair (S. Morris, 2012). Similarly, Stutts et al. (2003) reported a case of a 13-year-old boy who was forced by his mother to feign a disability to settle a court case.

Originally called the Munchausen syndrome by proxy, the abuse of children by pretending the children are ill or have a condition requiring medical treatment is called by a number of different terms, including 'fabricated or induced illness', which is used in the UK in *Working Together* (Department for Children, Schools and Families, 2010). 'Munchausen syndrome by proxy' is still a useful term when searching international literature, although 'factitious disorder by proxy' appears to be one of the most common internationally used phrases (Dye et al., 2013; Ferrara et al., 2013; Squires and Squires, 2013).

Munchausen syndrome was a term first coined by Asher in 1951, and was named after Baron Hieronymus Carl Friedrich von Münchhausen, who was a German aristrocrat. He travelled across Eastern Europe fighting in the Russio-Turkish War (1735–39). When he returned to his German estates he regaled his dinner party guests with fantastic and exaggerated tales of his exploits.

The condition Munchausen syndrome, according to Kinns et al. (2013), refers to a particularly severe manifestation of factitious disorder. Those suffering from the syndrome appear to have a compulsion to seek medical treatment and adopt the patient role when they have no physical condition warranting the treatment.

It is distinguished from 'malingering' because people with that condition have a clear objective, usually to avoid an unwanted situation. People suffering from Munchausen syndrome have such an overwhelming need for treatment that they will produce symptoms so convincingly that experienced medical practitioners can be deceived. Munchausen syndrome *by proxy*, as the name suggests, is when a child is presented instead of the adult, mostly by people who are suffering from Munchausen or would do so if they could not use their child instead.

The perpetrator is usually the mother, although other people, including fathers, can be the offenders. The non-abusing parent is often distant, insecure or has a job which means that they have to be absent for long periods. There are instances where one parent appears to be too attentive to their child and the partner feels jealous (Morrell and Tilley, 2012). While many non-abusing parents appear to ignore what is happening, some do raise questions. In rarer cases, both parents conspire to present the child as ill. The offending parents' motivation is often a craving for attention, and the sympathy and concern that caring health professionals provide to parents of ill children. They may also have a need to create dramatic situations in which they are the centre of attention.

Spotlight on research

Kucuker et al. (2010) Pediatric condition falsification (Munchausen syndrome by proxy) as a continuum of maternal factitious disorder (Munchausen syndrome).

This case study is of a mother aged 32 living in Turkey. She had been married at the age of 15 years and then lived with her husband and mother-in-law who had diabetes mellitus.

The mother was repeatedly assessed and treated for fainting and dizziness and was found to be hypoglycaemic, i.e. having low blood glucose. She was diagnosed with a heart defect, which was repaired. However, she continued to have hypoglycaemic episodes and complained of menstrual abnormalities and abdominal pain. Investigations found no obvious cause.

The mother gave birth to seven children. Six children died, aged between birth and 9 years, and most had suspected or confirmed hypoglycaemia. The seventh child, a daughter, was admitted to hospital aged 13 years. Eventually, she disclosed that her mother had frequently injected her with her grandmother's 'sugar' solution. Her mother eventually admitted that she had injected her surviving daughter with her mother-in-law's insulin. To make the child appear more seriously ill, she had contaminated her daughter's urine with samples with her own blood. This girl had learning disabilities and a seizure disorder, which was probably caused by repeated injections with insulin.

The mother's reasons for her behaviour were that she had a very difficult relationship with her mother-in-law and wanted to escape her influence. Also, she wanted more attention from her husband.

The case study above is an extreme case which constitutes physical as well as emotional abuse. It illustrates that Munchausen syndrome and the 'by proxy' conditions are not mutually exclusive. The two do not necessarily occur together, but can do so.

Even when the child is not physically harmed, the emotional impact of being presented as ill, being lied to and being forced to lie can be profound. Conway and Pond (1995), for example, describe a child whose mother claimed she had cystic fibrosis and who went on to maintain she had the condition in adulthood.

Concluding this chapter and looking towards the next

This chapter and the previous two have explored several forms of neglect and emotional abuse, including terrorising, singling-out for abuse and imposing inappropriate roles on children. They have also highlighted assessment issues. The next chapter looks more specifically at assessment and prepares the foundation for the later chapters on intervention.

Further resources

Department for Children, Schools and Families (2008) *Safeguarding Children in whom Illness is Fabricated or Induced*. Nottingham: DCSF.

Forrester, D. and Harwin, J. (2011) *Parents Who Misuse Drugs and Alcohol: Effective Interventions in Social Work and Child Protection*. Chichester: Wiley-Blackwell.

Barnados has a number of projects to help young carers in the UK. Information is available from: www.barnados.org.uk

Alcohol Concern produces a range of leaflets for parents, children and families, available from: www.alcoholandfamilies.org.uk

8

From assessment to response

This chapter contains both aspects relevant to assessment and ones which are important when planning or providing a response. Some interventions, such as communicating effectively with children, are equally important whether assessing or intervening strategically.

Chapter overview

- Pointers and obstacles to the recognition of child emotional abuse and neglect
- Obstacles to recognition
- Reflective practice
- Power issues in assessment and response
- Focusing on the child
- Overcoming barriers to communication
- Play-based work: assessment or therapeutic tool?
- Reflecting the child's cosmos
- Working together

As the cosmological model of children's development (see Figure 1.2, p. 7) indicates, a child lives not just with close family members or even a local community, but also within a larger, state-wide environment. The ability of practitioners to assess and respond to potential neglect and emotional abuse will depend on the protective approach of the state. Chamberland et al. (2011, p. 852) explain that these forms of maltreatment are often overlooked if policy is:

> focused on the assessment of risk and specific behaviors, the cessation of danger, and limiting the powers of government to intrude in the private lives of families in severe situations in which evidence is often required in a legal context.

This chapter therefore has to be set against the prevailing social policy within which practitioners work and this is explored further in Chapter 12.

Pointers to recognition and obstacles to recognition of child emotional abuse and neglect

There is no golden bullet, no checklist which will guarantee an accurate assessment. This point is eloquently summed up by Long et al. (2012, p. 9):

> Neglect is not absolute. It is not scientifically measurable. It is always relative and relies on a series of complex interagency judgements about 'normal' or 'average' levels of parenting in families.

This chapter therefore does not contain a long checklist of information that must be obtained and evaluated, because, as Daniel et al. (2010, p. 249) stated, they could identify 'little research into their effectiveness in leading to improved outcomes for neglected children'. Moreover, we espouse the view of Houston and Griffiths (2000) that we need to move away from objective and mechanistic risk assessment tools to understanding concerns.

Nevertheless, there are useful frameworks that can help professionals gather appropriate information, check that they have not missed important areas of inquiry and organise their material (Holland, 2010; Martin, 2010). In England and Wales, practitioners from all helping professionals involved with children can use the Common Assessment Framework (CAF). This is useful because it means professionals from various disciplines are using the same language, although an insightful critique of the CAF is provided by White et al. (2009). Daniel and Baldwin (2005) suggest that professionals explore various areas rather than using a series of tick boxes. For example, when practitioners explore the internal state of the family's accommodation, they suggest that if the property is rented, then a distinction has to be made between factors that are the responsibility of the landlord and those that are the responsibility of the householders. However, as Glaser et al. (2012) comment when evaluating training for an assessment framework for emotional abuse and neglect called FRAMEA, 'it is difficult to introduce new thinking into already established procedures and ways of working' (p. 7).

We have resisted providing a checklist, but there are some pointers which can suggest emotional abuse and neglect. Therefore, the next three sections look at some of the facilitators and obstacles related to recognition.

Factors relating to the child

There appears to be no specific type of child who is neglected or emotionally abused. For example, in terms of gender, boys and girls are equally vulnerable but there are some cultural practices that mean that either girls or boys are more likely to be targeted in terms of specific abusive practices. Children of all ages can be neglected and emotionally abused, although Dent and Cocker (2005) note that neglect is the greatest cause of fatality from maltreatment in children from birth to 5 years old. Nevertheless, adolescents can suffer from neglect and particularly from emotional abuse (Rees et al., 2011). Birth order again is not generally significant, although often the youngest members of a family are more vulnerable to neglect.

Doyle (1998) found that children from a wide range of cultures and backgrounds were emotionally abused, and the literature demonstrates that neglect can occur in any family in terms of ethnicity and religion. However, children from minority ethnic groups will often be more affected by neglect and emotional abuse because they have the double vulnerability from abuse within the home and discrimination outside. Children living in poverty who are neglected and emotionally abused similarly suffer from multiple disadvantages (Ridge, 2011). Children with disabilities are also susceptible to double emotional abuse and distress from both within and without the home (Iwaniec et al., 2006). Furthermore, as Kennedy and Wonnacott (2005) explain, there is more potential for children with disabilities to suffer physical neglect because, for example, an incontinent child might be left for long periods in soiled pads. They are also more easily emotionally neglected if carers do not compensate for some disabilities, such as sight-impaired children who cannot see a smile. A further problem facing children with communication disabilities is that practitioners may feel that they do not have the skills to communicate with them and therefore overlook their views and opinions.

Information needs to be obtained about all the children in the family, and, if possible, any absent ones for whom cohabitees or other carers might have responsibility. The information can usefully be gathered and evaluated on the basis of the child's cosmology, which includes 'temporal' or time-related aspects, namely:

- Their *past* condition and behaviour: for example, Heidi Koseda (Chapter 2) was reported to be a happy child until her father moved out and a new cohabitee moved in. If possible, events around a child's birth should be sought because, as Darren's case (see p. 85) demonstrated, negative experiences during pregnancy and birth can adversely influence the parental bond.
- Their *present* state, situation and behaviour, including physical, emotional, cognitive and, where relevant, spiritual well-being. This includes the impact of their extended family and their environmental situation.
- Their *future* prospects, opportunities and aspirations, and how far their carers are facilitating or obstructing them.

Factors in the family and wider environment

There are no particular types of carer who can be readily identified as emotionally abusive or neglecting. Nevertheless, some carers have more of a challenge to meet their children's needs than others. Dufour et al. (2008) found single, female-headed families were more vulnerable to neglect. Carers coping with multiple stressors, especially when personal, relationship and environmental stressors are combined, are more likely to perpetrate emotional abuse (Doyle, 1998). One constant theme is that carers with problems of drink and drug misuse and mental health problems are more likely to be neglectful or emotionally aggressive (Donohue et al., 2010; Freisthler and Holmes, 2012; Laslett et al., 2012). However, not all carers struggling with these issues are abusive and, equally, parents without these problems can maltreat their children.

There is a considerable debate around whether neglect and emotional abuse are the fault of mothers or fathers. Should mothers always be held responsible when a small child lacks food, warmth and the essentials of life? Do child protection professionals ignore fathers? These debates have a place in the welfare discourse. However, in practice, if neglect and emotional abuse are sufficiently serious to warrant the intervention of professionals it is because all parent figures, particularly if they live in the same household, are failing to provide effective care. If there is one strong, reliable and caring parent figure present in the child's life, then significant harm to the child is unlikely. In contrast, physical abuse can occur apparently 'out of the blue' and in some rare cases it can cause death or permanent damage. The television presenter, Richard Madeley (2008, p. 167) describes how his father viciously caned him 'as last reflex stirrings of the abiding resentment my father felt about his own childhood. I was quite literally his whipping boy.' Both father and son hid this from his mother and everyone else for a considerable time. Sex offenders can abuse children in secret without their partners being aware of the problem. But neglect and emotional abuse sufficient to cause significant harm to a child can rarely happen surreptitiously. A thin, small child with ragged clothing and poor hygiene cannot be overlooked by another adult resident in the household, and nor can one being denigrated or locked away for long periods.

Emotional abuse will rarely cause harm if one parent figure is committed and caring, even if another parent is emotionally abusive, ineffective or distant. An example is Harry in Chapter 5 (see p. 68), whose mother was, for part of his early life, emotionally distant because she was suffering from post-natal depression. Harry was cared for by his father and grandfather and he thrived.

However, harm can occur when one parent becomes neglectful or emotionally abusive and all other parent figures in the child's life are disempowered. This can be because of absence due to the need to earn a living, which takes a parent away from home most of the time. Other ways a parent can be disempowered are through significant disability and illness, or by becoming a victim of the other parent's violence. Furthermore, new mothers' capabilities can be substantially diminished by perinatal psychiatric disorders including postnatal depression (Oates, 2003; Oates et al., 2004).

In the UK, the concept of 'parental responsibility' is enshrined in law under the Family Law (Scotland) Act 2006, the Family Law Act (NI) 2001 in Northern Ireland, and the Children Act 1989 in England and Wales. Part of the assessment needs to be about the attitude to the child of each person with parental responsibility. Their power in relation to the child needs to be ascertained and then how they are using it evaluated. The same is true of anyone else who is a parent figure, even one without parental responsibility, such as a cohabitee, who might be a powerful influence in the family.

With all actual or potential carers, based on the child's cosmology, including the time element noted above, it is important to find out about and then evaluate:

- Their *past* behaviour: questions to explore include have they a criminal record for violence or abuse or did their behaviour change after a significant event, such as the arrival of a new baby or a new cohabitee?
- Their *present* attitude and behaviours, from their own account and that of others, including, if possible, the children.
- Their *future* intentions, wishes and potential to care for the child: this needs to take into account how much power they have in relation to the children and the time issues in the child's cosmology – children cannot wait too long for their parents to mature into effective carers.

Obstacles to recognition

The inquiry cases in Chapter 2 show that children were seriously maltreated, yet with hindsight there was ample evidence of neglect and abuse which was overlooked. When child protection practitioners see the excoriation of their colleagues in the popular media, many will look back at their case-load and think 'it could have been me'. Few professionals working in child protection can reflect on their work over the years and be clear that they always recognised what was happening to the children. This is because in order to undertake accurate assessments practitioners have to surmount a considerable number of obstacles to recognition. Doyle (2014) explores these, particularly in the case of young children. In relation specifically to neglect and emotional abuse obstacles include the following:

- *Appearance, behaviour and developmental problems* occurring because of neglect and emotional abuse might be attributed to another cause.
- *Children have difficulty communicating* that they are being abused, especially in cases of neglect and emotional abuse. As Daniel (2005, p. 15) comments, 'children who are neglected are particularly unlikely to seek help in their own right'. Additional communication obstacles include children's language limitations due their developmental level or a disability, or because English might not be their first language.
- *The Stockholm syndrome* can mean that children are entrapped in abusive situations and actively hide any maltreatment and do all they can to protect their abusers.
- *Neglect and emotional abuse can occur in every type of family or family substitute*, including apparently 'respectable' families (see Brabbs, 2011).
- *Children are sometimes singled out for abuse* when other children in the family are well cared for. The good care of siblings can obscure the abuse of one child in the family.

- *Professional issues* are particularly relevant in cases of neglect and emotional abuse. In particular, Dent and Cocker (2005) describe how selective perception means that professionals make an initial judgement and then notice evidence to support their original judgement.

Reflective practice

In an evaluation of intervention in neglect cases, Long et al. (2012, p. 40) noted that 'complex circumstances, vulnerable families, and the breadth of factors to include in decision-making provide a challenge to any worker'. Among the challenges is the requirement to intervene in ways that are both effective and ethical. A service which is exploitative, dishonest and manipulative will not serve anyone well.

One consideration when making an assessment is for the practitioner to determine their partiality. Singh (2013), who defines himself as a 'Black British South Asian', explains this: 'Where I am positioned socially, culturally and politically will influence how I experience the social world and the types of theories and literature I draw upon to explain and make sense of it' (p. 26). Meanwhile, Crofts (2013) and Kennedy (2013) reflect on what it means to be white practitioners. An associated aspect of any intervention is to ensure that it adheres to the concept of anti-discriminatory practice. Important relevant works on the topic include Bartoli (2013), Laird (2008), Millam (2011) and Thompson (2012).

Spotlight on research

Ards, S.D. et al. (2012) Racialized perceptions and child neglect.

The authors conducted an exercise in the USA whereby they provided vignettes with pictures strongly suggesting physical neglect. They altered the photographs to be exactly the same apart from the inclusion of a black child or a white child or no child at all. They found that the inclusion of black children in the photograph significantly raised the likelihood of the case being defined as reportable neglect.

Some caution has to be exercised about generalising this research because BME (black and minority ethnic) populations have very different attributes in different countries and cultures. Furthermore, awareness of discrimination and prejudice among welfare professionals will vary across different countries, depending on training and cultural attitudes. For instance, Stokes and Schmidt (2011) did not find that race was a statistically significant factor in their study conducted in Canada. Furthermore, care has to be taken not to be so concerned about negatively judging BME parents that their children are left at greater risk and suffer more harm than non-BME ones.

Power issues in assessment and response

Table 8.1 suggests how issues of power, which are the basis of any form of abuse or oppression, can be considered.

Table 8.1 Assessment of the use of power by carers

Assessment – what to explore and evaluate	Response
How do the carers behave towards the child?	Can a strategy be introduced to improve the carers' negative conduct or enhance positive behaviours?
What powers do carers have in relation to the child and in what forms?	Is it possible to share with the carers your analysis of the powers they possess? How do they respond?
How effectively do carers use their power in relation to caring for the child?	Can carers be helped to use power more effectively for the welfare of the child?
Are carers misusing any of their powers in relation to the child?	Is it possible to stop carers misusing the power?
Are carers disempowered in any way?	Can any disempowering factors be neutralised and carers be empowered in a way that helps their child?

Again, if we think back to the case of Miranda (see p. 84), her mother Heather was misusing her power but was also disempowered by her husband, Hugh. The options for the child protection team were:

- Option 1. Change Hugh and Heather's behaviour

  o Even if this was possible, the change would take too long and Miranda needed good care as soon as possible

- Option 2. Ensure Heather changes her behaviour and disempower Hugh to enable Heather to be a 'good enough' parent

  o As above, even if this could be achieved, it would take too long for Miranda

- Option 3. Heather to leave Hugh and be empowered to be a 'good enough' single parent

  o Heather showed no inclination to leave Hugh and if coerced into doing so could resent Miranda, believing her to be the 'cause' of the marital breakdown

- Option 4. Explore the situation of Miranda's alternative parent figures

  o Miranda had no grandparents or other extended family members who were able to care for her. Could the birth father be found, the reason for his absence evaluated, and his potential as a carer assessed?

- Option 5. Find alternative substitute carers

  o Miranda had already had several homes and because she was now a young teenager it was unlikely that she would move straight into a permanent foster home. She would suffer further changes, moving from short- to longer-term foster carers, compounding her view of herself as unlovable and worthless.

Outcome: Miranda's father, Mike, and his new wife were willing to be assessed as Miranda's carers and proved suitable.

The reality for most children in Miranda's situation is that there is no birth parent searching for them. The missing birth parent may be dead, unknown, in prison long-term, abusive or simply not interested. Often child protection workers are left with few options, and rather than choosing the best one, they have to decide on the least worst.

Had Mike not been available for Miranda, which of the options would have been the next best? Can you think of an alternative option which would have been more appropriate?

REFLECTION

Focusing on the child

A distinguishing feature of neglect and emotional abuse is that children are less likely than in cases of physical and sexual abuse, to recognise their carers' behaviour as abusive or, if they do recognise what is happening, they find it difficult to describe any mistreatment (Daniel et al., 2010). This is because neglect and emotional abuse are nebulous and one small but corroding incident merges into another. Therefore, a child is unlikely to be able to give a coherent account of what has been happening to them, particularly when they are very young.

Communicating with children

Children and young people communicate in a holistic way. This means that practitioners trying to find out what has been happening need to use most of their senses. A urine-soaked baby will unquestionably feel damp and also smell. The boniness and light weight of an infant or young child can be felt beneath loose-fitting clothes that may disguise malnutrition.

A note of caution, however, is that care has to be taken not to make hasty assumptions when exercising powers of observation. A young child might have an undetected disability, especially if a parent has been unable or unwilling to attend developmental checks. An infant showing visual unresponsiveness or holding her head at strange angles might have a visual impairment (Brodsky, 2010). Babies over about 9 months who seem to lack any social responsiveness, rarely gesture and do not gaze at their parents' faces might not be emotionally neglected but instead could be showing early signs of autism (Bolton et al., 2012; Ozonoff et al., 2010). A young child who seems unresponsive may have a hearing impairment, which may have developed since his newborn hearing screening (Lok et al., 2012; Lu et al., 2011).

Care also has to be exercised when working with children and families from minority groups who may not share majority norms. For example, some young people may not look directly at their parents, or maintain eye contact, not because they are cowed or have a poor relationship with their parents, but because in some cultures making eye contact with someone with a senior status is not deemed appropriate. Koramoa et al. (2002, p. 420), for example, explain that in West African culture 'as a sign of respect, a young person should not look straight into the face of an adult talking to him or her. To do so is considered rude or even confrontational.'

Bearing in mind the caveats above, the use of professional observation to assess what the child is trying to communicate is used in three ways. The first is to observe the child. For example, is there consistency between what the child is saying and her appearance and facial expression? Children with unhappy or blank, inexpressive faces who say that they are absolutely fine are probably not fine and some exploration of what is troubling them is required, although the very fact that they say they are OK may mean that they will be resistant to any further probing of their true feelings.

The second is to observe the child in context. This means that the appearance, demeanour and behaviours of a young person are observed within a particular environment. A child who is only dressed in a thin shirt and shorts in cold, wintry weather may be neglected. Account needs to be taken of the family circumstances. For example, a child from a very poor household looking for food in bins may be behaving pragmatically, supplementing the limited diet the parents can provide. However, a child from a more affluent family searching through bins for scraps of discarded food is giving out a very different message. In the case of Daniel Pelka, who was starved and beaten to death in Coventry in 2012, school teachers saw him stealing food from children in his class or scavenging food from the school dustbins (*Coventry Telegraph*, 2013). This was a clear sign that he was being inadequately fed at home.

The third way visual observation is used is to enable children to show what has happened to them or what they think about a situation. Working and communicating through play is discussed later in this chapter, but 'showing', particularly with older children and young people, can be through illustrations and symbols. For example, practitioners can produce buttons or counters. One is chosen to represent the young person, who then selects others to represent each person of significance.

Illustration: Melvin

Melvin was oppressed by domestic violence in his family. He used counters to portray his family, placing himself, his three sisters and his mother very close together with his father slightly further out. When asked what the ideal situation for him would be, he simply threw his 'father' counter across the room. He explained that this was because his father hurt his mother. When asked where his family members would be if his father could be helped to stop hurting his mother, Melvin separated out the five counters representing himself, his sisters and mother so that they were very slightly further apart and then put his father alongside them so that the family members were in a circular formation. This demonstrated that it was his father's violence rather than his father himself that Melvin rejected.

Diagrams and illustrations can also be employed. An example of a drawing used with Miranda, discussed above, is given in Figure 8.1 to illustrate this.

Figure 8.1 Illustration of a decision diagram

Overcoming barriers to communication

There are various barriers to communication but in order to undertake an effective assessment and respond to both the carers and children in neglect and emotional abuse cases these barriers, as far as possible, need to be overcome. If the child, or adult, has a disability or language issue, it is useful to prepare by talking to those who know the person well because each person is an individual with their own specific abilities.

Very young children

Younger children will not have developed full command of a language and therefore will not communicate clearly. They may also not have sufficient confidence in their skills to continue to explain or describe anything for very long, particularly if they have been neglected or emotionally abused. However, early years workers communicate with the youngest children with ease and guidance from their profession can help other child protection practitioners. The 'Mosaic Approach' (Clark and Moss, 2011) was introduced to help children aged under 5 years to give their opinion of their early years settings. It shows that practitioners should use more than one method of communication. The authors employed observation and talking to children, but also enabled children to take photographs of what they liked and disliked, used map-making of their photographs and drawings, and the children conducted them around the site showing what they thought about it. The important message of this research is that children are encouraged not just to tell, but also to show, using a variety of media.

Winter (2011), in her guide to communicating with young children, also alerts practitioners not to show shock when they describe or replay distressing and disturbing incidents. Winter's description of work with a child who was severely neglected offers excellent guidance on how insight into the reality of the child's experiences can be gained. One suggestion is the use of boxes. On the outside of the box children can stick materials or draw pictures to illustrate how they would like to be seen; on the inside of the box they can show how they feel. Alternatively, it is possible to have time shifts: how they are now on the outside and how they once were on the inside, or how they are now and how they would like to be in the future.

Children and adults with physical difficulties

It is difficult to give precise guidelines because no two people with a disability are the same. However, there are some general approaches that are applicable to some conditions. Sight-impaired children can still show and tell, but by harnessing touch. For example, they can be offered small cubes or balls covered with different materials, such as soft fluffy wool, metal foil and very fine sandpaper, which they subjectively define as feeling 'good', 'OK' and 'bad'. They can then be asked to imagine a significant person in their life and say which touch best describes the person.

Communication with children with conditions such as cerebral palsy, which might impair speech, may require the assistance of augmentative and alternative communication tools, such as talking mats, communication boards or touch pads. Similarly, with some deaf children and adults, it will be necessary to use sign language, possibly through an interpreter when there are complex issues to exchange.

The basic principles, whatever the disability of the adult or child, are to be aware, sensitive and harness empathetic imagination. For example, if children or adults depend on lip-reading, it is important to avoid mumbling or being silhouetted so that the mouth cannot be seen.

Children and adults with learning difficulties

Some people with learning difficulties also have physical problems, so account needs to be taken of any sensory impairments. When people have little or no speech, alternative tools, such as Makaton, which utilises signs and simple symbols, can be employed. For many people with learning disabilities the principle of show and tell is relevant. It is important to give clear messages so that facial expression, body language, speech and gestures all match. Giving people time to gather their thoughts and to express themselves is necessary, as is checking that what is being communicated has been understood.

People with minority languages

If people do not have command of the majority language, they are at a considerable disadvantage, but this need not be a reason to avoid communication. Again, sometimes professional interpreters have to be used, although Koprowska (2010) and Kriz and Skivenes (2010) outline the difficulties that can be encountered when using them. Children, however, can be encouraged to employ pictures and other materials to demonstrate what they want to say so that verbal exchanges are minimised.

Emotional difficulties

Children who have been neglected and emotionally abused might be very fearful of any communication. They may have become accustomed to being told to 'shut up', and have stopped drawing attention to themselves in order to minimise any aggressive and abusive response. Some might have developed selective mutism as a way of avoiding distressing situations (B.J. Young et al., 2012). Patience is needed and, initially, the children can be given toys and materials just to explore and enjoy. Then they can be encouraged to show with drawings, models, gestures and other materials. If there is selective mutism combined with a sensory disability, then the difficulties are compounded. However, they can often understand what is communicated to them and so can be encouraged to nod, shake the head and, if they have sufficient sight, to point.

Play-based work: assessment or therapeutic tool?

Play-based work is sometimes seen as a highly specialist skill that ordinary child protection practitioners cannot exercise without attending equally highly specialised training courses. There are specific types of play therapy that do need training and supervised acquisition of skills. However, as Bywater et al. (2012, p. 83) explain, 'children and young people find it easier to express themselves through creative media rather than interviews that rely on verbal interchanges'. We define this use of creative media, particularly with pre-adolescents, as 'play', and this is a normal and often essential way of communicating with children and young people.

Another aspect of using creative media is that children, like adults, have experiences and emotions that go beyond words. Words can never describe a scream and all its attendant emotions as brilliantly as the painting by Edvard Munch, 'The Scream'. As we have indicated, when assessing children and trying to understand what has happened, they may well 'describe' their experiences through pictures, models and other media such as the movement of play figures (Landreth, 2012).

As Novotny (2010) elucidates, emotionally abused children may, as a result of their maltreatment, develop communication and speech difficulties. She advocates the use of puppets, although other play and representational methods can be used. VanFleet and Faa-Thompson (2010) outline the benefits of animal-assisted play therapy. Coholic et al. (2009, 2012) demonstrated the usefulness of art-therapy in raising the self-esteem of children in foster care.

When children give descriptions of trauma, there are considerable benefits if they can follow up their descriptions in further sessions. Interviewing children for assessment purposes may start them on a therapeutic journey that can usefully be followed through until the child finds some healing. VanFleet et al. (2010), for example, describe a boy called Kirk who was suffering from post-traumatic stress. He started in a small way, crashing toy cars into each other. Then, during subsequent play therapy sessions, he built cities and scenarios which were wracked by any manner of disaster, from major road accidents to hurricanes and bombings. Eventually, the initial helplessness in the face of catastrophe started to change and an element of mastery and problem solving began to emerge, with the forces of the police and army fighting and helping to resolve the various misadventures.

Children can be helped individually or in groups and the place can be at a therapeutic centre, but nursery and school-based programmes are effective. Play-work organisations such as KidsAid in Northampton, UK, may offer play therapy, art and drama therapy, as well as Protective Behaviours work and child/adult relationship counselling. KidsAid has a play centre but also take their work out to children's schools. Mishna et al. (2012) reflect on the difficulties and benefits of school-based therapies. Problems include stigma and missed lessons for children involved in therapy sessions. However, there can be both direct benefits to the children and also indirect ones, such as changing teachers' attitudes towards sometimes 'difficult' children. Their recognition of the 'stresses the children experienced at home appeared to increase the teachers' empathy' (p. 80).

Reflecting the child's cosmos

It is helpful to know how far the child's cosmos is meeting or can meet their needs. Diagrams are particularly effective and can represent complicated histories and concepts simply and vividly. For example, it is difficult just using words to explain to a visitor to London how to travel across the city on the underground. The task is both easier and more effective if the London Underground map is used. Diagrams can be drawn from information in case records, from and with significant people in the child's life or, most importantly, created with the children themselves. It can be diagnostically interesting to ask the child and the parents to draw the same diagram separately. For example, ecomaps can show how the child is placed within their cosmos on the basis of their relationships.

Illustration: Munira

Munira, a 13-year-old, was asked to draw herself as a circle in the middle of the piece of paper and then to draw other circles around herself to indicate the significant people in her life. She was then asked to link these to her own circle with lines. Strong firm lines meant a beneficial relationship, dotted lines signified a weak one, and jagged lines denoted relationships that upset her.

Munira was being emotionally abused by both parents. They had wanted a son to carry on the family business, but her mother's ovarian cancer soon after Munira's birth meant they could not have more children, so their dream of a son vanished. They provided Munira with the physical basics to keep up the appearance of a happy family unit, but they constantly told her how useless she was and blamed her for any family misfortunes. In the past year she had attempted suicide three times and had recently described her home life to a teacher. Subsequently, a social worker asked her and her parents to draw a diagram of how they saw her relationships.

Munira's relationships

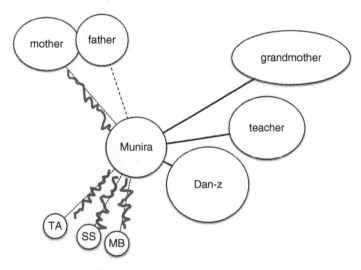

Figure 8.2 Munira's diagram

Munira drew her relationship with her father as weak and the relationship with her mother as one causing distress. Her grandmother had died three years ago and Dan-z was a well-known rap artist whom she had only seen on television and the internet. She evidently had considerable trust in her teacher because she was able to talk to him about her home life. MB, SS and TA were two girls and a boy in her class who were bullying her. The ecomap reveals an isolated child with no real friendships. If she had

(Continued)

(Continued)

not been asked to texture the lines, it might have been assumed that she had good relationships with her parents and had at least three firm school friends. Figures 8.3 and 8.4 show the diagrams drawn by Munira's parents.

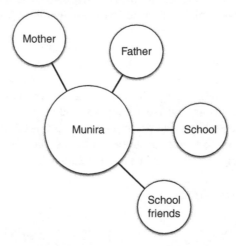

Figure 8.3   Munira's mother's diagram

Munira's mother appreciated that her daughter was relatively isolated because she could not identify any individuals other than herself and her husband who had a relationship with Munira, although she assumed she had school friends.

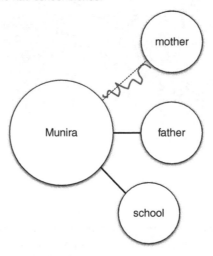

Figure 8.4   Munira's father's diagram

Munira's father understood how isolated his daughter was and recognised that the mother–daughter relationship was troubled, although he portrayed his own relationship with Munira as strong. He thought she must have some relationships at school but did not know the names of any friends or teachers.

There are very many other diagrams which can be drawn to obtain an understanding of the child's history, life and emotions. These include simple family geneograms, flow charts such as squares representing different homes and schools that a child has experienced, and roads to show where a child has come from and where they hope to go to.

Working together

One essential point made by Howe (2009, p. 180) is that 'social work is about *inter*-dependence not independence'. This is a profound statement and one which should perhaps be written large at the start of all social work textbooks. Many of the reasons for poor interagency communication are laid at the door of differing professional attitudes, language and priorities. White (2009) provides an engaging and perceptive description of the tensions between a consultant paediatrician and social workers, with the latter making 'routine ironic references to "medical power"...' (p. 103). However, there is evidence of inadequate communication even when practitioners are from the same profession. Monds-Watson et al. (2010), for example, examine the case of Madeleine O'Neill, who killed her 9-year-old daughter, Lauren, and committed suicide. One problem was differences in definitions of 'at risk' and 'in need' between different teams of social workers, such as those in the Community Mental Health Services versus those in Family and Child Care teams.

Conversely, sometimes it is when a number of different professionals hold the *same* misconceptions that difficulties arise. In the Newcombe-Buley case described in Chapter 2 (Brabbs, 2011), the fact that the adoptive parents were reasonably wealthy and both bore the title 'doctor' seems to have been an impediment to any vigorous intervention and led to a subliminal consensus between several different agencies and professionals that abuse could not exist.

In the process of assessing cases and intervening, practitioners from a range of professions and agencies will meet together in several formal forums. In child protection cases this is most likely to be in case conferences and family court proceedings.

Case conferences

Case conferences are by no means any guarantee of children's safety. Hammond (2001), in the report of the inquiry into the death of Kennedy McFarlane in Scotland, comments: 'the difficulties experienced by professionals in effectively sharing their concerns at case conferences, particularly where they conflict with others' views or where parents are present, are again a common theme' (p. 41). Furthermore, if professionals do agree, there is the danger of 'group think'. This is where group members can become overly cooperative and individuals have difficulty dissenting. As Nouwen et al. (2012, p. 2102) explain, 'opinions that are divergent from the team culture ... and/or shared opinions, are considered dumb, stupid, wrong, abnormal or even aggressive'.

Another concern about case conferences is that in England the 'family' has a right to participate. However, in reality this often means that the parents attend and, unless they are adolescent, the children do not. Baynes and Holland (2012, p. 59) noticed that 'very few children attended the initial child protection meeting, only one had completed a child consultation document and none had an advocate. In general, children's contributions were very limited.' There is the danger that the needs of the parents will dominate case conferences and any assessment will be skewed if the participation of children is not encouraged.

Nevertheless, case conferences are often an important and effective forum. A key factor in the effectiveness of case conferences is the skill of the chairperson. Individual practitioners can assist by ensuring that, if they are involved with the family, they make every effort to attend and prepare carefully so that they can deliver a succinct but informative report. Because neglect and emotional abuse can be ill-defined, it is important for practitioners in such cases to be clear about concerns prior to the conference so that their information can be conveyed with confidence.

Court proceedings

Inevitably some cases will reach family courts but, unlike sexual and physical abuse, fewer instances of neglect and emotional abuse will reach criminal court proceedings. This can be an advantage because it is easier to keep the focus on the child and plan more effectively around the child's needs when free of the necessity of obtaining uncontaminated evidence in order to achieve a successful prosecution of the perpetrators. Nevertheless, family court proceedings may be necessary to ensure the welfare of the child, and only by ensuring that the case is well founded, prepared and presented can practitioners help safeguard the child appropriately.

Spotlight on research

Masson (2012) What are care proceedings really like?

In order to discuss the realities of care proceedings in English courts, Masson drew on three research projects that she and her colleagues conducted. Masson states that 'an overwhelming conclusion in all three studies is that the process leading to care proceedings is long and tortuous' (p. 6). She explores the reasons for some of the length and complexity. One reason is the overwhelming number of people involved. For example, one mother was represented by two solicitors and three barristers. She also itemised all the other barriers, such as poor recording, poor preparation and the failure of some local authorities to support their social workers.

Masson then turns her attention to cases of neglect, commenting: 'Neglect is one of the most difficult problems for professionals to deal with because it is chronic rather than acute' (p. 9). She notes that in these cases lawyers rarely advise the parents to concede the case. She concludes by exploring ways that the system could be improved, especially to ensure that the needs of children do not become 'subsumed by an over-whelming concern with process' (p. 11).

There are lessons to take from Masson's study about the need for careful recording, preparation for court, the production of reports which are well expressed and presented without grammatical errors and, finally, an anticipation of the points other parties' solicitors might raise in order to respond to them. Nowadays there are some excellent guides for practitioners who are uncertain about court conventions and how they should present their evidence. Davis (2007) and Seymour and Seymour (2011) have both written explicitly for social workers. For medical staff, Clements et al. (2001) should prove helpful. When report writing is required, consulting Bogg (2012) and Watt (2013) is advised, and for more general writing there is Healy and Mulholland (2012). For practitioners who may be going to court themselves and who may also have to counsel children or other vulnerable witnesses, Bond and Sandhu (2005) offer sound advice.

Concluding this chapter and looking towards the next

This chapter has explored some of the issues to consider when undertaking assessments of neglect and emotional abuse. The next chapter and the following three explore interventions based on the child's cosmology.

Further resources

Barlow, J. and Schrader McMillan, A. (2010) *Safeguarding Children from Emotional Maltreatment*. London: Jessica Kingsley.

Daniel, B., Taylor, J. and Scott, J. (2011) *Recognizing and Helping the Neglected Child*. London: Jessica Kingsley.

Nichols, J. (2012) *Conducting the Home Visit in Child Protection*. Maidenhead: Open University Press.

Scaife, J. (2012) *Deciding Children's Future*. Hove: Routledge.

Books on communication include:

Dunhill, A., Elliot, B. and Shaw, A. (2009) *Effective Communication and Engagement with Children and Young People, their Families and Carers*. Exeter: Learning Matters.

Winter, K. (2011) *Building Relationships and Communicating with Young Children*. Abingdon, Oxon: Routledge.

Further details of KidsAid can be found at: www.kidsaid.org.uk/About-the-Charity

PART 3
Response

Part 3 comprises four chapters examining intervention in all aspects of a child's cosmos. It moves from attachments with close carers to work with their families and supports in their wider systems. Finally, the role of society, which can influence intervention and the prevention of neglect and emotional abuse, is explored.

9
Attachment issues

Attachment to one or more close relationships from birth is seen as the foundation for future development and the application of this concept in instances of emotional abuse and neglect is explored in this chapter.

Chapter overview

- The relevance of attachment theory
- The case of Candace Newmaker: 'attachment therapy' under scrutiny
- Theraplay
- Parent and Child Therapy in Action (PACT)
- Attachment theory in other relationships

Given what we have learnt of the damaging effects of neglect and emotional abuse on the young child's brain architecture and development, there may seem little point in intervention, especially with older children. However, the brain continues to evolve throughout the lifespan, and is dynamic, ever changing and 'plastic' in that new experiences can change its functioning. Having said that, as Karmiloff-Smith (2010, p. 938) points out, 'there is no such general thing as "the brain's plasticity"'. By this, she means that plasticity is region-specific. Furthermore, the nature of plasticity changes over time, with certain processes, such as synaptic strength, able to alter throughout the lifespan whereas others, such as myelination (the accumulation of a fatty layer, myelin, around nerve cells), are only available to the earlier developing brain.

The consequence of our increasing understanding of brain plasticity is that intervention with children to reverse the effects of neglect, in particular, is worthwhile. As we have seen, developmental damage, even at the foetal stage, can have life-long results and, because it can harm the eggs in the ovaries of the developing female foetus, even impacts on later generations. Extreme early neglect or exceptionally disrupted early attachments can result in damage which is irreversible or very difficult to reverse. However, positive experiences can do much to change the way a child's brain functions, even when they have had adverse early experiences.

The relevance of attachment theories

Attachment figures, as suggested by Bowlby (with Ainsworth, 1965), are important throughout the lifespan and have four key features (Ainsworth, 1989):

- proximity maintenance, which is a wish to be in the presence of the other;
- separation distress, when there is disruption in the relationship;
- in times of difficulty the attachment figure is a safe haven;
- the attachment figure is a secure base from which the world can be explored.

To develop satisfactorily, infants need at least one attachment figure and, although in adulthood individuals can be more independent and self-contained, there are benefits in having at least one close relative, friend or partner who can represent a centre of safety and support.

Prudence dictates that we should not espouse attachment theory uncritically. Few theories are perfect and they are designed to be questioned, tested and developed. Even if the basic tenets bear up to rigorous testing, there are often modifications or additions required to make further sense and use of the theory.

Bowlby's attachment theory was first postulated in the early 1950s in Western society. This was a time in the West when women were expected to be full-time mothers. Fathers were required to earn a wage to support his whole family. He often came home grimy and tired after long hours in heavy industry, seeking refuge in a quiet, clean home. The expectation was for a close mother–child bond, with a much more distant father–child one. Nowadays, the reality for many families throughout much of the industrialised world is for parents to share the task of financial support for the family, with child care being divided between the parents, other family members and day carers. Children might therefore have different attachment patterns from those originally perceived by Bowlby, but ones which are equally beneficial.

An aspect of attachment theory that has to be regarded with reservations is Ainsworth's classification of attachment. First, there is the question of the ethics of the Strange-Situation Procedure (SSP) experiment, which deliberately causes distress to children who cannot give informed consent and, unlike medical injections, there is no direct link between the distress caused to children and an intention to protect them from a greater harm. Furthermore, a study by Fraley and Spieker (2003) supported the idea of a continuum of attachments rather than categories of attachments. It is better to view attachment not as a 'type', which is fixed by the time a person reaches toddlerhood, but rather, as Rutter et al. (2009, p. 537) state, a model of 'a dynamic, transactional process that begins in infancy but which is influenced by later experiences'.

Nevertheless, it is possible on a continuum to create categories. For example, age is a continuum but, for convenience, we divide time into years and then link years together to create different categories of age using terms like 'infancy', 'adolescence' or 'old age'. We can therefore similarly talk about the relationship behaviour of children and adults as 'secure', 'insecure', 'disorganised' and 'disinhibited'. There is a condition called reactive attachment disorder (RAD) which is classified as a disorder in the American Psychiatric Association (2000) DSM-IV and the World Health Organization (1996) ICD-10 classification. This can be 'inhibited', where there is an absence of expected initiations of, and responses to, social interactions, or 'disinhibited', which is characterised by a lack of shyness with strangers. These labels are, however, 'constructed' and are only valid in certain contexts.

Partly because attachment categories tend to be based on patterns of behaviour, we cannot be certain that a particular group of behaviours have the same cause. It is, moreover, doubtful that the cause is inevitably the mother's degree of sensitivity. An example is the disinhibited attachment behaviour of a child with William's syndrome. These children show over-friendliness, and seem compelled to greet and interact with strangers excessively and inappropriately (Doyle et al., 2004; Klein-Tasman et al., 2007). The origins of this syndrome and its associated behaviour are a genetic abnormality caused by a deletion of genetic material from a portion of chromosome 7 (Haas et al., 2009). As well as characteristic physical features, there are cognitive ones and the disinhibited behaviour seen in people with William's syndrome is associated with functional abnormalities of the amygdala. Importantly, the deletion on chromosome 7 is a chance mutation and is not hereditary, nor is it caused by anything the mother has done either before or after her baby's birth.

There are also questions about whether the categories of attachment formulated by Ainsworth are useful beyond a description of the child's behaviour at about the age of 2 years. This is doubtful, and as Rutter et al. (2009) comment in their evaluation of attachment theory: 'Long-term longitudinal studies have clearly shown that the predictive value of SSP measurements in the infancy period is very weak' (p. 537).

Given what we know about the plasticity of the brain, children whose early life is one of disruption, neglect and abuse are not necessarily doomed to a lifetime of poor relationships. Work, particularly between the parent and child, to improve their rapport is very valuable. The dynamic and plastic nature of attachment means that if positive relationships can be developed even in later childhood and beyond, then very real benefits accrue. This chapter therefore examines therapies that attempt to improve children's attachment experiences. But before an exploration of some interesting positive developments in attachment-based therapies, the next section looks at how therapy arising from attachment theory can be misused. This is important because the history of child welfare has been riddled with the uncritical application of theory which has damaged children or has been misused by those willing to exploit and abuse children. In recent years, for example, not only was there the Pindown regime, but there was also the case of Frank Beck (Kirkwood, 1993), who gained admiration for his 'regression therapy' with children in care. The idea of regression meant he could groom children for sexual abuse by recommending cuddling them and sought opportunities to punish them physically by provoking them to have 'toddler' temper tantrums.

The case of Candace Newmaker: 'attachment therapy' under scrutiny

The term 'attachment therapy' can be used very broadly to indicate any therapy based on attachment theory. However, particularly in the USA, it refers more specifically to a type of therapy which involves holding and provoking a child to experience a range of feelings, including anger and frustration. Once the child becomes more quiescent, she experiences re-parenting by being held, cuddled and generally 'babied', such as being given a feeding bottle.

On 18 April 2000, 10-year-old Candace Newmaker was killed by two social workers in Colorado, USA, who were undertaking attachment therapy with her.

Her story starts with 16-year-old Angela, who had been labelled emotionally disturbed, had been in foster care and had given birth to a son who was removed and placed in care. The following year Angela married Todd Elmore and gave birth to Candace and then had two further children. There was domestic violence and Candace spent her third birthday in a women's refuge. Subsequently, there was an investigation when injuries were found on one of the children. All three children were taken into care and then released for adoption. Consequently, when Candace was 6 years old she was adopted by Jeanne Newmaker, a paediatric nurse.

The account of the years that followed can be seen as a combination of emotional abuse by her adoptive mother, and physical and emotional abuse through a range of therapies by medical and social work professionals. Despite reports from her schools and among her neighbourhood friends that Candace's behaviour was respectful, pleasant and sociable, her adoptive mother saw her as psychiatrically disturbed and having a 'learning disorder' (Mercer et al., 2003, p. 21).

A short while after her adoption, Candace's mother had taken her to two psychiatrists, who diagnosed attention deficit disorder (ADD) and prescribed Ritalin. This was then changed to Dexadrine and she was also given Prozac. Bear in mind that during this period Candace was aged between 6 and 8 years old. In May 1999, a psychiatrist added oppositional defiant disorder (ODD) and post-traumatic stress disorder (PTSD) to the diagnoses and she was given a further medicine, Zoloft. Other drugs, such as Tenex and Effexor, medication for depression and anxiety disorders, were tried. A possible diagnosis of bipolar disorder was then suggested and Candace given an antipsychotic drug, Risperdal.

Towards the end of 1998, Jeanne Newmaker attended a workshop held at the Guildford Attachment Centre in North Carolina and learnt about reactive attachment disorder (RAD). Candace was diagnosed with the disorder and was subjected to attachment therapy at the Guildford centre. She was held over the therapist's lap, immobilised, her face grabbed and she was shouted at to obey commands (Mercer et al., 2003). Candace's behaviour became worse, so her mother took her to an Attachment Centre in Colorado on 10 April 2000. As well as the attachment therapy she had experienced at the Guildford centre, she was subjected to compression therapy, where her mother laid on top of her and licked her face. On 18 April, Candace was forced to take part in a re-birthing, with the idea that she would be born again as her adoptive mother's true child. She was wrapped tightly in a red sheet, had pillows on top of her, and the adults pressed against these to simulate vaginal contractions. For 40 minutes Candace struggled, choked and screamed that she could not breathe. For the next 30 minutes she made no sound. When the therapists eventually unwrapped her, she was dead. She had been suffocated.

Having looked at what can go wrong, we now provide two examples of attachment-based therapies that are being used ethically and to good effect: Theraplay and PACT. They are by no means the only therapies effectively using attachment theory. They are two with which we have some links, and therefore have understanding and knowledge of the ethical and reflective approach of some of the practitioners using the methods described.

Theraplay

The origins of Theraplay lie in the Headstart programme, which aimed to help disadvantaged young children in the USA. In 1967, Ann Jernberg set out to develop a programme which could be implemented by specifically trained professionals and paraprofessionals to provide children with the ingredients that Jernberg identified as constituting 'good-enough' parenting. She saw that the essential ingredients were:

- *Structure*: setting boundaries to provide emotional security
- *Engagement*: to increase a child's feeling of being a unique individual
- *Nurture*: this includes calming and soothing touching
- *Challenge*: to enhance feelings of competence

Unlike some therapies, it is avowedly directive, with the therapist being responsible for the management of sessions. However, both child and carer are involved in the therapy. There is an emphasis on play and fun rather than on intense verbal exchanges. It is designed to be of relatively short-term duration. A major feature is that it can be used in very many different situations. Because it is about fun, play, touching but limited verbal exchanges, it is particularly appropriate with babies and young children (Munns, 2008). Equally, Jernberg (1988) reports using Theraplay effectively in a residential setting with a 92-year-old emotionally distressed woman. Other studies have established its effectiveness with older people in South Korea (Kim, 2011).

So often articles mention 'parents' and mean 'mothers'. However, Theraplay can be a valuable approach with fathers and their children. Sherman (2009) writes about sessions with father–son dyads and describes the dyads mirroring each other, which leads to the fathers appearing to be more in tune with their sons. The intervention can also be used with adoptive and foster carers.

Theraplay can be adapted to a wide range of cultures and is appropriate in multi-cultural environments. Atkinson (2009), for example, suggests a game for ethnically diverse populations where coloured paper is distributed to children in a Theraplay group and the children choose a sheet matching their skin colour, help each other to draw around their hands and then discuss the varieties of skin colour in the group. Theraplay can be effective in Eastern as well as Western cultures. For example, Siu (2009) has evaluated its effectiveness in China because, as she explains, 'interpersonal harmony is an important characteristic of Chinese communication. Emotional restraint and indirect communication, as opposed to confrontation, are often preferred' (p. 9).

There are a number of evaluations which demonstrate the effectiveness of Theraplay (e.g. Wettig et al., 2011). However, good therapeutic ideas can be hijacked by people wanting to earn money, kudos or power by misusing them. Therefore, although Theraplay is meant to be accessible to professionals from a range of professions, attempts are made to ensure that practitioners are properly informed and trained (Theraplay Institute, 2013).

Parent and Child Therapy in Action (PACT)

There is some confusion about the use of the acronym PACT because there are several organisations and projects that claim it as their own, such as a family support charity called PACT Parents and Children Together (2013) inaugurated in the Diocese of Oxford and, indeed, the PACT Animal Sanctuary in Norfolk, England.

Parent and Child Therapy in Action (PACT) was developed in New Zealand by Heather Chambers, a psychotherapist who observed how mothers enjoyed looking at their new babies. As currently practised, this is a therapy used by qualified practitioners who have experience of working with children whose behaviour is so concerning that they tend to attract psychiatric labels. It focuses on the mother–child relationship and is designed for use with children aged between 4 and 12 years. It is suitable when other therapeutic attempts appear to have failed. It covers a relatively lengthy period, comprising over 20 sessions plus a follow-up appointment several months later. It also demands considerable resources, including the attendance of two therapists for all this time, plus a play room and a parent's room divided from the playroom by a one-way screen (Allison et al., 2006).

A feature of PACT therapy is that it is structured around four stages. First, there is the *Parallel Parent Child Narrative*, when the mother and child, supported by a therapist, each try to identify the good intentions of each other. The second stage is *Preparing to Look*. Here the child is in the playroom with a therapist and the mother is in an adjoining room. She can see her child through a one-way screen but she does not need to watch him and the child can pull a curtain across the screen. The third stage is *Looking before Doing*. The mother now spends half the session looking at her child through the screen, although the child can still shut the curtain. For the other half of the session, the child and mother receive therapy separately. The final stage *Looking After* is when the mother joins the child in the playroom to care for him directly and the child is able to try out new ways of relating to his mother.

Illustration: Susan and Kevin

Amos et al. (2007) present the therapy in the form of a case study. The mother, Susan, became pregnant when she was 17 years old and received no support from either the child's father and his family or her own family. She had suffered considerable emotional abuse and neglect at the hands of her alcohol- and gambling-addicted parents. Just before her pregnancy with her son, Kevin, she contracted glandular fever, which left her with chronic fatigue syndrome and post-natal depression until Kevin was aged about 2 years. Consequently, Kevin was left alone for many hours. During this time they suffered extreme instability and poverty. Then Susan formed a partnership which turned out to be violent and abusive, although she eventually managed to escape with Kevin to a women's shelter.

Kevin, meanwhile, had become an angry, bewildered child who not only attacked his mother but was out of control in school. He was offered considerable support, including one-to-one supervision in school, a group for children who witness domestic violence, and specialist behavioural support. Susan and Kevin together were offered parent effectiveness training and behaviour management strategies. The situation continued to worsen, which is when the therapeutic team decided to propose PACT. Amos et al. (2007) then describe and analyse the process through the sessions of the PACT therapy, which seemed at last to offer Susan and Kevin a resolution of their relationship issues.

The case descriptions of PACT involve the mother–child dyad and Amos et al. (2011) explore why mothers who have been abused can become predominantly emotionally abusive and neglectful. However, PACT could work well when there are relationship difficulties between any of a child's main carers, including fathers, and it could potentially help long-term foster carers and adoptive parents.

Attachment theory in other relationships

There are instances of children who are neglected and abused by their mothers but who do not display distressed behaviours, appear to make loving parents and bring up children who appear to have few problems. One answer to this is that children manage to form attachments to alternative protectors. One of the most important yet often overlooked relationships is an attachment to a sibling.

Attachments to siblings

Children can form attachments to other people where parents are unavailable. There is evidence that siblings, especially twins, can become attachment figures and support each other during adversity (Ainsworth, 1989; Fraley and Tancredy, 2012; Samek and Rueter, 2011). The case of Muriel and Sylvia, the sisters we first encountered in Chapter 6, illustrates how a sibling can become an alternative attachment figure.

Illustration: Sylvia and Muriel

Muriel was the fourth of five sisters, and 'a disappointment'. Her parents had desperately wanted a son. Muriel's birth was a difficult one because she was a large baby and became a rather stolid, ungainly child. The fifth daughter was petite and pretty and, despite her being yet 'another disappointment', both parents were enchanted by her whereas they rejected Muriel. The family was wealthy and as each daughter reached 7 years old they attended boarding school. However, Muriel was sent off to school when she was 4 years old. The boarding school catered for girls aged 4–18 years. This meant that for many years she was in the same school as her sisters.

Muriel did not get on with her younger sister but had good relationships with her three older ones. Sylvia, the second eldest daughter, had always felt especially close to Muriel from the time she was born. Sylvia looked after and protected her younger sister both at home and at school. She left school aged 18 years. Therefore, despite being academically able, Muriel insisted on leaving school when she was 16 and moved into a flat with Sylvia. Eventually, Muriel became independent, trained as a nurse, gathered around her a good group of friends and had her own family. As a parent she was able to bond with her children and nurture them with affection.

Relevance in adoption and fostering

With reference to the above section, one essential aspect of fostering and adoption which, until recently, was often overlooked is the importance of assessing the degree of attachments between siblings and, where there is any strength of attachment, ensuring that the children are placed together. This should not just be a desirable objective '*if* we can find foster carers prepared to take more than one child', but should be an absolutely essential prerequisite. Arguably, it could be better for closely bonded siblings to remain in residential care together rather than being separated into different adoptive or foster ones. This is particularly true in the case of twins, where there is evidence that they are likely to be strong attachment figures for each other (Fraley and Tancredy, 2012).

The second aspect relates to children's ability to attach to foster and adoptive carers when they have suffered a considerable degree of neglect and emotional abuse.

There is mounting evidence that this is possible, even when the children had no original attachment figure. Much of the current evidence is from studies of children from Eastern European institutions who have been adopted by parents in both their own country and abroad. One of the complications of this research is that some children also suffered from malnutrition and lack of stimulation before and during their time in the institutions. Other children from institutions might have had enough nutrition in terms of calories, and therefore their growth initially appears normal, but might have had a restricted diet in terms of nutrients (Sonuga-Barke et al., 2008). Disentangling the impact on brain development of the various deprivations, including basic nutritional ones, is challenging. Therefore, that which pertains specifically to attachment is difficult to establish. Nevertheless, there is evidence to show that later high-quality caregiving can largely compensate for early neglect and deprivation.

Spotlight on research

McGoron et al. (2012) Recovering from early deprivation.

Rutter et al. (2007) Effects of profound early institutional deprivation.

The McGoron et al. (2012) study looks at 136 children abandoned at or shortly after birth by their parents. They were recruited from six institutional care settings in Bucharest, Romania. Children with conditions such as foetal alcohol syndrome were excluded. The selected children either remained in institutional care or were placed with foster or adoptive parents and some returned to their birth families. The quality of the caregiving they received was evaluated at 30 months using assessment factors such as their caregivers' sensitivity, their stimulation of the child's development and the degree of positive regard for the child. The children were tested at 30, 42 and 54 months old. Those children, whatever their setting, who were given high-quality care showed far fewer cognitive, behavioural and emotional difficulties at 54 months than those with lower quality care. The authors conclude that this attests to the plasticity of the young child's brain because although many suffered deprivation and lack of attachment for much of their early life up to 30 months, those with subsequent high-quality care made good progress.

Similarly, Rutter et al. (2007) assessed, at ages 6 and 11 years old, 144 children who had spent their earliest years in Romanian institutions and 21 Romanian non-institutionalised children adopted by UK parents before the age of 42 months, plus 52 non-institutionalised UK-born children adopted by UK parents before they reached 6 months old. In all three samples, the children had suffered a substantial level of physical and psychological neglect prior to their adoption. By the age of 11 years, children adopted before they were 6 months old were showing fewer problems. In general, the majority of children made good developmental and emotional progress. Rutter et al. (2007, p. 340) comment that the children's improved 'psychological functioning post-adoption provides a powerful testimony' to the importance of the care given by the adoptive families.

Concluding this chapter and looking towards the next

This chapter has looked at the relevance of the immediate attachments and interventions based on attachment theories. The next chapter moves out a little further into the child's cosmos to explore working with the child's family.

Further resources

Books on attachment theory include:

Howe, D. (2011) *Attachment Theory across the Lifecourse*. Basingstoke: Palgrave Macmillan.
Pearce, C. (2009) *A Short Introduction to Attachment and Attachment Disorder*. London: Jessica Kingsley.
Shemmings, D. and Shemmings, Y. (2011) *Understanding Disorganised Attachment*. London: Jessica Kingsley.
The Theraplay Institute can be accessed on: www.theraplay.org

10

Family support and intervention

This chapter focuses on intervention with families because the family is integral to any consideration of the child's welfare, even when it is a small one.

Chapter overview

- Defining 'family'
- Working with families
- Working with marginalised families
- Looked-after children

Defining 'family'

The family is here defined as the unit of carers and close relationships in the child's cosmos that surround the developing child. Some children may have more than one family or one family divided into several units, as in the case of parents who divorce and have shared care. Furthermore, as Stobart (2009) explains, in many cultures 'the head female in the household is called "mother", and the head male "father"; other adults are called "aunties" or "uncles"...' (p. 158).

One concern is that sometimes fathers are excluded from therapeutic work. Fathers have both a right and a responsibility for being engaged in cases of emotional abuse and neglect, and guidelines for involving fathers is given in Cabrera and Tamis-Lemonda (2013).

When undertaking direct work with children, a valuable strategy is to ask them to describe their 'family' using drawing, play figures or moulding clay. This can lead to some unexpected revelations, such as Cody (p. 57), who was unable to identify a coherent family unit but rather drew a disjointed mass of acquaintances.

Practitioners also need to be aware of the significant role that members of extended families can play. There are children with no apparent extended family, like Emer, who, when asked to draw her family, outlined her mother and four dogs which she described as her 'brothers'. We investigated whether there were other relatives, but could find none. On the other hand, there may be very dominant and important grandparents or a plethora of uncles, aunts and cousins who all play a part in the child's cosmos, as Vernon's story illustrates.

CASE STUDY

Vernon

Vernon was the elder of two half-brothers. His mother and step-father, the father of his brother, were white British. Vernon's birth father, who had worked as a 'bouncer' and had been killed trying to intervene in a nightclub brawl, was black British. Vernon's father had been brought up in care and had no known close relatives.

Vernon's mother and step-father loved both boys but they worked long hours in poorly paid jobs and so the boys were looked after for much of the time by their extended family. Both Vernon's maternal relatives and those of his step-father rejected him because they held racist attitudes and he had inherited his father's black skin and features. When he was in their care, they were emotionally abusive, using extreme racist terms which cannot be recorded here. They constantly compared him unfavourably with his younger brother.

REFLECTION

What intervention might help Vernon? How useful would it be to try to challenge the racist attitudes of the relatives? Would confronting the relatives have positive results for Vernon? Is there any strategy that would directly help Vernon?

COMMENT

It is unlikely that any forceful confrontation of the relatives would achieve anything other than a reinforcement of their views, although some non-aggressive challenge to their racist views is indicated. Deep-seated prejudices are usually hard to change, but they can be helped to understand that although some of Vernon's personality and features are inherited from his father, approximately half of these are inherited from his mother. Therefore, to reject Vernon is also to reject his mother.

One strategy would be to discuss the issues with Vernon's parents and, even if they could not change either the child care arrangements or their relatives' attitudes, they might be able to identify other people in Vernon's life who could give him positive affirmation and a favourable image of his father.

A second strategy might be to find a black mentor for Vernon to provide him with a positive role model and to explore positive aspects of his identity. Garraway and Pistrang (2010) described and evaluated a project with African-Caribbean boys aged 12–17 who were allocated a mentor, i.e. an adult who was not a relative, but who provided guidance and encouragement to the young people.

Working with families

There is no one appropriate way of working with families and intervention can vary from intensive psychodynamic family therapy to a complex web of provisions tackling different aspects of family problems. Alternatively, a straightforward, single therapy may be enough to resolve a particular problem that is causing a myriad of difficulties that are out of proportion to the underlying issue. One chapter cannot outline in any depth all the various family interventions. The United Nations (UNODC, 2010) has produced an ebook reviewing various forms of family work around the world, which can provide insight and suggestions about ways of working. There are also detailed descriptions of family intervention, such as Long et al.'s (2012) report about the Action for Children's intensive support programme for families where children are neglected. Macdonald (2005) discussed interventions in neglect cases, including cognitive behavioural programmes and family therapy. In this chapter, rather than list initiatives, we look at some of the key family-related issues that relate to emotional abuse and neglect and suggest some intervention approaches which can help to address these issues.

The case of Paul, summarised in Chapter 2, shows how ineffective even relatively intensive family work can be if practitioners fail to analyse the family dynamics, largely ignore the emotional welfare of the children and respond reactively rather than taking the initiative and intervening proactively. The social services were involved for 15 years. However, social work activity was largely providing financial and material help for the parents and preserving a relationship with them that even the practitioners described as 'superficial but better than none' (Bridge Child Care Consultancy Services, 1993, p. 49).

Using a SLOT analysis

Professional values include identifying and developing strengths, but the 'rule of optimism' and overly sanguine perspectives have to be avoided. One way of assessing families is by undertaking a SLOT analysis. This was developed as a management tool for analysing organisations in which the strengths, weaknesses, opportunities and threats of organisations are identified. In a SLOT analysis, the terms 'strengths', '*limitations*', 'opportunities' and 'threats' are preferred. When working with families, the idea is to build on strengths, minimise limitations, grasp opportunities and develop strategies to cope with threats. An example of its use is given in the case study below.

The Green family

Table 10.1 Composition of the Green family

Father	Alan	38 years
Step-mother	Emily	26 years
Subject child	**Myra**	11 years
Half-brother	Oliver	5 years
Half-sister	Tilly	5 years
Step-maternal grandmother	Reine	56 years
Step-maternal aunt	Coral	30 years

The Green family were relatively wealthy and had few financial stresses. Myra's mother had died of an overdose when Myra was 4 years old. Myra's maternal grandparents blamed Alan for his wife's death and would have nothing to do with him or his daughter. Alan himself had no siblings and his parents lived abroad. Myra was not helped to understand what had happened to her mother, and in his grief Alan had emotionally neglected her. Shortly after Myra's fifth birthday, her father married Emily, who was unable to bond with Myra. A year later twins, Oliver and Tilly, were born (see Table 10.1 for the composition of the Green family).

Alan and Emily plus Emily's widowed mother, who moved into the home, increasingly denigrated Myra. The only relative to develop a fondness for her was her step-aunt, Coral. After a series of suicide attempts by Myra, a child psychiatrist and social worker became involved. They identified the emotional abuse and neglect of Myra as well as unresolved mourning in both Alan and his daughter. The social worker engaged the parents and Myra in creating a SLOT analysis (see Table 10.2). Oliver, Tilly and Reine also joined them for some of the sessions.

Table 10.2 The Green family SLOT analysis

	Internal	External
Positive	**Strengths** • No financial stresses • Good standard of accommodation • Home in good social environment • Coral, aunt, very fond of Myra • Tilly and Oliver happy to be with Myra	**Opportunities** • Myra starting secondary school • Continuing help from family specialists • Bereavement counselling available for both Alan and Myra
Negative	**Limitations** • Adults in household united in their negative attitudes to Myra • No support from Myra's grandparents • Myra herself extremely dejected, angry and confused • Alan still feels some guilt about his first wife's death	**Threats** • Myra's primary school tending to label Myra 'a problem' • Myra starting secondary school • General financial downturn; family income might diminish

Sometimes points are put in more than one section. In this instance, Myra's move to a secondary school could be an opportunity for her to divest herself of the 'problem' label and have a positive, fresh start. However, a new school is another emotional challenge for Myra and the negative label could follow her from one school to the next. Therefore, starting a new school could be an opportunity if Myra is helped to cope with the changes and her new school is willing to support and encourage her; it could, however, be a threat if the transition is not made successfully.

Examine the points in the four sections of the SLOT analysis in Table 10.2. Then, one by one, determine how the family could be helped to capitalise on the strengths and opportunities, improve the limitations, and minimise the impact of any threats.

REFLECTION

There are neither obvious solutions nor any clearly 'right' or 'wrong' answers. There are some interventions which can help, such as working with the schools to ensure that Myra's transition to secondary school is as smooth as possible. Building a relationship with her aunt Coral may help to raise Myra's self-esteem. Exploration with Alan of his relationships with his own parents and those of Myra's mother may reveal whether or not Myra could establish links with her grandparents. Direct work with Myra can also help her to make sense of her life.

COMMENT

Working with marginalised families

There is evidence that emotional abuse is more likely to occur in families where there are several sources of stress (Doyle, 1997a). There are families with specific needs because they belong to groups which are marginalised in society. These include black and minority ethnic (BME) families, those where the parents suffer from mental ill-health, those with children with disabilities, traveller families, and the very poor and dispossessed. In some areas, single parents or same-gender parents might be socially shunned or excluded or find that mainstream services do not meet their needs. Children in these families are not necessarily abused. However, if maltreatment occurs, then meeting the requirements of both parents and children is often challenging. Similarly, marginalised families who are struggling to cope might not receive the help and support they require to prevent child neglect and emotional abuse.

In the UK, there are initiatives to ensure the inclusion of some of these groups. For example, the Children's Society (2013) and the Afiya Trust have together developed Engage, a web-based toolkit which helps to address the barriers that BME young carers face when accessing services. This is particularly welcome because children and young people who act as carers for family members can find their needs neglected and suffer a form of inadvertent emotional abuse. The situation is compounded if they come from BME families because all too often there can be obstacles, such as language, unfamiliar cultural practices and the absence of services which really meet their needs.

Families and substance misuse

Parents can function as loving carers even if they are addicted to alcohol or other drugs. However, as Forrester and Harwin (2008, 2011) point out, it is the families in which alcohol is part of a complex interplay of factors that are most likely to be referred to welfare agencies. They highlight how an assessment of the parents is skewed if the substance abuse is minimised as a subsidiary problem to all the other complexities faced by disadvantaged families. They also point to the problem of inadequate responses to the very real problems faced by children in these families if professionals avoid acting because they believe they are making moral judgements about the parents' behaviour. Uncontrolled and excessive consumption of alcohol and other substances by parents can lead to the neglect and emotional abuse of their children and, if there is evidence of abuse, then the substance use issues need to be addressed. Kroll and Taylor (2003) assert that while there has to be a holistic view of the family problems, the approach has to highlight the effect of the parental behaviour on the children.

Parents with physical ill-health or disability

There are parents who have readily identifiable health problems yet meet their children's needs despite conditions such as sensory impairment or mobility limitations. However, parental disability and poor health are often associated with poverty because of barriers to employment and the added costs of the condition. For example, it is more difficult for parents who use a wheelchair to go quickly around several different shops to find the cheapest bargains. This section examines, by way of exemplars, conditions such as dental decay, anaemia and hypothyroidism.

Stevenson (2007) provides an example of a young mother who was very fearful of dentists; consequently, her teeth and those of her son were in a parlous state. Decaying teeth, although perhaps considered a minor problem, can be incapacitating. First, there is the constant physical pain which can profoundly affect mood. Taking painkillers to dampen the pain costs money that a poor family cannot afford and can have adverse side-effects. Eating healthy foods, such as fruit, nuts and salad vegetables, is challenging, while there is undue sensitivity to very hot or cold food and therefore diets become restricted. This can in turn lead to a loss of appetite and consequent loss of energy and general physical well-being. Decaying teeth can lead to isolation. The person does not want to smile broadly, may have difficulty speaking, may worry about bad breath and be reluctant to take meals with others. The family presented by Stevenson (2007, p. 70) was attending a centre and, as she comments, the 'work at the centre included dealing with [the tooth decay] as a priority'.

Anaemia is due to the diminished ability of the bone marrow to produce enough red blood cells and/or their accelerated destruction and loss (Smith, 2012). For some people, a diet that is inadequate in available iron, excessive alcohol or heavy menstrual bleeding can be the reasons for anaemia. However, the condition can signify an underlying pathology, such as coeliac disease or bowel cancer. The symptoms of anaemia vary but often it causes tiredness, lethargy and a general lack of energy. Children, particularly younger ones, require reasonably alert, active parents. Undiagnosed anaemia means that coping with work is difficult, resulting in unemployment and the subsequent loss of living standards and poverty. Balarajan et al. (2011, p. 2124) note that there is a close association between maternal and child anaemia. Children with substantial iron deficiency in infancy 'score lower on measures of mental and motor functioning and are at risk for long-lasting developmental disadvantages, such as learning difficulties and socioemotional problems' (Pala et al., 2010, p. 434). Relatively straightforward treatment for anaemia for family members and dietary guidance for parents can result in a marked improvement in what seem to be neglecting families.

Other conditions also cause not only parental ill-health, pain and loss of energy, but, if present in the mother, lead to difficult pregnancies, birth complications and children with disabilities. Therefore, parents who are already disadvantaged by illness have children who require particularly skilful and energetic nurture. When working with black families, it is worth bearing in mind that people with an African inheritance can suffer from sickle-cell disease (SCD), involving episodes of acute illness and progressive damage to the organs (Bölke and Scherer, 2012; Rees et al., 2010). For mothers with SCD, there are concerns that taking oral contraceptives can increase the physical complications, although Haddad et al. (2012) report that this is unlikely. There is, however, a greater likelihood of complications in pregnancy, including pre-eclampsia, lung disease, and heart disease in the mother, emergency caesareans and low weight or premature babies (Barfield et al., 2010; Chase et al., 2010). All these added stresses can adversely influence bonding and the mother's ability to cope with parenthood. Good pre-natal care and monitoring by health professionals can help minimise any complications. One concern is that women who have been trafficked illegally or are seeking asylum may not obtain the pre-natal care they need.

The signs of maternal hypothyroidism can be suggestive of neglect. An underactive thyroid can develop slowly so may not be readily recognised, but the sufferer will generally become increasingly tired, overweight and have difficulties sleeping, remembering and concentrating. Hair loss, low libido and heavy periods can add to the difficulties. The infants of women with hypothyroidism can show signs of developmental delay (Henrichs et al., 2010; Smit et al., 2000).

Hormone-replacement tablets and good antenatal care can resolve what might appear to be a complex neglect case.

Parents with mental health issues

There are very many parents who have mental health issues with no adverse effects on their children, especially if they can rely on their health professionals and have support from other adult members of their family. However, this does not mean that where parents are well supported, the children should be ignored or excluded. An example of problems which can occur is provided by Rowena, who as a young girl overhead her father, who had schizophrenia, telling his mother that he was to be a 'guinea pig', leading her to believe that he was to be turned into a small animal. Rowena became deeply distressed but because she knew she should not have over-heard 'adult business', she felt guilty for having listened to the conversation and was unable to share her distress with anyone. This shows how important it is for adults to give children age-appropriate information. More importantly, children need to feel that they can ask questions without meeting with anger or their concerns being brushed aside.

Reupert et al. (2006) explored statistical estimates of parental illness from a range of countries throughout Europe, Australia and North America, and estimated that about one in five families have at least one parent with a mental ill health issue. Many studies show an association between parents with mental health issues and children with difficulties (Baulderstone et al., 2012; Gladstone et al., 2006). However, the severity of the mental health problem is not correlated to the severity of the difficulties. Often there are other stresses, such as poverty, unemployment, racism and isolation, associated with mental ill-health, therefore children may equally be psychologically damaged by those other factors.

Post-partum psychosis, usually in the form of post-natal depression, causes concerns (Oates, 2003; Oates et al., 2004). This is because of the risk of attachment problems if mothers are only able to provide mechanical caring for their infants and severe depression may lead to substantial neglect. Barr (2008) suggests that 10–15 per cent of mothers suffer from post-natal depression.

Baulderstone et al. (2012) explore ways in which GPs can help families where there is parental mental illness, including post-natal depression. Many of their suggestions are useful for other child protection workers. For example, they recommend enhancing insight without increasing stigma and explain this can be done by providing appropriate information, discussing the strengths and resources the parent has, and explaining that they are not alone in that many parents have conditions such as arthritis which make parenting a greater challenge. Rather than supplying the parents with suggestions, the advice is to encourage them to explore their own solutions to problems that arise. They also recommend trying to engage the children and, with older children, guiding them towards helpful websites and resources.

Despite the importance of not increasing stigma, child protection practitioners need to recognise that sometimes parental mental ill-health contributes to the neglect or emotional abuse of their children, as the following case study illustrates.

Illustration: Reheela

Reheela was the daughter of Aisha and Andy. Aisha's relatives lived far away but Andy's mother and father, Edna and Eric, lived locally. Andy, like his father, was a long-distance lorry driver, so was away for long periods of time. Shortly after Reheela was born, Aisha seemed very keen to hand over her care to Edna. Reheela did not seem to be putting on much weight and appeared an unhappy baby.

Edna and Eric, both experienced parents, were concerned about how thin Reheela was. Edna's close neighbour was a retired health visitor. She had some scales and weighed Reheela when she arrived to stay with her grandmother for a few days and again just before she left to go home. They realised that Reheela put on weight while at her grandparents and lost some when she went home. The neighbour alerted the family GP practice. Reheela was referred to hospital for investigations and Aisha admitted that she had not been feeding Reheela. She explained that during pregnancy she had become obsessed with cleanliness and desperately anxious about any dirt. She subsequently found changing Reheela's nappies repulsed her. To avoid dirty nappies, she was starving her daughter. Aisha was diagnosed with post-natal depression and an obsessive compulsive disorder (OCD).

The family rallied around Aisha. Andy arranged to change Reheela's nappies whenever he was at home. The grandparents agreed to look after Reheela on a routine basis and at other times Edna visited to help with nappy changing. Meanwhile, Aisha received therapy and counselling for her depression and OCD. This was designed to help her cope not only with the nappy changing, but also later with toilet-training and the messy toddler stage. Andy was also helped to understand his wife's difficulties so that he could support her appropriately.

This was a case of mental health problems which, had Aisha been an isolated lone parent, could have had disastrous consequences. However, intervention mostly by the family and supplemented by skilled therapeutic help meant that the problem was resolved satisfactorily.

Bereavement in the family

Loss in general can cause stress and suffering in the family. In focusing on bereavement, we are not dismissing the effects of the loss of a partner through divorce, which can also be deeply troubling. Similarly, when parents experience redundancy and job loss there can be negative effects on the family. However, with bereavement, any hope is extinguished; the beloved person is lost, never to be seen, held or embraced ever again. The only positive prospect is that the bereaved person will find a new way of living without the person who has died.

For parents, the loss of a partner, particularly where the partner is also the children's parent, can be profound because it involves a complete change of lifestyle. On a purely practical front, there is so much that has to be managed – telling the children and all the family acquaintances, managing the finances, arranging the funeral, plus sorting out probate. Childcare arrangements might have to be altered if the couple shared these or care was provided by the deceased parent.

Although there are fewer practical issues when a child in the family dies, the emotional impact can be profound. Most parents have strong, protective and nurturing feelings towards their children and if a child dies, then the challenge to these emotions can be devastating and can leave a parent completely numb or overwhelmingly depressed. Parents expect to die before their children and therefore the natural order is turned on its head. Even comparatively simple tasks, such as answering the box on a form that says 'Number of children', can be unbearably poignant. In families of more than one child, there is the problem of how to tell the dead child's siblings about the death and worries about their well-being.

For an adult, the eventual death of one's own parents has to be expected and many people can cope with equanimity, particularly if their parents live into old age and have had, in the expression of one older person, 'a good innings'. However, if a beloved parent dies when comparatively young or in tragic circumstances, then the impact can be devastating.

While there are no simple solutions to significant bereavements, there are supportive resources, such as Cruse or Winston's Wish, for all members of the family, and counselling and therapy can be helpful.

Parents lacking knowledge and understanding

Sometimes neglect and emotional abuse can occur because the parents simply lack knowledge of child development and how to run a household. This might be due to over-protection or infantilisation in the parents' own childhoods. Moreover, nowadays few families are large so that children do not learn about child development by watching younger siblings or the offspring of older siblings grow up. If young parents do not have knowledgeable friends and relatives to guide them or are unable to learn readily from books, then even good parental instincts may not be a match for the demands of parenthood. This is especially true if the parents are isolated and have other pressures in life, such as poor accommodation and financial stresses.

One group of parents who may be at a particular disadvantage are ones brought up in care, especially if they were not placed in affectionate foster homes. Some have grown up with no loving supportive relatives and might have spent long periods in institutions where there were no opportunities to learn skills such as cooking or how to manage finances. Rutter and Quinton (1984), for example, reported that the outcomes for women from London who grew up in institutions were worse than a matched group who had remained at home. However, even those who experienced institutional care fared comparatively well if they had supportive partners in adulthood. Fortunately, because provision for looked-after children has changed in the UK from large residential institutions to foster care or to smaller units where 'independent living' can be taught, parents struggling because they have had no learning or nurturing opportunities while in care are now less frequent.

A similar disadvantage, however, is experienced by children who remained at home but in chaotic, neglectful and poorly managed households where the only models they were presented with was poor child care, unsafe home environments and very low standards of hygiene and home comfort. For these parents, a period of skill learning, especially through family centres, is helpful.

Another group which is at a disadvantage are parents with substantial learning or intellectual disabilities. As with all parents, how well they cope with the demands of parenthood depends on how much support they have and how complicated their environment is. Therefore, a mother with learning disabilities who can live with others who are able to support her, provide a warm, comfortable home, help with finances and provide acceptable guidance and advice will have few difficulties. However, parents who do not have such advantages may struggle more than most.

Illustration: Tara

Karen and Martin were a couple in their 30s with a 2-year-old daughter, Tara. Both parents were designated 'learning disabled'. They had no relatives nearby. With midwife, health visitor and family worker support they had coped well with Tara as a baby and clearly adored her. However, as she became a toddler they needed substantial advice about safety and started to struggle a little. Local changes meant that the family had both a new health visitor and family worker and neither visited regularly. Neighbours reported that they had not seen Tara, but had heard her crying. A social worker visited and when he asked to see Tara he found that she was very thin and pale and was being kept in a poorly furnished back bedroom that was devoid of toys and had torn wallpaper.

A sensitive and careful investigation revealed that when Tara was a baby, the parents followed the family worker's advice on how to stimulate her. However, as she reached toddlerhood they did not know how to look after her. Neither parent had any memory of playing as children, nor did they know where to look for advice. Tara became bored and had started to be destructive, picking at wallpaper, finding scissors and cutting furnishings, and getting into food cupboards and then making a mess with cooking ingredients. Her parents had started to lock her in her bedroom for longer and longer periods, partly to keep her safe and partly to stop her from damaging the rest of the house.

A play worker was designated to help them. They went to a therapeutic centre where they were able to watch Tara interacting with the play worker. The help also continued in the family home, where the play worker demonstrated how the parents

(Continued)

(Continued)

could interact with Tara and keep her occupied at home with simple, cheap materials. After a few weeks of play work there was a dramatic difference in Tara, who was now clearly thriving. It was recognised that as she developed her parents would continue to need guidance on how to devise interesting experiences for her, although as she grew older the parents' efforts could be supplemented by nursery and school.

Countering domestic violence

When there are children in the family, domestic abuse is not just an issue for the partners; it is a family affair and a form of psychological abuse of the children. Eriksson (2011), commenting on the response to domestic violence in Sweden, notes that the children in these situations are witness, victim and competent participant. Each of these roles has interlacing but different requirements that need to be addressed. They might be witnesses in ensuing court proceedings and so need to be supported in that light. If not formal witnesses, they will still need opportunities to describe what they have experienced, to be believed and to be helped to reconcile any divided loyalties. As victims, they may be suffering from post-traumatic stress or the Stockholm syndrome, with all the impacts on their emotions and mind that these conditions imply. In any event, they will need opportunities to resolve the feelings of fear, helplessness, guilt, and even shame that victimisation produces. As participants, they have the right for their views to be heard and to contribute to decisions about their family and their own lives.

The other feature of domestic violence which relates to the emotional abuse of children is that there seems to be less of a response in terms of offers of service where the violence is verbal and does not involve a direct physical assault (Stanley et al., 2011a, 2011b).

A longstanding response to domestic violence has been the provision of refuges, so that a woman can leave the abusive situation with her children and has somewhere to go. Refuges tend to do more than simply accommodate women. First, they will provide safety and security by ensuring the refuges are hidden from the perpetrators. For this reason, in Ireland only one traveller woman is accommodated at a time so that the escaping wife will not find herself accommodated with a member of her husband's family who might disclose her whereabouts (Allen, 2012). Depending on their available resources, refuges may provide therapeutic services to help the women and children at an emotional and psychological level. They will help the women with re-homing and facilitate the establishment of a new life free of abuse. However, the impact of the Stockholm syndrome means some women are psychologically tied to the partner and so return to be re-abused after a short respite. On occasions, an abusive partner is determined to track the victim down when she is re-homed. The impact of the disruption of moving to and from refuges on the children's emotions, friendships, schooling and sense of security can be negative.

Another feature of refuges is that few cater for men who are abused and, consequently, victimised fathers' options may be very limited.

One often overlooked problem that can have a profound impact on the children is a threat by the abusive partner to family pets, especially if they are seen to belong to the victimised partner. First, the partner may not want to leave the home because of fears for the pet, as reported by Tiplady et al. (2012). Second, if they do escape with the children to a refuge, they and their children may be deeply worried and distressed about the pet left in the family home.

All parties involved in domestic abuse can benefit from therapeutic intervention. The victimised partners can profit from counselling to help them overcome issues about the loss of a partnership and emotions such as the guilt that some victims feel. Where the abuse is female against male there can be greater difficulties, although ideas such as workplace provision can be implemented (Pollack et al., 2010). Another response to domestic abuse is to deal directly with the violent partner's aggression (Akoensi et al., 2012; Hamilton et al., 2012). These programmes can motivate them to change their behaviour, by recognising 'a specific event or situation which constituted a turning point. These included criminal sanctions, fear of losing their partner or family, and an awareness that they were becoming like their abusive father' (Sheehan et al., 2012, p. 36). The evidence that such programmes are successful tends to be equivocal, partly because of the difficulty of determining what is meant by 'success' (Westmarland and Kelly, 2012).

There are some projects that help to strengthen relationships between the non-abusing parent and their children (e.g. Dodd, 2009). Another form of provision is direct work with children, such as the Australian Safe from the Start project, which can be conducted by non-specialist workers and parents, given the right training and tools (Spinney, 2012). Other options include art therapy, inspiringly described by Mills and Kellington (2012), and well-established groupwork with children witnessing domestic abuse (Thompson, 2011). Direct therapeutic work can take place in refuges, special centres and in school. Thompson and Trice-Black (2012), for example, describe the effectiveness of school-based programmes. Arguably, what is essential from the children's point of view is that something should be offered which will alleviate their distress because, as Stanley et al. (2012, p. 192) write, '[p]rofessionals who appeared ineffective in the face of domestic violence could reinforce children's and victims' own sense of powerlessness'.

Looked-after children

In England and Wales, the term 'looked-after child' (LAC) was introduced in the Children Act 1989, section 22 (1), and refers first to children whose parents might ask for them to be accommodated on a voluntary basis; in England in 2012, about 29 per cent of children are looked-after on this basis (Department of Education, 2012). Other looked-after children are the subject of court orders, including care orders, interim care orders and emergency protection orders. There are also looked-after children who, under the criminal law, are subject to a supervision order, incorporating residence in local authority provision, are bailed to such provision, or are in secure accommodation which is not under the auspices of the Home Office. In Northern Ireland, the term is used to refer to a child accommodated for 24 hours or longer under Part 4 of the Children (Northern Ireland) Order 1995. In Scotland, the term means children who are accommodated under the Children (Scotland) Act 1995, section 25, are subject to supervision by a Children's Hearing, or are subject to an order according to which the local authority has responsibilities under sections of the Children (Scotland) Act 1995. In the UK, the vast majority of looked-after children – approximately 75 per cent – are in formal foster care (Department of Education, 2012; DHSSPS, 2012; Fostering Network, 2012; Scottish Government, 2012; Welsh Government, 2012). Some are placed formally or informally with relatives, which is referred to as 'kinship care'.

Some children in the care of people other than their parents are not 'looked after' in the legal meaning of the term. A number are in long-term hospital care – their parents still have parental responsibility but they are cared for on a day-to-day basis by other adults. Others are privately fostered, for example, children who come to the UK to study and are accommodated with a family rather than a boarding school, or when parents have to work abroad for a while and cannot take their children with them. The local authority should be informed of the arrangements and they will make sure that the child is receiving minimum standards of care.

Unfortunately, trying to identify which factors lead to an enhanced experience for children who are looked after is extremely difficult. Jones et al. (2011) undertook a systematic survey of the research and identified a key factor was placement stability. However, what is not clear is whether less emotionally distressed children are more likely to settle in substitute care. Therefore, they will appear on any measure as doing well compared to children who come into care in a very distressed and disturbed state. These latter children, whose behaviour may well reflect their upset, may push one placement after another beyond the point that carers can tolerate, thereby requiring frequent changes of carer.

There are many programmes which can help to support foster carers. These are reviewed by Kinsey and Schlösser (2012), who identified 20 different programmes which fell into five categories: 'wraparound services; relational interventions; non-relational interventions for carer and child; carer training programmes; and interventions for the foster child' (p. 28). They found that the outcomes were mixed, although some were very positive. They observed that because most were based in the USA, there needed to be more studies undertaken in the UK where there are markedly different health and social care provision and cultural factors.

There is a type of chicken and egg dilemma in trying to decide what works in substitute care. For example, children who are looked-after tend to do less well in education. But what is uncertain is whether this is due to conditions in substitute care or the results of events before they became 'looked after'. To illustrate this in England, looked-after children do far worse than their non-looked-after peers in national exams. However, the official statistics include a substantial proportion of looked-after children who have special educational needs and some may have acquired these needs as a result of neglect and abuse before becoming looked-after.

Spotlight on research

McMurray et al. (2011) Shards of the old looking glass.

The authors explored the links between the identities of young people in need and how these are shaped by their relationships. The researchers tracked the short- and long-term outcomes for 52 children who have been deemed 'in need'. From this group they interviewed 13 young people aged 12–16 years. Six lived in residential care, one in foster care and six with a birth parent but were at risk of being looked-after children. Their case-accountable social workers were also interviewed.

First, the researchers found that extended family members were often a source of support. They also discovered that professionals were mindful of enhancing the young people's identity by encouraging their relationships with positive role models from both extended families and professionals, such as outreach workers. Some professionals, however, viewed the extended family as a negative influence. More worryingly, some talked about the parents and family members in negative terms in front of the young people. Another worrying feature was that while the young people saw their friends as important and affirming their identity, social workers did not discuss the young people's friends and simply mentioned 'the community'. Finally, while they were waiting for decisions about their futures many young people felt their identity was 'on hold'.

Six of the young people interviewed by McMurray et al. (2011) were in residential care. Sometimes there is a view that residential homes are a poor substitute for foster care. However, as O'Loughlin and O'Loughlin (2012) observed, although there are some disadvantages in residential homes, such as inconsistency of care because staff work shifts, young people may prefer a residential placement because they can no longer cope with family life, particularly if they have had a series of disastrous experiences with families. Conversely, they may still have bonds with their family and reject any form of alternative which may compete with their own family for their loyalty and affection.

Returning children home

Some children are taken into care and then returned home. In the case of neglected children there is now mounting evidence that this will not benefit the children unless there is careful preparation, available support and the original reasons for the children's removal, such as parental drug misuse, are resolved. Farmer (2012) examined 180 children who were returned home after being in care. She found that after a two-year period, 46 per cent of the returned children were abused or neglected. Nearly half of the returns had broken down. Lutman and Farmer (2012) followed up 138 neglected children and found that after five years, two-thirds of the returns had failed. The worst outcomes were those for children who had suffered the most severe neglect.

Concluding this chapter and looking towards the next

This chapter has explored intervention with the children's more immediate families. The next chapter moves out into the child's cosmology to explore ways of helping children and increasing their resilience by harnessing resources in their broader environment.

Further resources

Cleaver, H., Unell, I. and Aldgate, J. (2010) *Children's Needs: Parenting Capacity* (2nd edition). Norwich: The Stationery Office.

Farmer, E. and Lutman, E. (2012) *Effective Working with Neglected Children and their Families*. London: Jessica Kingsley.

Forrester, D. and Harwin, J. (2011) *Parents Who Misuse Drugs and Alcohol: Effective Interventions in Social Work and Child Protection*. Chichester: Wiley-Blackwell.

Kroll, B. and Taylor, A. (2003) *Parental Substance Misuse and Child Welfare*. London: Jessica Kingsley.

Below are some books designed to explain foster and substitute care to children:

Daniel, R. (2009) *Finding a Family for Tommy*. London: British Association for Adoption and Fostering.

Foxton, J. (2001) *Nutmeg Gets Adopted*. London: British Association for Adoption and Fostering.

Sambrooks, P. (2009) *Dennis Duckling*. London: British Association for Adoption and Fostering.

Bereavement counselling services include:

Cruse (for adults): www.cruse.org.uk/
Winston's Wish (for children): www.winstonswish.org.uk/

11

Promoting resilience in children

This chapter focuses on the child and explores how their needs can be met. It draws on a range of resources that are available within the child's cosmos, from immediate family to the wider environment.

> ## Chapter overview
> - The nature of resilience
> - Direct work with children
> - Supports and lifelines for children

The nature of resilience

Gardner (2008, p. 49) noted in her research that 'some respondents were concerned that poorly understood theories of resilience were being used as a basis for allowing children to cope with insufficient support in emotionally harmful situations'. This is a very real danger because children who have to handle situations for which they do not have the emotional resources or knowledge will suffer from chronic stress. Therefore, drawing on available resources within the child's cosmos, resilience has to be actively promoted; this is the main focus of this chapter.

Resilience is defined in various ways, including the 'capacity of a dynamic system to withstand or recover from significant challenges that threaten its stability, viability, or development' (Masten, 2011, p. 494), or 'a dynamic process by which individuals adapt successfully to an adverse experience' (Kim-Cohen and Turkewitz, 2012, p. 1297). As Rutter (2012a, p. 1) explains, 'some individuals have a relatively good outcome despite having experienced serious stresses or adversities'.

Our understanding of resilience in children is itself in a dynamic state, constantly changing and developing (Rutter, 2012b). Early psychologists and psychiatrists noticed that while some children who were subjected to abuse or trauma developed mental illnesses, others seemed to enjoy buoyant mental health, formed positive relationships and became what could be described as productive adults. Freud (1916/2001) and Bowlby (1951; Bowlby, with Ainsworth, 1965) argued that deficits in childhood, particularly in the mother–child relationship, led to mental ill-health, distress and relationship problems in later life. Others, such as Carl Rogers (1961), Werner and Smith (1982) and Michael Rutter (1981, 1985), noticed that if people had alternative attachments and positive high regard from others, they could avoid or recover from mental health and relationship problems despite childhood adversity.

Subsequently, there was an impetus to identify the factors which seemed to promote resilience. As well as people who could form positive bonds with the child, other features were:

- helpful schooling, supportive teachers and a sense of achievement;
- partners and other supportive relationships in adulthood;
- religion, spirituality and a positive belief system.

These features can all be described as 'environmental' or forming part of the individual's outer systems in cosmological theory. There was the recognition that some personality features were also associated with resilience, including:

- an ability to self-regulate;
- an ability to tolerate delayed gratification;
- high intelligence and problem-solving skills.

Awareness that a combination of external and internal factors were associated with resilience led to an interest in 'gene–environment interactions' (Kim-Cohen and Turkewitz, 2012). Studies associated with this showed that 'there is not, and cannot be, a single universally applicable resilience trait' (Rutter, 2006, p. 6). For example, there is allelic variation in the gene that regulates monoamine oxidase A (MAOA), an enzyme that breaks down neurotransmitters, such as dopamine, which are responsible for reward-driven learning. Monoamine oxidase A inhibitors (MAOI) are largely effective in treating major clinical depressions because MAOA levels in the brain are raised in people with severe depression. There is evidence that maltreated children with greater MAOA activity are more likely to display disruptive behaviour (Rutter, 2006). Similarly, in maltreated children variations in levels of the serotonin transporter gene can be associated with different susceptibilities to depression. Individual factors profoundly influence what strategies might be best for each child and there can be no one-size-fits-all strategy. Additionally, people can be resilient in one or two domains and not others. However, there are potential positive factors in a child's environment that can be harnessed to help promote resilience and some of these are examined later in this chapter.

Before concluding this section, mention needs to be made of the groups of children with additional vulnerabilities. Peek and Stough (2010) explain that marginalised groups are more vulnerable to disaster and have the hardest time recovering. Neglected and emotionally abused disabled children often have to cope with additional challenges, although it is not really possible to generalise because children with disabilities are not a homogeneous group and their personalities, conditions and environments vary substantially. Nevertheless, parental denigration and neglect may confirm the subtle, although erroneous, messages inherent in many cultures about people with disabilities being of less value than people without. Secondly, their medical condition might already have meant periods of hospitalisation and separation from their family, thereby straining the bonds of attachment. Thirdly, their education may have been customised to their needs and if they move or are fostered too far from their school, it may be difficult to arrange similar provision.

Direct work with children

It is here that Figure 1.3 (p. 11), 'Rungs of children's developmental needs', proves useful. Direct work with children can be geared to meeting their needs on each rung. A feature related to each need, which concerns promoting recovery or resilience, is investigated.

Physiological needs

This section examines children who have been deprived of food, and the need, when helping them to recover, for practitioners to be aware of the 're-feeding syndrome'. It highlights the dire consequences for children deprived of food and why immediately feeding such children, in the absence of medical supervision, might jeopardise their survival.

Malnourishment and the re-feeding syndrome

An important constituent of our metabolic system is phosphofructokinase (PFK), an enzyme that attaches phosphate to glucose. Phosphate is needed by children for physical growth. It is a component of adenosine tri-phosphate (ATP), which transports chemical energy within our cells as an essential part of our metabolism. When children are starved, there is a decrease in the secretion of insulin because there is a reduced intake of carbohydrates. The body starts to 'catabolise', i.e. breakdown fat and protein stores to produce energy, and this process results in a loss of electrolytes, especially phosphate from the cells. When a malnourished person is given a lot of carbohydrates there is an insulin surge in the body which results in a substantially increased uptake and use of already depleted phosphate in the cells. This can lead to insufficient phosphate available to service all the body systems. A word closely associated with the re-feeding syndrome is hypophosphataemia ('hypo' means 'too low', 'phosphate', and 'aemia', which means 'in the blood'). Other elements, such as magnesium and potassium, are similarly depleted.

The introduction of too much carbohydrate can also lead to a decrease in the excretion of sodium and water. To correct this, more fluids might be given but it can still result in cardiac problems and pulmonary oedema.

This general imbalance in the systems of the body can lead to cardiac or respiratory failure, seizures and delirium. The blood is disrupted with the occurrence of haemolysis (rupturing of the red blood cells), and leukocyte (white blood cells) dysfunction, which can lead to greater susceptibility to infection. There might also be rhabdomyolysis, the breakdown of muscle cells into the blood resulting in kidney failure (Burns, 2012; Hearing, 2004; Mehanna et al., 2008).

Safety and security needs

The second rung is meeting safety and security needs, with physical safety being a priority. For some parents, knowing how to keep their children physically safe in the home is not easy and they require support and assistance.

Use of computer programs to enhance child safety

There are computer programs to help parents improve their children's safety, such as *Supervising for Home Safety*, which is aimed at parents of children aged 2–5 years. It comprises a video presentation, a structured follow-up discussion, followed by a one-month series of activities that are designed to enhance parental supervision of their children. The outcome appears to be increased appropriate supervision, which, according to researchers, could be extended to small groups of parents in order to be more cost-effective (Morrongiello et al., 2013).

The immediate problem that springs to mind is that some families who could benefit from the resources described above cannot afford technology such as home computers or DVD players. However, this can be overcome by the loan of equipment or using facilities in family or community centres.

While parents should have a primary responsibility for their children's safety, children can be helped to keep themselves safe. Morrongiello et al. (2012) have evaluated a fire-safety computer game for use with children aged 2–6 years, while Padget et al. (2006) evaluated a similar game for children aged 5–7 years who had foetal alcohol syndrome and suffered some degree of emotional or cognitive impaired functioning. Playing the games improved the children's ability to correctly identify fire-safety components and perform safety steps such as leaving a blazing building. Simply encouraging children to play safety games does not, however, guarantee their safety. Schwebel et al. (2012) reported on the effects of the dog safety game, The Blue Dog. Although the game gave the children increased knowledge, they did not behave in a safer way when exposed to a strange dog. The authors therefore conclude that carers and other adults still need to supervise young children carefully.

Moving away from purely physical protection, the provision of consistent care that the child can trust is also an important aspect of meeting children's safety and security needs. The young child needs to be able to form attachments to a consistent group of carers. As children grow and develop, they continue to need connections to people who are trustworthy and provide unconditional positive regard.

Belonging needs

The next rung is around belonging needs. Attachment, particularly to parent figures, is again important for a sense of belonging. However, children require more than this. Particularly as they grow and develop, they need a sense of belonging to a family and community. As the cosmology of the child (see Figure 1.2, p. 7) shows, there is also the temporal dimension in that children need to know where they came from, their personal and family histories, and the nature of their cultural roots. This section therefore looks at kinship care, although the life-story work explored in the next section can also help to enhance belonging needs.

Kinship care

The requirement to meet children's belonging needs is the reason why fostering and adoption agencies emphasise children's rights to have opportunities to enhance their understanding of their roots, and the culture and inheritance of their birth families. This is far easier if the substitute parents come from the same cultural background, although matching children is not the only way. Some children have such a diverse heritage that finding substitute carers with the same heritage would be difficult. Nevertheless, the more familiar the environment and culture of the substitute home, the more likely it is to meet the child's needs.

This is one of the reasons why 'kinship care', despite its drawbacks, is viewed as a positive option. NICE (2010, p. 98) comments that kinship care is a 'term formerly used to describe care provided by family and friends'; recent government guidance uses the term 'connected care'.

One drawback is the fact that professionals tend to provide less support and supervision to kinship or connected carers than non-kin ones (O'Brien, 2012). Another disadvantage of kinship care is that in instances of abuse and neglect the treatment of the children can reflect the wider family culture. Particularly in the case of neglect, there are often complex difficulties within the extended family. There is therefore a concern, as expressed by Kate Morris (2012, p. 913), that 'these "high-risk" families and "kinship care" families may well be the same families'.

There is perhaps an assumption that children in substitute care are placed formally with foster carers. However, Nandy and Selwyn (2012) revealed that of the children in kinship care, the overwhelming majority, maybe as high as 95 per cent, were in informal connected care. Many were with elderly grandparents or siblings. Children from minority ethnic groups tended to be over-represented in informal kinship care. Unfortunately, there was evidence of poverty associated with this type of care.

Despite all the potential problems of kinship care, it is worth recording the conclusion of Farmer et al. (2013, p. 31) in their engaging study of children looked after by informal family or friend carers:

> [M]ost of the children felt they belonged in their kin families and that they would remain there as long as they wanted. They were also well attached to their kin carers, in spite of their past adversities, including maltreatment and parental rejection.

Esteem needs

The fourth rung is esteem needs, which means self-respect, feeling valued by significant others and having an ability to respect others. Esteem is particularly important for children who are at risk of stigmatisation. Probably one of the first strategies is to help victimised children understand that they are not to blame for the abuse. Howe (2011, p. 82) makes the important observation that 'even people who have suffered childhood abuse and neglect can achieve a secure status if they can recognize and understand why a parent might have maltreated them'. This section therefore looks at life-story work, which helps children gain this understanding as well as enhancing a sense of belonging. The second way of helping children's esteem needs is by enhancing lifelines, mentors and supports that give them positive, high regard. These are explored further in the section on lifelines and support later in this chapter.

Life-story work

Life-story work started as a simple concept but over the years there has been an accumulation of expert voices which has shrouded this essential work in mystery and made it appear as if only those with consummate skills can work with children on their life story. However, anyone who has the sensitivity to relate positively to distressed children can undertake or at least assist in life-story work.

Nevertheless, practitioners need to be aware of potential difficulties if children cannot cope with the powerful emotions engendered by learning about their history. Some children face particular issues. For example, unaccompanied asylum seekers may have very little tangible information about their history and any memories about their family may be extremely traumatic. They might have witnessed their parents and siblings being tortured or murdered, experienced hiding in extreme fear and could themselves have been tortured. Such children will need additional support from specialist professionals.

Survivors of abuse may have few truly positive memories and what they do remember can be distorted by their minds to help them survive emotionally. We recall the Stockholm syndrome from Chapter 5, where children may form deep attachments to abusers and therefore may not be able to understand why they are in care or why a parent has been imprisoned or excluded from their life. The research of Owusu-Bempah (1995) showed that children who have negative or no knowledge of their missing parent do less well than those who have positive knowledge. It is difficult to give a positive construction to parents who have shown no affection towards their children and appear to have no redeeming features. Sometimes children turn the abuser into an unreal figure, to whom they cling, and bitterly resent the fact that they have been removed from their care. Children's anger in these instances needs to be acknowledged and absorbed. Additionally, it is sometimes possible to emphasise that *at that particular stage in his or her life* their parent could not offer them adequate care.

Cultural sensitivity is also required. For example, collecting photographs is often advocated in life-story work but some religions and cultures do not accept photographs or representations of people. There can also be emotional issues, such as when dual heritage children completely reject anything about the appearance or culture of the parent whom they hold responsible for abuse. Similarly, Vernon (see case study in Chapter 10, p. 132) rejected his black identity, inherited from his father. It would have been inappropriate to force him to face the black part of his identity and history. Nevertheless, positive aspects of his paternal cultural heritage were collected and made available to him when he was ready to explore them.

A further consideration is the need to adapt life-story work for children with certain disabilities. Learning difficulty is no barrier to helping children to understand who they are in the fullest sense, how and why they are in their present situation, to gain a sense of belonging and to look forwards to fulfilling who they might be. But materials may require adaptation. One of the key advantages of this work is that it is person-centred. Throughout the work, the child is seen first as a child with a personal story, before someone with disabilities (Hussain and Raczka, 1997).

Similarly, children with certain physical disabilities might need alternative resources and this includes sight-impaired children. Vernon's father's family was Ghanaian and once Vernon was able to accept information about his paternal inheritance, he was shown where Ghana is on a map and learned about its geography, people, cultures and traditions. A sight-impaired child would not have access to visual representations of Ghana, but could instead hear traditional sounds, receive and record verbal reports and maybe have opportunities to the taste some traditional foods.

Hearing-impaired children or those with speech and communication issues will also benefit from imaginative strategies. A deaf child might 'have countless experiences of not understanding what is being said to him or of others not understanding what he is saying' (Plummer and Harper, 2007, p. 32). A central feature of life-story work is that the child is in control. Where communication is difficult, it might be tempting to take over the work and speak for the child, but work has to be taken at the children's pace and in a way that is meaningful to them.

Fulfilment needs

The final need is to have the potential for fulfilment, which can lead to a sense of gratification and contentment. Early fulfilment needs are met by the provision of enough food and warmth and safety and secure attachments. However, as children grow older their fulfilment needs become more complex. Life-story work and play work can help them feel they belong and can raise their self-esteem. Nevertheless, many neglected and emotionally abused children, particularly in adolescence, may still hold on to negative scripts and can quickly become undermined by their experiences and overwhelmed by the pressures of growing up and having to cope with independent life.

For some, the route to fulfilment lies in education. A number of emotionally abused children work hard academically and become the classic 'A' grade student. In some ways, these young people are fortunate because they can go on to have fulfilling careers. However, this is not to say that all high academic achievers were emotionally abused; many non-abused young people find intellectual challenges and the pursuit of knowledge intrinsically rewarding.

Children whose cognitive development was adversely effected by neglect or whose education was unsatisfactory or disrupted do not have this source of fulfilment. Nevertheless, they may be fortunate if they have a talent, perhaps for music, art, business acumen or other creative skill. However, this often depends on there being someone who will help them to develop their skills. Others might find fulfilment in relationships, perhaps being able to engage young children, connect with older people or build a rapport with animals.

Among some of the most disadvantaged young people, for whom fulfilment seems a long way off, are care-leavers. In recent years in the UK, initiatives to improve their prospects have been introduced. In England and Wales, prior to the Children Act 1989, children in care who reached the age of 18 years were, in effect, left to their own devices. Now, as identified by NICE (2010), local authorities in the UK have Leaving Care Teams. Ofsted and the Care Quality Commission are responsible for inspecting provision for care-leavers. One important recommendation is to enable young care leavers over the age of 18 years 'to return to the care of the local authority for support, including to the previous placement if available … [and they are] helped to maintain contact with past foster or residential] carers they value' (NICE, 2010, p. 54). This provision helps to meet their attachment and belonging needs. Mentors can also provide support for care-leavers and other young people who have to cope with emotional challenges.

Mentors

In terms of fulfilment needs, mentors can be hugely beneficial. Often they are young people who are a little older than their mentees, but are in a similar situation, or have a similar cultural background or reflect the aspirations of the child. As Dolan and Brady (2012) point out, there are circumstances where professional help is preferable, and they illustrate this with the example of having a qualified dentist sort out a troublesome tooth rather than a friend using string tied to a door handle. However, mentors who are informal befrienders can offer children and young people considerable benefits.

First, the mentor is a role model, but not one such as a football star, celebrity or pop idol, whose lifestyle might seem unattainable. Mentors may also have experience of overcoming difficulties commonly met by young people and so can offer emotional or practical advice in solving the problems. They might be able to help a young person to follow their interests through the contacts they have. On an emotional level, mentors can reduce loneliness, give a sense of belonging and enhance self-esteem.

There is a converse advantage in that some young people can benefit by becoming mentors themselves. Those who were themselves emotionally abused and neglected, or suffered another adversity, can turn their experiences into something positive by drawing on them to empathise and help younger children who are having similar experiences. As Pawson et al. (2004, p. 91) observed, 'the evidence indicates that it pays to use mentors who have been there and done that'. Happer et al. (2006) interviewed Natalie, who had been looked-after and was now mentoring other young people. She commented: 'I do think I've done well myself. I didn't used to but now I do. Being a mentor means I'm helping other people and that's a good feeling – very good' (p. 41).

When vulnerable children and young people build relationships with professionals and volunteers, there is always the concern that they could be abused, particularly sexually. Predatory sex abusers are particularly adept at targeting the susceptible and overcoming obstacles to obtain positions where they can take advantage. Conversely, the children and young people might misinterpret their mentors' intentions and make accusations of abuse or inappropriate conduct. The mentors should therefore choose to meet up where they will not be closeted too privately.

Another problem is the possible distrust of mentors by family members, particularly parents and older siblings who may resent the mentor, feeling he or she has taken over their role. Similarly, as Dolan and Brady (2012) point out, if the young person is in care, then foster carers or residential workers might be mistrustful of mentors, believing they are undermining the good work the carers are doing. It is therefore as important for the mentor to form trusting relationships with the mentees' family and carers as with the young people themselves.

Supports and lifelines for children

This section looks at the various lifelines that can help children compensate for emotional deficits or counter emotionally abusive messages. It is not possible to point to one or two factors which contribute more to resilience than others because, as Eriksson et al. (2010) explain, some factors are more protective for boys than girls and vice versa, and others are more important at certain ages and stages of a child's development. A number of factors, such as good schooling, can produce a cascade effect, so that a child who is helped to succeed in education will have supportive teachers and peers, and enhanced qualifications leading to better job prospects, which improve self-esteem and provide a more satisfying adult lifestyle. Ultimately, the efficacy of resilience factors will also depend on culture and context (Clauss-Ehlers, 2008; Ungar, 2012).

One of the differences between emotional abuse and neglect and the two other main forms of abuse, namely sexual and physical abuse, is that within the household there is often no available 'non-abusing' parent. This is because emotional abuse and neglect are hard to hide from others living in the family.

The sections in Chapter 10 on PACT and Theraplay demonstrate that sometimes parents can be helped to improve their relationships with their children, but parents cannot be forced to love their children. Chapter 10 on family work suggested how family functioning can be improved, but while parents can make a commitment to stop hitting their children or sexually exploiting them, they cannot guarantee that they will love them after years of failing to bond with them. Child care practitioners will ideally try to work with parents and improve the relationships between children and their parents. However, there are times when this intervention is going nowhere or not progressing quickly enough to meet the child's needs. In these instances, practitioners need to look elsewhere.

Extended family members

We have already detailed how siblings can support each other so we will not revisit that here, apart from to offer a reminder about the importance of siblings. Older siblings can help younger ones to learn, while younger siblings can give older ones a sense of being admired and respected (Tucker and Updegraff, 2009).

Grandparents often have a role in supporting children (Griggs et al., 2010). Many have a caring role, either while parents are out at work or as kin carers because the parents are dead or not able to provide day-to-day care. There can, however, be difficulties if they were abusive or neglectful towards their own children, as this only serves to perpetuate and reinforce the abuse into the next generation. Where there is partnership tension and domestic violence, grandparents can find themselves taking sides. They may also collude with parents who use their children as scapegoats or weapons.

Nevertheless, they can be attractive as lifelines for children because they have experience and wisdom to share. Many report having more patience with their grandchildren than the children's parents, and those who are retired often have time to give. Unlike parents, many do not have to buy essentials for the children and so are a source of treats and little luxuries. In a study by Doyle et al. (2010), 2,220 children aged 9–13 years were asked to suggest supports for two fictitious children who were being emotionally abused by a housekeeper while their parents were absent. Grandmothers received the highest number of nominations with 79 per cent of participants selecting them, and grandfathers were nominated by 72 per cent. This demonstrates the importance for many children of their grandparents. Moreover, as Griggs et al. (2010) revealed, there is a significant role for many grandparents in enhancing the welfare of their grandchildren, who often found it 'easier to open-up to their grandparents than to their parents, often because grandparents had shown themselves to be better listeners' (p. 209).

One group of relatives who reoccur in survivor accounts, reviews, biographies and literature are aunts and uncles. Again, not all provide support for their nieces and nephews. The account of Sarah Reed, Jane Eyre's aunt (Brönte, 1847), is of a cruel figure, although interestingly Jane's uncles were positive figures in her life.

McMurray et al. (2011) interviewed a child in care whose mother gave her 'crap' and whose father was absent. They ascertained that the girl was given a more positive identity by an aunt: 'She sees herself as part of the [town name] community; her aunt in [town name] gives her a really good sense of belonging' (p. 214). The study involving 2,220 children noted above by Doyle et al. (2010), revealed that 65 per cent of the respondents nominated aunts and 61 per cent nominated uncles as supportive in instances of emotional abuse.

In discussion with survivors of emotional abuse, Doyle (2001) found that for some the term 'aunt' included an 'honorary' family member, such as the mother's best friend or a close neighbour. On occasions, small gestures had a substantial impact, such as the survivor who explained that her parents had been very strict, dressed her in plain clothes and made comments that made her feel unattractive. Her aunt sent her pretty underwear which her parents did not really notice. Wearing the underwear beneath her plain clothes made her feel that, whatever her parents' views, she deserved lovely clothes and was pretty underneath the façade that her mother and father imposed.

In her account of neglect by her father and emotional abuse by her step-mother, Mah (2002, p. 67) recalls that when she was 7 years old she wrote an essay set by her teacher, opening with:

> My aunt and I share a room. She is my best friend and cares about me in every way. Not only about my hair, my clothes and how I look but also about my studies, my thoughts and who I am. Though I am really nothing, she makes me believe I am special.

In the serious case review into the death of 11-year-old Child S, who killed himself with the lead of a mobile phone, the authors noted that 'an Uncle with whom he was understood to have a close relationship' was invited to give evidence to the review (C. Murphy, 2011, para 3.3). Given that 'Child S's biological father had not had any contact with him for the majority of his life', practitioners involved in the family could perhaps have harnessed the uncle's support to help a young person who probably felt uncared for and abandoned.

Teachers and helping professionals

Adults who are not part of their family, such as teachers and youth workers, can also provide assistance to emotionally abused and neglected children. As with adult relatives, there can be problems. Some adults working with children can be insensitive and emotionally abusive, while a number of sex offenders seek jobs with access to children. However, very many people who work with young people can offer valuable support. In the Doyle et al. (2010) study, teachers were nominated as a lifeline for emotionally abused children by 55 per cent of the respondents, while school nurses and family doctors were nominated by 31 per cent. Youth leaders were nominated by 24 per cent, although this might well have been higher had the survey been extended to include young people aged 14–18 years.

Teachers, educational psychologists and other helping professionals can experience considerable doubts when faced with the knowledge that a child is being abused, as described by Ellis (2012) in relation to the stresses they face when confronted with pupils suffering from domestic violence. Frederick and Goddard (2010) explained that insufficient resources could hamper the roles of schools in supporting abused children. However, the survivors of emotional abuse interviewed by Doyle (2001) talked about the benefits they derived from teachers or educational psychologists who spotted a talent or potential in them when they were children and encouraged them, thereby making them feel valued and in some ways 'special'.

Peer friendships

There is a considerable literature on peer bullying of children which might give the impression that vulnerable children are often very isolated. There is also the theory that children who fail to attach to their mothers as babies go on to fail to attach to other people throughout their lifespan, including having friends in school. Certainly, abused children can become isolated, as can other vulnerable young people, such as young carers, especially those from BME families (Jones et al., 2002; Mills, 2003). Sometimes, as in the case of Khyra Ishaq (see Chapter 2), the parents deliberately isolate the children (Radford, 2010). Where emotionally abused and neglected children are able to make friends, there is also a problem if the child's peer group engage in risky or socially problematic behaviour, because this may have a negative impact on the child's welfare (Perkins and Jones, 2004).

Nevertheless, after grandmothers, peer friends were the next highest group nominated by the children in Doyle et al.'s (2010) study, at 77 per cent. Peers can be major attachment figures, as demonstrated by six very young children rescued from a 'ward for motherless children' in the Tereszin concentration camp in 1945. They had lost their parents but became deeply attached to each other. Despite appalling experiences at the camp, they subsequently showed better than expected development and appeared to have a capacity to make positive attachments (Freud and Dann, 1951). Doyle (2001, 2003) found that distressed children sometimes linked up with other vulnerable children, reminiscent of the English folktale of the 'babes in the wood', where two abandoned children cling to each other for comfort in a hostile environment.

Religion and spirituality

In many discussions of child abuse, religions do not fare well. Abuse and exploitation of children in the name of religion is perpetrated in various cultures and spiritual traditions throughout the world, including children being branded as witches (Mercer, 2012; Tedam, 2013) or being sexually abused by clergy (Y. Murphy, 2011; Ryan, 2009).

However, Sapienza and Masten (2011) identified that a belief, faith and spirituality can help enhance children's resilience. Walker et al. (2009) found that religiousness or spirituality can diminish the development of post-traumatic symptoms. Tedam (2013) explains how for some ethnic minorities places of worship minimise isolation and in 'church, families are not judged and not ill-treated; they have the opportunity to worship and to be "British" and "Christian", irrespective of their immigration status and situation' (p. 62). Doyle (2001) found that religion and religious communities offered support for children who had been emotionally abused, while a belief in a God who gives unconditional love is a powerfully positive message. In Doyle et al.'s (2010) research, over a third of the respondents identified God, Allah and religious leaders as a source of support for emotionally abused children, while 20 per cent nominated a 'guardian angel'.

For many practitioners, there is little training either on how to address religious beliefs which are important to service users or on how to reconcile their own beliefs with the dilemmas that they face when agency policy is in sharp contrast to their own beliefs. Gilligan (2009) has researched practitioners' approach to spirituality and religious beliefs and found that there were polarised views, with some highlighting their importance whereas others felt that 'beliefs of service users were something to be ignored and avoided' (p. 103). This latter group of practitioners is likely to overlook important potential supports for some children.

Exploiting technology

In the UK, ChildLine is a well-established telephone helpline for children in distress, and in Doyle et al.'s (2010) study, 65 per cent nominated it as a supportive resource. Meanwhile, there are developments of more recent technologies, such as Skype, computer programs and social networking sites, that all have potential. Timms et al. (2013) surveyed young people with chronic illnesses and they reported that they would be willing to accept help from professionals delivered through social networks sites rather than having to have repeated hospital visits. Other researchers (March et al., 2009; Morland et al., 2011; Rothbaum, 2009) have endorsed internet-based and virtual therapy.

Pets and companion animals

There is mounting research that contact with companion animals has beneficial effects for children generally (Daly and Morton, 2009; Wedl and Kotrschal, 2009) and in relation to those with a range of disabilities and challenges (Burrows et al., 2008; Somerville et al., 2009) as well as relieving pain (Braun et al., 2009). The available neurobiological evidence suggests that the release of neuropeptides, which contribute to feelings of security in children, is activated by proximity to companion animals (Yorke, 2010).

Barlow et al. (2012) engaged in research with young adults who had been neglected in childhood and discovered that neglected females reported more attachment to companion animals than non-neglected ones. The findings for males were less certain because of small sample sizes. For children who were emotionally abused, Doyle (2001) found that pets were a major source of support.

The importance of this is that animal-assisted therapy can be useful for neglected and emotionally abused children, and when practitioners are thinking of removing children from home, consideration has to be given to children's attachments to their pets.

Concluding this chapter and looking towards the next

This chapter has shown that resources in the middle and wider environments of the child's cosmos can be used to help enhance their resilience. Ultimately, the wider and widest parts of a child's cosmology (see Figure 1.2), the environment of the greater community, state and society, will also impact on their welfare and this is examined in the next and final chapter.

Further resources

Dolan, P. and Brady, B. (2012) *A Guide to Youth Mentoring*. London: Jessica Kingsley.

Books for children coping with parental issues include:

Centre for Addiction and Mental Health and Rudebjer, L. (illustrator) (2011) *Wishes and Worries: Coping with a Parent Who Drinks Too Much Alcohol*. Toronto: Tundra Books.
Johnstone, M. (2007) *I Had a Black Dog*. London: Constable & Robinson.

12

Society, prevention and future directions

Important elements of the child's cosmos (Figure 1.2, p. 7) are located in the wider and widest environment, that is society beyond family, close friends, school or any of the other immediate supports towards which the child can reach. The child will be affected by matters such as social policy and socio-economic factors as well as societal attitudes to children and their families, matters which are investigated in this chapter.

Chapter overview

- Social policy contexts, including:
    - o Laissez-faire
    - o Parent First
    - o Parenting Norms
    - o Children's Rights

- Constructions and representations of children
- The child's world: chaos or ordered cosmos
- Prevention and community-based initiatives
- Professional resilience
- Valuing the lay voice
- The role of news and entertainment media

Social policy contexts

Intervention in neglect and emotional abuse cases is heavily influenced by the social policy in a society because there is often a very wide interpretation of the threshold for state involvement, which the social policy context will influence (Chamberland et al., 2011). As Graham (2011, p. 1542) observes: 'Professional groups such as social workers are firmly positioned in a range of social and political processes that enact a particular discourse of childhood and practices in line with welfare models.' The schema of social policy contexts outlined here is based on Fox Harding (1997), but has been adapted to apply specifically to cases of neglect and emotional abuse.

Laissez-faire

In the 'Laissez-faire' approach to social policy there is a general consensus that the state should not interfere with families unless maltreatment is extreme and cannot be overlooked. The implication for neglect and emotional abuse is that there is very little intervention. There will be involvement by state authorities only if children are so severely neglected that their lives are threatened or children's behaviour becomes so disturbed that it impinges on society's composure. In the latter instance, concerns will be raised about predatory and 'feral' children, leading to intervention based on criminal processes or mental health services rather than child protection measures.

Parent First

In this approach, children's rights and welfare are subsumed under those of the parents, and the child's interests are seen as the same as the parents. It is assumed that parents will inevitably provide good care for their children if they have the wherewithal to do so. Any maltreatment is defined as a problem with the family's circumstances or with the child. If the child is suffering from neglect or emotional abuse, then the solution is to provide the parents with extra support. It is easier to hold to this policy perspective in cases of neglect and emotional abuse because, unlike instances of sexual and physical maltreatment, parents rarely appear to be behaving in an overtly criminal or uncontrolled manner. However, when a child's behaviour reflects his or her distress, the compassion is extended towards the parents. This is illustrated in the case of Candace Newmaker (see Chapter 9), where her adoptive mother was given every sympathy, and Candace was defined as 'the problem'. Services therefore tend to be geared towards giving material relief to the parents where neglect is detected or towards 'solving' the disturbed behaviour of the child in instances of emotional abuse.

Parenting Norms

Here the parents are seen as being responsible for their children's welfare. The emphasis is on parents meeting their children's needs and maintaining basic standards. Intervention is focused on parental ability to provide for their children. The discourse is of 'family support', meaning assistance for the parents to enable them to meet a standard of 'good enough' parenting. Neglect and emotional abuse is defined in terms of whether or not the child will become a damaged adult. The views of the children are not sought and if their behaviour becomes disturbed or they are seriously neglected, and if, with help, the parents cannot reach the required standards, the children will be removed and placed with parents who can.

Children's Rights

Within this policy approach there is the recognition that children and their parents may have separate needs and, ultimately, it is the state that ensures that these needs are met. As with vulnerable adults, if carers cannot safeguard the welfare of dependent children, then intervention is required. The threshold of neglect and emotional abuse is judged primarily on how far the children are suffering in the present. Any involvement is focused on the child and given directly to the child, although if help to the carers can improve matters that is also provided. Again, like vulnerable adults, children have a right to participate, speak out about their experiences, and share in decisions about their future.

Constructions and representations of children

Depending on the prevailing social policy perspective, children are viewed in different ways which might hinder or help any intervention. If, for example, a Laissez-faire approach dominates, then children tend not to have a high profile. There are education and health systems to cater for children's essential needs but little impetus to provide leisure activities or youth services. Children are given attention if they break the law, but they are viewed not as victims, but as delinquent youth who must be controlled.

The Parent First perspective assumes that the child is a happy, small appendage of their parents. Viewing them rather like domestic super-pets, the family provides for their children. There might be projects to support parents and, in some circumstances, again like pets, their children can be brought along. Any child whose behaviour causes difficulty is labelled 'disturbed' or 'mentally ill'.

The Parenting Norms perspective similarly assumes that children are appendages of their parents and if the parents function well, their child will be happy, secure and 'adjusted'. If, however, the child cannot be thus labelled, he or she becomes insecure, acquires a 'victim' status and needs to be rescued.

The Children's Rights perspective sees children as individuals with the same rights as adults. In some of the more extreme Children's Rights perspectives, there is the danger that they are viewed as little adults and are therefore not protected. However, many people who espouse the Children's Rights perspective also acknowledge that, like vulnerable adults, their needs for protection and guidance are recognised.

Objectification of children

Closely associated with all the perspectives, except the Children's Rights one, is the objectification of children, where children are seen as parental accessories and not quite fully human. They are potential human beings, but have to spend many years in a state of limbo while they develop to full personhood. Ominously, if children are viewed as 'not-yet-persons', there are very many ways, as described by Lancy (2013), of using children to meet adult needs, for example 'the uncontaminated soul of an infant can save a bewitched adult' (p. 11).

Although we will not 'name and shame', we have found repeated instances of modern social science textbooks referring to infants and children as 'it'. One author writing a recent social work book states: 'it is important that the child is supported at this stage of its life so that it does not develop a sense of inferiority'. Readers might spot the irony of this statement. Viewing children as 'its' is to collude with those who abuse children because, as explained in Chapter 1 (see Figure 1.4, p. 14) the objectification of victims is a prerequisite for abuse.

The child's world: chaos or ordered cosmos

Poverty, exclusion and discrimination can all contribute to neglect and emotional abuse. Doyle (1997a, 1998), in her analysis of emotional abuse cases both from a population survey and from cases officially recorded as 'emotional abuse', found that stress, particularly multiple stressors, was strongly associated with emotional maltreatment. Family burdens can accrue from many different sources. However, there are some stresses that tend to cluster together. When these feature in the cosmos of children, they render the child particularly vulnerable and intervention particularly challenging. They include: poverty or financial difficulties; accommodation problems; illness, disability and bereavement; and discrimination, stigma and exclusion.

Poverty

This section needs to be prefaced by the statement that neglect and emotional abuse are not confined to poor families. Doyle (1998) found that the income distribution profile of cases officially recorded as 'emotional abuse' was equal to that of the general population profile. Nevertheless, concerns about money and income were a key factor in instances of emotional abuse. Hearn (2011) and Spencer and Baldwin (2005) point out that poverty is often one of the most important contextual factors in neglect cases. Financial worries, in general, and poverty, in particular, create stress because in most societies money or currency is a source of power as well as well-being. Money can buy access to valued resources, influence and, most important of all, to comfort and cleanliness. There is a marked difference in the effort required to keep a house clean when we compare a family that is able to afford to buy and run goods such as a washing machine with one where everything has to be cleaned by hand.

Importantly, the lived experiences of poorer children are those of missing out on experiences, which, in some senses, mirrors parental neglect. For example, Wager et al. (2010) describe the problems facing children living in poverty, such as the child who wanted to learn to swim but could not afford arm bands. Many of the children they interviewed relied on extended families for help. If, however, poorer children are neglected or emotionally abused by their family, including their extended family, the dual impact of poverty and abuse is substantial.

There is no one solution to family poverty because there is no single cause. Doyle (2012) gave the example of Becky, a young single mother who was managing on welfare payments. When her block of flats was taken over by a gang who took most of her welfare money, she was plunged into complete poverty and forced to borrow money and engage in prostitution. When Becky and her baby were moved away from the flats and into a small house with a garden, she was able to cope adequately on welfare benefits again. Many people in poverty have a limited income which might give them a basic standard of living, but if they encounter any adverse circumstances, they rapidly fall well below the poverty line.

Child protection practitioners will encounter families who have no income because they are not entitled to benefits and cannot work. For example, in the UK, people who are in the country illegally or whose asylum application has been rejected but who are too frightened to return to their country of origin, might be struggling to survive on charitable hand-outs.

Poor families may always hover on the brink of neglect because if parents encounter emotional problems, they cannot purchase themselves any comfort. A very stressed but wealthier parent may be able to buy the family a holiday, use spare cash to relieve stress through leisure pursuits or pay for child care to supplement their own efforts. Parents living in poverty have none of these advantages and if, to relieve stress, they engage in even moderate drinking and smoking, their provision for their children is likely to fall below what is acceptable. Furthermore, their stress-relief activities may be viewed as evidence that they prioritise their own needs over those of their children.

Others are like the Page family outlined in Chapter 2: the family potentially had a good income but Mr Page gave his wife a very small proportion of his earnings for the children and household bills and spent the rest on his own pleasures. Consequently, his family lived in poverty.

The social workers in the case of Paul in Chapter 2 can be criticised for constantly giving the parents material goods. However, the criticism is not for supplying the goods, but for doing so while ignoring the children and failing to assess their well-being. Material provision has to be given in a holistic way with adequate follow-up.

Another aspect of poverty which Gringeri and Vogel-Ferguson (2012) highlight is that abuse in childhood can often lead to a life of poverty because of the numbers of losses the child suffers, including the loss of educational opportunities. As the authors found when they interviewed women on a low income who had suffered from childhood maltreatment, 'the participants talked about being at school physically, but not being present mentally' (p. 12). They could rarely concentrate in school and stress caused memory impairment. Their fear and unhappiness at home led them to feel disconnected with peers and therefore they were more likely to suffer bullying in school. Many low-income parents may be struggling with multiple issues in their cosmos, including past maltreatment and present emotional and material stress. In such circumstances, managing without neglecting or emotionally abusing their own children will require considerable personal resources and resilience.

Accommodation problems

Another area of stress relates to inadequate accommodation. Thoburn et al. (2000) found that in 59 per cent of cases where neglect or emotional abuse were a concern, people lived in over-crowded conditions. Doyle (1998) identified accommodation and conditions in the home as significant stressors. For example, in one case of emotional abuse, the parents and five children under 7 years of age lived in a two-bedroom council flat. Although neglect and emotional abuse are associated with chaotic home conditions, Doyle's research revealed that sometimes the homes are too tidy: 'the family's maisonette is kept in an immaculate state and no toys are allowed because of the mess they might make' (p. 160). Equally, and just as ominous, was the observation that the 'house [was] kept in an immaculate condition except the child's room, which is just a store room and dumping ground with no proper bedding' (p. 160).

One aspect is that high rents lead to poverty because there is little additional money left for food and other living costs. In other instances, the accommodation is unsuitable for a family. Flats with nowhere for children to play can lead to parents requiring their children to be still and quiet. Damp conditions with mould in the house and environmental pollution can overwhelm a parent struggling with household chores. Thin walls in a noisy, traffic-filled neighbourhood may result in lack of sleep, which can lead parents, and indeed children, to act irrationally.

Sometimes accommodation problems are less obvious but no less significant. Allen (2012), whose research is described below, explored the issues facing Irish traveller women trying to escape domestic violence.

Spotlight on research

Allen (2012) Domestic violence within the Irish travelling community: the challenge for social work.

This was a mixed-methods exploration of the issues facing women subject to domestic violence in the Irish traveller community. This community is a distinct group in Ireland which has strong, extended family networks. Although some members live in settled housing, most still travel in caravans, often staying in 'halting sites' where several families have access to some basic facilities. A postal survey was distributed to service providers and interviews were conducted with five traveller women who had suffered abuse, and fifteen traveller women took part in a focus group.

As in many communities, the women were isolated and had difficulty trusting the police response. They also had accommodation difficulties if they wanted to escape abuse, particularly when escaping with their children. The options open to other women are not available to traveller women. Because of the complexities of the extended family networks, for safety reasons, Irish women's refuges can only take one traveller woman at a time. The owners of bed and breakfast provision often overtly discriminate against travellers. Married traveller women tend to live with their husband's families and can rarely return to their mother with their children because there will be no room. To be given settled housing and having to break off contact with the extended family will only increase their isolation. If the woman is able to move to another caravan, the husband can be barred from approaching the caravan, but cannot be stopped from moving on to the same halting site.

The Irish traveller women faced many of the prejudices, barriers, problems with finances and inadequate legal protection common to other victims of domestic violence. It was, however, the many barriers to finding alternative accommodation, thereby escaping the abuse, which stood out as a major factor distinguishing traveller women from many others who suffer domestic violence.

Illness, disability and bereavement

The impact on children of parental or their own disability and illness has been explored throughout the book. However, what can profoundly influence the impact of any disability or illness is how society views these conditions. Disability can 'impose on children and families a lifestyle that is not of their choosing' (Carpenter and McConkey, 2012, p. 351).

Many mental health problems can either be treated or the family organised to protect the child – as happened when Harry's mother had post-natal depression (p. 68) – as long as there is societal acceptance of mental illnesses and a belief that they can be managed. If, however, there is the belief that ill-health or misfortune is caused by the child through witchcraft, there can be dire consequences for the child (Mercer, 2012; Pearce, 2012; Tedam, 2013). Another issue is that of drug-taking. It is more difficult for parents to openly seek help for their own or a relative's addiction in societies where possession and consumption of many drugs is illegal.

Attitudes to children with disabilities can vary considerably depending on the child's social and cultural environment. Akilapa and Simkiss (2012) describe the different cultural attitudes to disability in children, including a belief that the child is a blessing or, in contrast in some cultures, a curse. Some societies hide disabled children, while others believe that through some form of ritual they can be 'cured'. Self-esteem may be damaged by societal attitudes to disabling conditions. For example, Beresford (2012, p. 238) found, when exploring the subjective well-being of a group of children with disabilities, that 'some of the young people used emotive and derogatory words to describe themselves', reflecting societal attitudes. In England, 'risk of exposure to bullying was three to four times higher among children with autistic spectrum disorders, children with speech language and communication needs and children with learning disabilities' (Emerson, 2012, p. 216).

Being the sibling of a child with chronic illness or a disabling condition can result in emotional distress which is not generally acknowledged by society. One questionnaire respondent whose brother had a learning disability wrote in response to Doyle's (1998, p. 164) survey: '[I] never felt loved – elder sister spoilt, brother needed a lot of attention.'

Another area of stress which receives little societal acknowledgement and support is family bereavement. Doyle (1998) found that among families in which emotional abuse occurred there was a significantly higher level of child losses compared to families where such deaths were absent. The death of a child is usually devastating for parents and this can lead to an inability to care for the remaining children. Sometimes the bereavement is hidden, as in the case of Shula.

Illustration: Shula

When Shula was 17 years old she became pregnant, but because she was not ready to have a child, she had an abortion. Afterwards, she started to imagine her lost baby, who became in her mind the ideal child. None of her subsequent offspring lived up to this ideal, and she vented her anger and disgust with herself on her children. Only a skilful and sensitive investigation enabled her to talk about the termination, which had not been disclosed to anyone else, including her parents and husband.

Society also often overlooks the devastating impact of perinatal death on fathers (McCreight, 2004), and also the dilemmas for members of minority ethnic groups. In some countries, the procedures to enable parents to mourn for and bid farewell to miscarried, aborted and stillborn children are being reviewed or enhanced (Miscarriage Association, 2013; Sanger, 2012).

The loss through death of a partner can have a profound effect on all the family. The remaining partner can be so devastated that care of the children becomes extremely challenging. The behaviour of the children may become disturbed at the same time as the remaining parent is depressed and disoriented. However, again, the rituals and support that society offers bereaved families may help or hinder.

Discrimination, stigma and exclusion

Many different groups in society find themselves subject to discrimination, stigma and exclusion. For example, Curran (2013) has written eloquently about the marginalisation, racism and disadvantage faced by some immigrant and asylum-seeking communities. In many cultures, certain conditions, such as mental illness (Cheon and Cheon, 2012; Mellor et al., 2012) or HIV/AIDs (Zaidi et al., 2012), are subject to greater stigma than others. Barr (2008), for example, makes the point that in many societies a 'good' mother is a happy one. Therefore, to add to the misery of women who suffer post-partum depression, is the stigma of being viewed as a 'bad' mother. Poverty too can lead to stigma and exclusion, such as poorer children who are 'stigmatized by the lack of the "right" designer clothing or because they are dependent on free school meals' (Spencer and Baldwin, 2005, p. 29).

One group of heavily stigmatised parents in most societies and cultures are those in prison. When fathers are imprisoned they have to endure separation from their children (Dyer et al., 2012), while their partners often develop depression because they both miss the person in prison and suffer stigma and socio-economic pressures (Wildeman et al., 2012). Children with imprisoned parents sometimes feel the stigma so much that they tell no one and the 'fear underpinning their secrecy could lead to a sense of isolation and withdrawal' (Losel et al., 2012, p. 96). Mothers in prison tend to suffer more stigma than men because they are seen as 'unfit and indifferent mothers' (Mignon and Ransford, 2012, p. 70). This isolation and humiliation can result in mothers being unable to mourn if their child dies just before or during their incarceration (Lewin and Farkas, 2012).

Anti-discriminatory practice and anti-oppressive practice are important professional principles. The police in the UK, for example, have worked to try to correct the 'institutional racism' identified in the Macpherson report (1999). However, the espousal and advocacy of a stigmatised group can lead to the professionals involved being equally stigmatised. An illustration is Urh's (2011) example of social work with societally denigrated Roma families in Slovenia. Similarly, an inevitable consequence of working with child protection cases is that, by association, practitioners will be viewed either as helpless and 'hopeless', like its victims, or alternatively depraved or irresponsible, like the perpetrators.

Prevention and community-based initiatives

Holland et al. (2011) attest to the rich jigsaw of assistance offered to parents and children from relatives, friends and neighbours. This can be help with childcare, but also covers personal and emotional support and material aid. The community and neighbourhood can be a powerful factor in preventing neglect and emotional abuse or in helping young victims who remain at home. Susan Young et al. (2012), for example, describe a number of community projects from Australia, New Zealand and Norway, where children are neglected or emotionally abused. Work is undertaken to minimise the difficulties and challenges in the community environments and cultural practices, while strengths within extended families and communities are identified and harnessed in order to protect and care for children who are 'at risk'.

Individuals have realised that initiatives based in communities and drawing on resources within those communities can provide assistance to children. Two examples are described here: the Penn Green Centre in Corby and Kids Company in London.

Penn Green Centre

Pen Green, in Corby, Northamptonshire, is a community provision for families with children under 5 years old, although over time this has extended to holiday and after-school clubs for older children. There is no stigma because the philosophy is that all families within its 'reach' should have access to its services. Many of its groups and facilities are suggested and run by the parents and children themselves. There are provisions for babies, children, mothers and fathers, including a Saturday baby massage group for fathers.

It has a preventative function in relation to neglect and emotional abuse because isolated parents are drawn into the provision and, by both direct services and the culture of the centre, they learn positive caring for their children. Although family-based, it is informed by a Children's Rights perspective because the children do not have to be labelled 'delinquent', 'disturbed' or 'disabled' to participate in the various activities.

Kids Company

There is a telling sentence in the report into the death of Child S (C. Murphy, 2011), whose family had longstanding problems, including the neglect of the children, domestic violence and alcohol misuse. Aged 11 years, Child S put a ligature around his neck and died from asphyxia caused by strangulation, although there was uncertainty about whether this was a deliberate act or unintentional suicide. The report catalogued inadequate assessments, a failure to make links between events, and closure of the case because the family appeared not to engage in the help offered. He had been referred to the Child & Adolescent Mental Health Service (CAMHS) but 'he was closed to CAMHS because he was not taken to appointments, although it was considered he still needed the service' (para 4.13).

A problem which is particularly pertinent to cases of neglect and emotional abuse is that neglectful, over-burdened or uncaring parents are less likely than most to take their children to assessments and therapeutic provision. This was something that Camila Batmanghelidjh realised early in her career and so she developed Kids Company. Kids Company takes services into the community to the children who need emotional, educational and material support. The children are from the inner-city and their parents have so many difficulties that they cannot nurture their children adequately. The children receive a range of help and services through their schools, in centres and a therapy house. Children often respond to neglect, emotional abuse and trauma by 'closing down' their emotions and Kids Company helps them by giving them sustained, caring relationships.

Professional resilience

Practitioners working with abused children are part of the children's cosmos and therefore need to be resilient to the stresses of the work. Stress is not always negative and many professionals thrive on demanding, challenging work. It will be recalled (see p. 77) that Ulrich-Lai and Herman (2009) observed that, physiologically, the stress response is very similar to that of positive stimuli, especially if these are new and not self-administered. This means that there is a relatively thin line between work which is full of interest and challenge and that which causes tension and undue strain.

Child protection work can be rewarding. The vast majority of families where the children are abused, after maybe some initial uncertainty or antagonism, welcome offers of assistance. Helping a tired mother to keep an appointment with her GP, who diagnoses and treats anaemia, may relatively easily resolve what, at first sight, appears to be a serious issue of neglect. Cases are settled and child protection practitioners, while not seeking gratitude, can nevertheless find themselves receiving appreciation. As Scourfield and Walsh (2003, p. 401) state: 'It is important to avoid the unrelenting negativity about social work from some authors.' There is a considerable amount of very positive child protection work undertaken. Nevertheless, from time to time workers may experience undue stress and some of the most committed and conscientious workers are likely to experience conditions such as burnout and compassion fatigue.

There are number of sources of advice about how to remain resilient. For example, Mathieu (2012) provides guidance on how to cope with compassion fatigue. Pomeroy (2012) explores how social workers can help people who are being bullied at work but her suggestions equally apply to child protection workers being bullied by colleagues.

Remaining physically healthy, eating nutritiously and exercising can also help. Eriksson et al. (1998) showed that the human hippocampus is able to generate neurons, a process called neurogenesis, throughout the lifespan. Exercise is associated with the generation of neurotrophic proteins in different areas of the brain. These are proteins which are responsible for the growth, maintenance and survival of neurons. Therefore, generally, exercise also promotes neurogenesis (Vina et al., 2012). Exercise can also help to regulate the levels of amyloid β (Aβ) in the brain (Foster et al., 2011). All these processes can be cognitively beneficial. Finally, exercise strengthens muscles, reduces 'bad' and raises 'good' cholesterol levels in the blood and helps the body take up and use oxygen (Myers, 2003).

Another strategy is to have 'time-out', a complete break from work, without feeling guilty. Additionally, 'buddies' who are not in the same work setting but understand enough about each other's job to be able to give mutual advice and support can be beneficial. Finally, humour (as long as cynical attacks are avoided) can serve as a release from emotionally demanding situations, and Howe (2008) noted that laughter can be infectious.

Supervision is also essential. Carpenter et al. (2010) examined the quality of supervision experienced by newly qualified social workers. They had both case management and reflective supervision. This was generally welcomed and one respondent commented: 'I have really valued the opportunities for quality supervision in order to reflect on my practice and development' (p. 26). The case of Victoria Climbié illustrates how essential good quality, trusting supervision is. Commenting on the case, Ferguson (2009) reflects:

> A crucial yet vastly under-analysed reason why professionals failed to get close to and protect her was because she was diagnosed as having scabies. At least one social worker could not get away from Victoria quickly enough when she came to the office, while two other social workers and a police officer, all independently of one another, refused to visit the home for fear of getting infected. (p. 475)

If these practitioners could have discussed openly with a supervisor their fear of Victoria's scabies, a supportive supervisor might have encouraged their supervisees to find out about scabies, whereupon they would have learnt that, although there is some evidence of transfer of the scabies mite via clothing or furnishing, this is very unlikely, and it generally takes 15–20 minutes of *close* contact to transfer the mites from one person to another (Hicks and Elston, 2009). Furthermore, there is now, and was in 2001, a number of effective treatments for scabies. Therefore, not only should Victoria and her great-aunt have received treatment, but in the unlikely event of practitioners catching it, they could also be treated (Strong and Johnstone, 2010; Walker and Johnstone, 2000).

Valuing the lay voice

In the analysis of reports in Chapter 2, we encountered the voices of parents, professionals and, occasionally, the faint voice of the child. However, there was another voice, one with important information and observations but which was all too often ignored. It was the voice of the lay person: the neighbour, the passer-by, the volunteer.

Health services have been using lay helpers for many years. They have, for instance, been found to be particularly helpful when drawn from minority ethnic groups to work with their communities, disseminating culturally specific messages and overcoming barriers which other workers cannot readily surmount (Lewin et al., 2010; South et al., 2012). Kennedy (2010) found nutrition and health lay workers were able to reach people with whom professional workers could not engage. As one worker reflected: 'Because we're all mums, they think "they're teaching their kids to eat healthy so we can do it and we can go and ask them"' (p. 168).

When people, including children, have sensitive information to impart, they may prefer to talk to people who are not professional, as illustrated in the research by Hogg and Warne (2012).

Spotlight on research

Hogg and Warne (2012) Ordinary people, extraordinary voices: the emotional labour of lay people caring for and about people with a mental health problem.

This research reports the narratives of four research participants: a bar worker, a parish priest, a hairdresser, and a beauty therapist. All these jobs bring the workers into contact with the public, and each occupation comprises an element of caring and listening while remaining impartial. Many people who come to the four workers are suffering from mental distress and talk to them about their personal problems. The beauty therapist found people disclosed their worries to her and she commented 'Well, I have lots of tissues ... [laughs]. We go through loads just with people crying. You've just got to let them talk ... until, like, they feel comfortable' (p. 300). The priest clearly offered his support unconditionally to distressed people. The barmaid saw listening to unhappy customers as part of her job and she did more. One customer was evidently lonely and when he was hospitalised, she visited him in hospital, explaining: 'Well, who else was there for him?' (p. 301). The hairdresser displayed the skills of a professional counsellor. She was adept at recognising the nuances that betrayed her customers' emotional turmoil, despite their initial presentation as well and happy. Tellingly, she also said: 'I just listen really, you can't tell them what to do because it's something they have to choose for themselves' (p. 302).

Hogg and Warne's study showed that lay people can show skills, empathy, sensitivity and caring equal to that possessed by primary helping professionals.

Despite the findings of Holland et al. (2011) that there was sometimes reluctance to report child abuse, their study results concur with Daniel et al.'s (2010) conclusion, from an extensive review of the literature, that people are often prepared to report their misgivings and observations. This was confirmed by Potter and Hepburn (2003), who examined lay callers who reported cases of possible abuse to the NSPCC child protection line.

All these examples show that the voice of the lay person is not one to be ignored. Their skills, basic understanding and empathy often mean that if they say they are worried about a child, there is good reason for practitioners to take notice.

The role of news and entertainment media

The news and entertainment media, whether through newspapers, magazines, television or the internet, are the link between the professional and the lay person. The media can distort or enhance the perspectives of the general public. They can also play a part in the construction of the professional worker. Our image of the health, legal, police and education professions comes not just through the news media but through fiction. We see law enforcers and health professionals heroically saving vulnerable people in police and medical dramas.

Child protection practitioners, especially social workers, are different. Few people have contact with them, even through relatives, and, if they do, it is often in circumstances about which they do not want to talk generally. They are rarely portrayed sympathetically in fiction, if they are mentioned at all. This means that child protection workers only come to public attention when they have obviously failed in their task, as when there is an inquest or inquiry following the death of a child. This is highlighted in a comment by Laming (2009, p. 45): 'There has been a long-term appetite in the media to portray social workers in ways that are negative and undermining.' Parton (2011, p. 867) similarly observed in England after the death of Peter Connelly: 'The intense and rancorous social and media reaction clearly engendered a sense of very high anxiety amongst government officials and children's services managers and practitioners.'

An example is the BBC, which in their popular soap *Eastenders* in October 2012, depicted a young mother, Lola, who clearly loved her baby but was slightly neglectful. A social worker intervened and took her baby away. There was no portrayal of any legislation used or the need to determine grounds, especially in cases of neglect. Instead, they justified their storyline with 'the social worker witnessed a series of unfortunate incidents, including Lexi wearing a tea-towel as a make-shift nappy, reports of Lola not taking Lexi to the mother & baby group, a messy and unclean flat and the discovery that Billy had lied to her about having a job' (Pemberton, 2012). This shows the depth of ignorance of some of the entertainment media. The storyline gave rise to comments on Twitter such as: 'I hate that social worker from Eastenders', and 'Lola's social worker needs a punch', 'I want to slap Lola's social worker so much, she has a face just made for slapping!' (Pemberton, 2012).

This is not just a problem in the UK. In the USA, Zugazaga et al. (2006) surveyed 665 social workers in Florida who believed they were portrayed negatively in the press. Californian practitioners complained about child welfare workers being scapegoats in high-profile child deaths (Spratt and Devaney, 2009). However, some news and entertainment media are less condemnatory. For example, Kuijvenhoven and Kortleven (2010) remarked on how much less hostile the Dutch press is compared to the British press.

News and entertainment media relations with child protection practitioners are not helped by the profession and its employers. Often, the response to the media is 'no comment'. Maier (2009) outlines ten reasons why social workers need to relate to the press. The points she outlines, although referring specifically to social workers, will also apply to other child protection professionals:

1. If social workers do not put their perspective, reporting in the media cannot be balanced.
2. A story will not go away just because social workers do not comment; rather, they will give the impression that they are hiding something.
3. Journalists need to be told about successes in all areas of social work and they will only know about this if social workers tell them.

4. Although local authorities may have PR and press liaison bodies, journalists will want accounts of frontline work, which is more engaging than just formal statements.
5. Most people know little about social work and therefore its practitioners need to explain the nature of their work via the news and entertainment media.
6. Most other professions are often portrayed positively, so they can survive stories that portray them negatively because they have a buffer of 'residual affection'. Social work needs to give the media plenty of positive stories in order to create this buffer.
7. The negative portrayal of social workers tends to go hand-in-hand with a negative portrayal of their service users. Social workers highlighted in child abuse cases might create an association that families needing social work help are potentially abusing ones. Yet, daily, social workers come into contact with service users who are fully deserving of the utmost respect; people who cope with some of life's most demanding challenges.
8. If social workers and other child protection professionals are portrayed as indiscriminately removing children or as mistake-prone fools, then service users will lose confidence in them.
9. Social workers have a right to accurate representation.
10. The future of the profession is in jeopardy if it is not publicly valued. Young people considering future careers will not be attracted into the profession and there will be problems with recruitment and retention. Having too few social workers to fill the posts means that those who are working are overstretched and are therefore more likely to make a mistake – which could be the next tragedy to hit the headlines.

Unfortunately, the representation of child protection professionals will never be entirely positive because they cannot readily engage with the news and entertainment media because of confidentiality issues and because it is difficult to evidence a negative, i.e. when, as a result of their intervention, a child is *not* harmed. The gaze of the media is usually only turned on child protection work when mistakes are made and there is a particularly heart-rending tragedy.

Nevertheless, it is essential to attempt to work with the entertainment and news media. As Tomlinson and Blome (2012) contend, in order give the general public reliable and important information promptly, it is necessary for children's welfare services and the media to forge a working relationship. Jones (2012) persuasively argues that through the media it is possible to explain the realities and complexities encountered in protecting children.

An example of skilful public relations is the training subcommittee of a safeguarding board in England, which arranged a half-day workshop for local newspaper and radio journalists. The course participants were given some case studies and asked what decision would be the best ones. The journalists began to appreciate the sheer complexity of child protection work and the need to make the least worst decision. The national press is unlikely to participate in such localised training, but local journalists are often more amenable to interesting community invitations. Among local journalists will be those at the beginning of their career, who will go on to become national journalists. Therefore, the seeds of understanding that are planted in early careers may later bear fruit. Furthermore, national media sometimes pick up stories reported locally and a local story treated with understanding and insight is more likely to set the tone for any national coverage.

Concluding comments

When the term 'battered baby syndrome' was coined (Kempe and Helfer, 1968), attention was drawn to the abuse of children by their parents. At the time, the focus of assessment and intervention was the child and the parent. Over time we have realised that the abuse of children encompasses much more than 'battering', i.e. physical abuse. Neglect and emotional abuse are now increasingly acknowledged. Furthermore, while attachment and the parent–child relationship remain important factors, we are now aware that understanding, assessment and response requires an appreciation of the dynamics in every aspect of the child's cosmos, from the mal-treated individual to the widest environment. A sound grasp of these dynamics will help practitioners who are faced with the challenge of helping neglected and emotionally abused children.

Further resources

Donnellan, H. and Jack, G. (2009) *The Survival Guide for Newly Qualified Child and Family Social Work*. London: Jessica Kingsley.
Gilbert, N., Parton, N. and Skivenes, M. (2011) *Child Protection Systems*. New York: Oxford University Press.

Further information about:

Penn Green can be found at: www.pengreen.org/
Kids Company at: www.kidsco.org.uk/about-us

References

Adinkrah, M. (2011) Child witch hunts in contemporary Ghana. *Child Abuse and Neglect* 35: 741–752.

Ainsworth, M.S. (1989) Attachments beyond infancy. *American Psychology* 44(4): 709–716.

Aizer, A. (2011) Poverty, violence, and health: the impact of domestic violence during pregnancy on newborn health. *Journal of Human Resources* 46(3): 518–538.

Akilapa, R. and Simkiss, D. (2012) Cultural influences and safeguarding children. *Paediatrics and Child Health* 22(11): 490–495.

Akoensi, T.D., Koehler, J.A., Lösel, F. and Humphreys, D.K. (2012) Domestic violence perpetrator programs in Europe, Part II. *International Journal of Offender Therapy and Comparative Criminology* 57(10): 1206–1225.

Alexander, S.M., Baur, L.A., Magnusson, R. and Tobin, B. (2009) When does severe childhood obesity become a child protection issue? *Medical Journal of Australia* 190: 136–139.

Allen, M. (2012) Domestic violence within the Irish travelling community: the challenge for social work. *British Journal of Social Work* 42: 870–886.

Alleyne, E. and Wood, J.L. (2012) Gang-related crime: the social, psychological and behavioral correlates. *Psychology, Crime and Law* 19(7): 611–627.

American Psychiatric Association (2000) *Diagnostic and Statistical Manual of Mental Disorders: DSM-IV-TR* (4th edition). Arlington, VA: APA.

Amos, J., Beal, S. and Furber, G. (2007) Parent and Child Therapy (PACT) in action: an attachment-based intervention for a six-year-old with a dual diagnosis. *Australian and New Zealand Journal of Family Therapy* 28(2): 61–70.

Amos, J., Furber, G. and Segal, L. (2011) Understanding maltreating mothers. *Journal of Trauma Dissociation* 12: 495–509.

Anderson, K.M. and Bang, E.-J. (2012) Assessing PTSD and resilience for females who during childhood were exposed to domestic violence. *Child and Family Social Work* 17: 55–65.

Anderson, V., Godfrey, C., Rosenfeld, J.B. and Catroppa, C. (2012) Predictors of cognitive function and recovery 10 years after traumatic brain injury in young children. *Pediatrics* 129: e254–e262.

Ards, S.D., Myers, S.L., Ray, P., Kim, H.-E., Monroe, K. and Arteaga, I. (2012) Racialized perceptions and child neglect. *Children and Youth Services Review* 34(8): 1480–1491.

Asher, R. (1951) Munchausen's syndrome. *Lancet* 257(6650): 339–341.

Atkin, K. and Ahmad, W.I.U. (2001) Living a 'normal' life: young people coping with halassaemia major or sickle cell disorder. *Social Science and Medicine* 53: 615–626.

Atkinson, N.J. (2009) Theraplay in multi-cultural environments. In E. Munns (ed.), *Applications of Family and Group Theraplay*. Lanham, MD: Jason Aronson, pp. 137–157.

Bakermans-Kranenburg, M.H. and van IJzendoorn, M.J. (2007) Research review: genetic vulnerability or differential susceptibility in child development. *Journal of Child Psychology and Psychiatry* 48(12): 1160–1173.

Balarajan, Y., Ramakrishnan, U., Özaltin, E., Shankar, A.H. and Subramanian, S.V. (2011) Anaemia in low-income and middle-income countries. *Lancet* 378: 2123–2135.

Bandura, A. (1977) *Social Learning Theory*. Englewood Cliffs, NJ: Prentice-Hall.

Bandura, A. (1999) Social cognitive theory: agentic perspective. *Asian Journal of Social Psychology* 2: 21–41.

Bandura, A. (2012) Social cognitive theory. In P.A.M.Van Lange, A.W. Kruglanski and E.T. Higgins (eds), *Handbook of Theories of Social Psychology* (Vol. 1). Los Angeles, CA: Sage, pp. 349–374.

Barfield, W.D., Barradas, D.T., Manning, S.E., Kotelchuck, M. and Shapiro-Mendoza, C.K. (2010) Sickle cell disease and pregnancy outcomes. *American Journal of Preventative Medicine* 38(4S): S542–S549.

Barker, D.J.P. (1997) Maternal nutrition, fetal nutrition, and disease in later life. *Nutrition* 13(9): 807–813.

Barlow, J. and Schrader McMillan, A. (2010) *Safeguarding Children from Emotional Maltreatment*. London: Jessica Kingsley.

Barlow, M.R., Hutchinson, C.A., Newton, K., Grover, T. and Ward, L. (2012) Attachment to companion animals, and stuffed animals as attachment objects in women and men. *Anthrozoös* 25(1): 111–119.

Baron-Cohen, S., Leslie, A.M. and Frith, U. (1985) Does the autistic child have a 'theory of mind'? *Cognition* 21: 37–46.

Barr, J.A. (2008) Postpartum depression, delayed maternal adaptation, and mechanical infant caring. *International Journal of Nursing Studies* 45: 362–369.

Bartholomew, K., Regan, K.V., White, M.A. and Oram, D. (2008) Patterns of abuse in male same sex relationships. *Violence and Victims* 23(5): 617–636.

Bartoli, A. (ed.) (2013) *Anti-racism in Social Work Practice*. St Albans: Critical Publishing.

Baulderstone, M.J., Morgan, B.S. and Fudge, E.A. (2012) Supporting families of parents with mental illness in general practice. *Medical Journal of Australia* Open 1(Suppl. 1): 11–13. DOI: 10.5694/mjao11.11146.

Baynes, P. and Holland, S. (2012) Social work with violent men: a child protection file study in an English local authority. *Child Abuse Review* 21: 53–65.

Beckett, C. and Taylor, H. (2010) *Human Growth and Development* (2nd edition). London: Sage.

Beesley, P. (2011) *Ten TopTips for Identifying Neglect*. London: BAAF.

Beresford, B. (2012) Working on well-being. *Children and Society* 26 (3): 234–240.

Berkshire County Council (1979) *Lester Chapman Inquiry Report*. Reading: Berkshire County Council.

Berresford Ellis, P. (2002) *The Mammoth Book of Celtic Myths and Legends*. London: Constable & Robinson.

Besharov, D.J. (1981) Toward better research on child abuse and neglect. *Child Abuse and Neglect* 5: 383–390.

Blomberg, M.I. and Källén, B. (2009) Maternal obesity and morbid obesity. *Birth Defects Research (Part A)* 88: 35–40.

Bogg, D. (2012) *Report Writing*. Maidenhead: Open University Press.

Bölke, E. and Scherer, A. (2012) Sickle cell disease. *Canadian Medical Association Journal* 184(3): E210.

Bolton, P.F., Golding, J., Emond, A. and Steer, C.D. (2012) Autism spectrum disorder and autistic traits in the Avon Longitudinal study of Parents and Children. *Journal of the American Academy of Child and Adolescent Psychiatry* 51(3): 249–260.

Bond, T. and Sandhu, A. (2005) *Therapists in Court: Providing Evidence and Supporting Witnesses*. London: Sage.

Bowlby, J. (1951) Maternal care and mental health. *Bulletin of the World Health Organization* 33: 534–535.

Bowlby, J. (1988) *A Secure Base*. Abingdon, Oxon: Routledge.

Bowlby, J. with Ainsworth, M. (1965) *Child Care and the Growth of Love* (2nd edition). Harmonsdworth: Penguin.

Brabbs, C. (2011) *Serious Case Review CE001: Child B, Child C, Child D: Executive Summary*. Cheshire East: Cheshire East Safeguarding Children's Board.

Brandon, M., Bailey, S., Belderson, P. and Larsson, B. (2013) *Neglect and Serious Case Reviews*. Norwich: University of East Anglia/NSPCC.

Brandon, M., Sidebotham, P., Bailey, S., Belderson, P., Hawley, C., Ellis, C. and Megson, M. (2012) *New Learning from Serious Case Reviews*. London: Department of Education.

Braun, C., Stangler, T., Narveson, J. and Pettingell, S. (2009) Animal assisted therapy as pain relief intervention for children. *Complementary Therapies in Clinical Practice* 15: 105–109.

Bridge Child Care Consultancy Services (1993) *Paul: Death by Neglect*. London: BCCCS.

Bristol Safeguarding Children Board (2011) *Serious Case Review: Child M Overview Report*. Bristol: Bristol SCB.

Brodsky, M.C. (2010) *Pediatric Neuro-Ophthalmology* (2nd edition). New York: Springer.

Bronfenbrenner, U. (1979) *The Ecology of Human Development*. Cambridge, MA: Harvard University Press.

Bronfenbrenner, U. (1994) Ecological models of human development. In *International Encyclopedia of Education* (Vol. 3). Oxford: Elsevier.

Brönte, C. (1847) *Jane Eyre: An Autobiography*. London: Simon, Elder & Co.

Burd, L., Klug, M.G., Li, Q., Kerbeshian, J. and Martsolf, J.T. (2010) Diagnosis of fetal alcohol spectrum disorders. *Alcohol* 44: 605–614.

Burden, M.J., Andrew, C., Saint-Amour, D., Meintjes, E.M., Molteno, C.D. Hoyme, H.E. et al. (2009) The effects of fetal alcohol syndrome on response execution and inhibition. *Alcoholism, Clinical and Experimental Research* 33(11): 1994–2004.

Burns, E.E., Jackson, J.L. and Harding, H.G. (2010) Child maltreatment, emotion regulation, and posttraumatic stress. *Journal of Aggression Maltreatment & Trauma* 19(8): 801–819.

Burns, L.A.K. (2012) Refeeding syndrome: an old problem with new challenges. *HIV Clinician* 24(1): 11–13.

Burrows, J., Adams, C.L. and Spiers, K.E. (2008) Sentinels of safety. *Qualitative Health Research* 18(12): 1642–1649.

Bywater, J., Hughes, J., Ryden, N. and O'Loughlin, S. (2012) Direct work with children and young people. In M. O'Loughlin and S. O'Loughlin (eds), *Social Work with Children and Families* (3rd edition). London: Learning Matters/Sage, pp. 81–106.

Cabrera, N.J. and Tamis-Lemonda, C.S. (eds) (2013) *Handbook of Father Involvement* (2nd edition). New York: Routledge.

Cain, M.A., Bornick, P. and Whiteman, V. (2013) The maternal, fetal, and neonatal effects of cocaine exposure in pregnancy. *Clinical Obstetrics and Gynecology* 56(1): 124–132.

Carpenter, J. and McConkey, R. (2012) Disabled children's voices: the nature and role of future empirical enquiry. *Children & Society* 26: 251–261.

Carpenter, J., McLaughlin, H., Patsios, D., Blewett, J., Platt, D., Scholar, H. et al. (2010) *Newly Qualified Social Worker Programme: Evaluation of the First Year: 2008–09*. Leeds: Child Workforce Development Council.

Caspi, J. (ed.) (2011) *Sibling Development*. New York: Springer.

Centre for Addiction and Mental Health and Rudebjer, L. (illustrator) (2011) *Wishes and Worries: Coping with a Parent Who Drinks Too Much Alcohol*. Toronto: Tundra Books.

Chamberland, C., Fallon, B., Black, T. and Trocméa, N. (2011) Emotional maltreatment in Canada. *Child Abuse and Neglect* 35: 841–854.

Chambers, H., Amos, J., Allison, S. and Roeger, L. (2006) Parent and child therapy: an attachment-based intervention for children with challenging behaviours. *Australian and New Zealand Journal of Family Therapy* 27(2): 68–74.

Chase, A.R., Sohal, M., Howard, J., Laher, R., McCarthy, A., Layton, D.M. and Oteng-Ntim, E. (2010) Pregnancy outcomes in sickle cell disease. *Obstetric Medicine* 3: 110–112.

Chatelain, P., Carrascosa, A., Bona, G., Ferrandez-Longas, A. and Sippell, W. (2007) Growth hormone therapy for short children born small for gestational age. *Hormone Research* 68: 300–309.

Cheon, B.K. and Cheon, J.Y. (2012) Cultural variation in implicit mental illness stigma. *Journal of Cross-Cultural Psychology* 43(7): 1058–1062.

Children's Society (2013) Engage Toolkit. Available from: www.engagetoolkit.org.uk/ (accessed 10/08/13).

Choi, J., Jeong, B., Rohan, M.L., Polcari, A.M. and Teicher, M.H. (2009) Preliminary evidence for white matter tract abnormalities in young adults exposed to parental verbal abuse. *Biological Psychiatry* 65: 227–234.

Chomsky, N. (1959) A review of B.F. Skinner's *Verbal Behavior*. *Language* 35(1): 26–58.

Christiansen, O. and Anderssen, N. (2010) From concerned to convinced. *Child and Family Social Work* 15: 31–40.

Clark, A. and Moss, P. (2011) *Listening to Young Children: The Mosaic Approach* (2nd edition). London: National Children's Bureau Enterprises.

Clauss-Ehlers, C.S. (2008) Sociocultural factors, resilience, and coping: support for a culturally sensitive measure of resilience. *Journal of Applied Developmental Psychology* 29: 197–212.

Cleaver, H., Unell, I. and Aldgate, J. (2010) *Children's Needs: Parenting Capacity* (2nd edition). Norwich: The Stationery Office.

Clements, R., Davis, N., Palmer, R. and Patel, R. (2001) *Medical Evidence: A Handbook for Doctors*. London: The Royal Society of Medicine Press.

Climo, S. and Heller, R. (1989) *The Egyptian Cinderella*. New York: HarperCollins.

Coholic, A., Fraser, M., Robinson, B. and Lougheed, S. (2012) Promoting resilience within child protection. *Social Work Groups* 35(4): 345–361.

Coholic, A., Lougheed, S. and Cadell, S. (2009) Exploring the helpfulness of arts-based methods with children living in foster care. *Traumatology* 15(3): 64–71.

Conway, S.P. and Pond, M.N. (1995) Munchausen syndrome by proxy abuse. *Australian and New Zealand Journal of Psychiatry* 29(3): 504–507.

Corby, B., Shemmings, D. and Wilkins, D. (2012) *Child Abuse* (4th edition). Maidenhead: Open University Press/McGraw-Hill Education.

Costantino, M. (2010) Parenting children with disabilities. *Journal of Creativity in Mental Health* 5(1): 87–92.

Coventry Telegraph (2013) Daniel Pelka's murder described as 'callous and wretched' by top detective. *Coventry Telegraph*, 31 July. Available from: www.coventrytelegraph.net/news/coventry-news/daniel-pelkas-murder-described-callous-5390789 (accessed 01/08/13).

Crofts, P. (2013) Critical race theory and exploring 'whiteness'. In A. Bartoli (ed.), *Anti-racism in Social Work Practice*. St Albans: Critical Publishing, pp. 103–124.

Curran, B. (2013) Backlash blues. In A. Bartoli (ed.), *Anti-racism in Social Work Practice*. St Albans: Critical Publishing, pp. 7–24.

Daly, B. and Morton, L.L. (2009) Empathetic differences in adults as a function of childhood and adult pet ownership and pet type. *Anthrozoös* 22(4): 371–382.

Daniel, B. (2005) Introduction to issues for health and social care in neglect. In J. Taylor and B. Daniel (eds), *Child Neglect*. London: Jessica Kingsley, pp. 11–25.

Daniel, B. and Baldwin, N. (2005) The outline format for comprehensive assessment. In J. Taylor and B. Daniel (eds), *Child Neglect*. London: Jessica Kingsley, pp. 302–309.

Daniel, B., Taylor, J. and Scott, J. (2010) Recognition of neglect and early response: overview of a systematic review of the literature. *Child and Family Social Work* 15: 248–257.

Daniel, B., Taylor, J. and Scott, J. (2011) *Recognizing and Helping the Neglected Child: Evidence-based Practice for Assessment and Intervention.* London: Jessica Kingsley.

Daniel, R. (2009) *Finding a Family for Tommy.* London: British Association for Adoption and Fostering.

Daniels, H., Cole, M. and Wertsch, J.V. (eds) (2007) *Cambridge Companion to Vygotsky.* Cambridge: Cambridge University Press.

Davies, C. and Ward, H. (2012) *Safeguarding Children across Services.* London: Jessica Kingsley.

Davis, L. (2007) *See You in Court: A Social Worker's Guide to Presenting Evidence in Care Proceedings.* London: Jessica Kingsley.

De Bellis, M.D. (2005) The psychobiology of neglect. *Child Maltreatment* 10(2): 150–172.

Delghingaro-Augusto, V., Ferreira, F., Bordin, S., Corezola do Amaral, M.E., Toyama, M.H., Boschero, A.C. and Carneiro, E.M. (2004) A low protein diet alters gene expression in rat pancreatic islets. *Journal of Nutrition* 134: 321–327.

Denham, A. (1981) *Malcolm Page.* Chelmsford: Essex County Council.

Denis, C., Fatséas, M., Lavie, E. and Auriacombe, M. (2006) Pharmacological interventions for benzodiazepine mono-dependence management in outpatient settings. *Cochrane Database Systematic Review* 3: CD005194.

Dent, R.J. and Cocker, C. (2005) Serious case reviews: lessons for practice in cases of child neglect. In J. Taylor and B. Daniel (eds), *Child Neglect.* London: Jessica Kingsley. pp.147–165.

Department for Children, Schools and Families (DCSF) (2008) *Safeguarding Children in Whom Illness is Fabricated or Induced.* Nottingham: DCSF.

Department for Children, Schools and Families (DCSF) (2010) *Working Together to Safeguard Children.* Nottingham: DCSF.

Department of Education (DofE) (2012) *Children Looked After in England (Including Adoption and Care Leavers) Year Ending 31 March 2012.* London: DofE.

Department of Health (2011) *Folic Acid: An Essential Ingredient for Making Healthy Babies.* London: National Health Service (NHS).

DHSSPS (Department of Health, Social Services and Public Safety) (2012) *Children in Care in Northern Ireland 2010/11: Statistical Bulletin.* Belfast: Community Information Branch, DHSSPS.

Dickens, C. (1837/2012) *Oliver Twist.* Penguin English Library. London: Penguin.

Dingwall, R., Eekelaar, J. and Murray, T. (1983) *The Protection of Children: State Intervention and Family Life.* Oxford: Basil Blackwell.

Dodd, L.W. (2009) Therapeutic groupwork with young children and mothers who have experienced domestic abuse. *Educational Psychology in Practice* 25(1): 21–36.

Dolan, P. and Brady, B. (2012) *A Guide to Youth Mentoring.* London: Jessica Kingsley.

Donaldson, M. (1978) *Children's Minds.* London: Fontana Press.

Donnellan, H. and Jack, G. (2009) *The Survival Guide for Newly Qualified Child and Family Social Work.* London: Jessica Kingsley.

Donohue, B.C., Romero, V., Herdzik, K., Lapota, H., Abdel Al, R., Allen, D.N., Azrin, N.H. and Van Hasselt, V.B. (2010) Concurrent treatment of substance abuse, child neglect, bipolar disorder, post-traumatic stress disorder, and domestic violence. *Clinical Case Studies* 9(2): 106–124.

Doyle, C. (1985) *The Imprisoned Child.* Occasional Paper No. 3. London: NSPCC.

Doyle, C. (1997a) Emotional abuse of children: issues for intervention. *Child Abuse Review* 6: 330–342.

Doyle, C. (1997b) Terror and the Stockholm syndrome. In J. Bates, R.G. Pugh and N. Thompson (eds), *Protecting Children: Challenges and Change*. Aldershot: Arena. pp. 103–114.

Doyle, C. (1998) Emotional abuse of children. Unpublished PhD thesis, University of Leicester.

Doyle, C. (2001) Surviving and coping with emotional abuse in childhood. *Clinical Child Psychology and Psychiatry* 6(3): 387–402.

Doyle, C. (2003) Child emotional abuse. *Educational and Child Psychology* 20(1): 8–21.

Doyle, C. (2012) *Working with Abused Children* (4th edition). Basingstoke: Palgrave Macmillan.

Doyle, C. (2014) Protecting and safeguarding children. In T. Waller and G. Davis (eds), *An Introduction to Early Childhood* (3rd edition). London: Sage. pp. 223–243.

Doyle, C and Oates, M.R. (1980) Effective methods for tackling child abuse. *Social Work Today* 12(5): 13–14.

Doyle, C., Timms, C.D. and Sheehan, E. (2010) Potential sources of support for children who have been emotionally abused by parents. *Vulnerable Children and Youth Studies* 5(3): 230–241.

Doyle, T.F., Bellugi, U., Korenberg, J.R. and Graham, J. (2004) 'Everybody in the world is my friend': hypersociability in young children with Williams syndrome. *American Journal of Medical Genetics (Part A)* 12A(3): 263–273.

Dufour, S., Lavergne, C., Larrivée, M.C. and Trocmé, N. (2008) Who are these parents involved in child neglect? A differential analysis by parent gender and family structure. *Children and Youth Services Review* 30: 141–156.

Dunhill, A., Elliot, B. and Shaw, A. (2009) *Effective Communication and Engagement with Children and Young People, their Families and Carers*. Exeter: Learning Matters.

Dunn, J. (1983) Sibling relationships in early childhood. *Child Development* 54: 787–811.

Dutton, D.C. (2012) The case against the role of gender in intimate partner violence. *Aggression and Violent Behavior* 17: 99–104.

Dye, M.I., Rondeau, D., Guido, V., Mason, A. and O'Brien, R. (2013) Identification and management of factitious disorder by proxy. *Journal of Nurse Practice* 9(7): 435–442.

Dyer, W.J., Pleck, J.H. and McBride, B.A. (2012) Imprisoned fathers and their family relationships. *Journal of Family Theory and Review* 4: 20–47.

Egeland, B. (1991) From data to definition. *Developmental Psychopathology* 3: 37–43.

Eitle, D., Gunkel, S. and van Gundy, K. (2004) Cumulative exposure to stressful life events and male gang membership. *Journal of Criminal Justice* 32(2): 95–111.

Elder, G.H. (1998) The life course as developmental theory. *Child Development* 69(1): 1–12.

Ellis, G. (2012) The impact on teachers of supporting children exposed to domestic abuse. *Educational and Child Psychology* 29(4): 109–120.

Emerson, E. (2012) Understanding disabled childhoods. *Children & Society* 26 (3): 214–222.

Enato, E., Moretti, M. and Koren, G. (2011) The fetal safety of benzodiazepines. *Journal of Obstetrics and Gynaecology Canada* 33(1): 46–48.

Erikson, E.H. (1995) *Children and Society*. London: Vintage.

Eriksson, I., Cater, A., Andershed, A.-K. and Andershed, H. (2010) What we know and need to know about factors that protect youth from problems. *Procedia Social and Behavioral Sciences* 5: 477–482.

Eriksson, M. (2011) Contact, shared parenting, and violence. *International Journal of Law, Policy and the Family* 25(2): 165–183.

Eriksson, P.S., Perfilieva, E., Björk-Eriksson, T., Alborn, A.M., Nordborg, C., Peterson, D.A. and Gage, F.H. (1998) Neurogenesis in the adult human hippocampus. *Nature Medicine* 4(11): 1313–1317.

Farmer, E. (2012) Improving reunification practice. *British Journal of Social Work*: 1–19. DOI:10.1093/bjsw/bcs093.

Farmer, E. and Lutman, E. (2012) *Effective Working with Neglected Children and their Families*. London: Jessica Kingsley.

Farmer, E., Selwyn, J. and Meakins, S. (2013) 'Other children say you're not normal because you don't live with your parents': children's views of living with informal kinship carers. *Child and Family Social Work* 18: 25–34.

Ferguson, H. (2005) Working with violence, the emotions and the psycho-social dynamics of child protection. *Social Work Education* 24(7): 781–795.

Ferguson, H. (2009) Performing child protection. *Child and Family Social Work* 14: 471–480.

Ferguson, H. (2010) Walks, home visits and atmospheres: risk and the everyday practices and mobilities of social work and child protection. *British Journal of Social Work* 40: 1100–1117.

Ferguson, H. (2011) *Child Protection Practice*. Basingstoke: Palgrave Macmillan.

Ferrara, P., Vitelli, O., Bottaro, G., Gatto, A., Liberatore, P., Binetti, P. and Stabile, A. (2013) Factitious disorders and Münchausen syndrome. *Journal of Child Health Care*, DOI: 10.1177/1367493512462262.

Field-Fisher, T.G.F. (1974) *Report of the Committee of Enquiry into the Care and Supervision Provided in Relation to Maria Colwell*. London: HMSO.

Fillmore, A.V. (1981) The abused child as survivor. Paper presented to the Third International Congress on Child Abuse and Neglect, Amsterdam, The Netherlands, April.

Fischer, J.L., Pidcock, B.W., Munsch, J. and Forthun, L. (2005) Parental abusive drinking and sibling role differences. *Alcoholism Treatment Quarterly* 23(1): 79–97.

Flach, C., Leese, M., Heron, J., Evans, J., Feder, G., Sharp, D. and Howard L. (2011) Antenatal domestic violence, maternal mental health and subsequent child behaviour. *BJOG* 118: 1383–1391.

Flintshire Local Safeguarding Children Board (2012) *Executive Summary in Respect of Siôn D. Mold*, Flintshire: Flintshire County Council Local Safeguarding Children Board.

Forrester, D. and Harwin, J. (2008) Parental substance misuse and child welfare: outcomes for children two years after referral. *British Journal of Social Work* 38: 1518–1535.

Forrester, D. and Harwin, J. (2011) *Parents Who Misuse Drugs and Alcohol: Effective Interventions in Social Work and Child Protection*. Chichester: John Wiley & Sons.

Foster, P.P., Rosenblatt, K.P. and Kuljiš, R.O. (2011) Exercise-induced cognitive plasticity, implications for mild cognitive impairment and Alzheimer's disease. *Frontiers in Neurology* 2(28): 1–5.

Fostering Network (2012) Statistics on children in care. Available from: www.fostering.net/about-fostering/statistics-children-in-care (accessed 17/01/13).

Fox, S.E., Levitt, P. and Nelson, C.A. (2010) How the timing and quality of early experiences influence the development of brain architecture. *Child Development* 81(1): 28–40.

Fox Harding, L. (1997) *Perspectives in Child Care Policy* (2nd edition). Harlow: Prentice Hall.

Foxton, J. (2001) *Nutmeg Gets Adopted*. London: British Association for Adoption and Fostering.

Fraley, R.C. and Spieker, S.J. (2003) Are infant attachment patterns continuously or categorically distributed? A taxometric analysis of strange situation behaviour. *Developmental Psychology* 39(3): 387–404.

Fraley, R.C. and Tancredy, C.M. (2012) Twin and sibling attachment in a nationally representative sample. *Personality and Social Psychology Bulletin* 38(3): 308–316.

Frankel, J. (2002) Exploring Ferenczi's concept of identification with the aggressor: its role in trauma, everyday life, and the therapeutic relationship. *International Journal of Relational Perspectives* 12(1): 101–139.

Frederick, J. and Goddard, C. (2010) 'School was just a nightmare': childhood abuse and neglect and school experiences. *Child and Family Social Work* 15: 22–30.

Freeman, D.J. (2010) Effects of maternal obesity on fetal growth and body composition. *Seminars in Fetal Neonatal Medicine* 15: 113–118.

Freisthler, B. and Holmes, M. (2012) Explicating the social mechanisms linking alcohol use behaviors and ecology to child maltreatment. *Journal of Sociology and Social Welfare* XXXIX(4): 25–48.

Freud, A. and Dann, S. (1951) An experiment in group upbringing. *Psychoanalytical Study of the Child* 6: 127–168.

Freud, S. (1916/2001) Introductory lectures on psycho-analysis. In *The Standard Edition of the Complete Psychological Works of Sigmund Freud*, Vol. XV (1915–1916): Introductory Lectures on Psycho-Analysis (Parts I and II). London: Vintage, pp. 1–240.

Frye, E.M. and Feldman, M.D. (2012) Factitious disorder by proxy in educational settings. *Educational Psychology Review* 24: 47–61.

Furnell, J. (1986) Emotional abuse of children. *Medical Science Law* 26(3): 179–184.

Gardner, R. (2008) *Developing an Effective Response to Neglect and Emotional Harm to Children*. Norwich: University of East Anglia/ NSPCC.

Garraway, H. and Pistrang, N. (2010) 'Brother from another mother': mentoring for African-Caribbean adolescent boys. *Journal of Adolescence* 33(5): 719–729.

Gass, K., Jenkins, J. and Dunn, J. (2007) Are sibling relationships protective? A longitudinal study. *Journal of Child Psychology and Psychiatry* 48(2): 167–175.

Gilbert, N., Parton, N. and Skivenes, M. (2011) *Child Protection Systems*. New York: Oxford University Press.

Gilligan, P. (2009) Considering religion and beliefs in child protection and safeguarding work. *Child Abuse Review* 18: 94–110.

Gladstone, B.M., Boydel, K.M. and McKeever, P. (2006) Recasting research into children's experiences of parental mental illness. *Social Science and Medicine* 62: 2540–2550.

Glaser, D. (2011) How to deal with emotional abuse and neglect. *Child Abuse and Neglect* 35: 866–875.

Glaser, D., Prior, V., Auty, K. and Tilki, S. (2012) *Does Training in Systematic Approach to Emotional Abuse Improve the Quality of Children's Services*. London: Department of Education.

Graham, M. (2011) Changing paradigms and conditions of childhood. *British Journal of Social Work* 41(8): 1532–1547.

Grattan, D.R. (2008) Fetal programming from maternal obesity. *Endocrinology* 149(11): 5345–5347.

Gray, D.D. (2012) *Nurturing Adoptions*. London: Jessica Kingsley.

Greaves, M. and Chamberlain, M. (1990) *Tattercoats*. London: Frances Lincoln Ltd.

Green, E. and Root, K.B. (1997) *Billy Beg and his Bull*. New York: Holiday House Inc.

Griggs, J., Tan, J.-P., Buchanan, A., Attar-Schwartz, S. and Flouri, E. (2010) 'They've always been there for me': grandparental involvement and child well-being. *Children & Society* 24(3): 200–214.

Gringeri, C. and Vogel-Ferguson, M.B. (2012) Childhood abuse and loss in the lives of low-income women. *Qualitative Social Work*. DOI: 10.1177/1473325012451481.

Haas, B.W., Mills, D., Yam, A., Hoeft, F., Bellugi, U. and Reiss, A. (2009) Genetic influences on sociability: heightened amygdala reactivity and event-related responses to positive social stimuli in Williams Syndrome. *Journal of Neuroscience* 29(4): 1132–1139.

Haddad, L.B., Curtis, K.M., Legardy-Williams, J.K., Cwiaka, C. and Jamieson, D.J. (2012) Contraception for individuals with sickle cell disease. *Contraception* 85: 527–537.

Hagan, J. and Rymond-Richmond, W. (2008) The collective dynamics of racial dehumanization and genocidal victimization in Darfur. *American Sociological Review* 73(6): 875–902.

Hague, G., Thiara, R. and Mullender, A. (2011) Disabled women, domestic violence and social
care: the risk of isolation, vulnerability and neglect. *British Journal of Social Work* 41:
148–165.

Hamad, M., Refaat, K., Fischer-Hammadeh, C. and Eid Hammadeh, M. (2012) The impact
of smoking on infertility, pregnancy outcomes and fetal development. *Teratology Studies*
2: 1e–10e.

Hamilton, L., Koehler, J.A. and Lösel, F.A. (2012) Domestic violence perpetrator programs in
Europe, Part I: A survey of current practice. *International Journal of Offender Therapy and
Comparative Criminology* 57(10): 1189–1205.

Hammond, H. (2001) *Child Protection Inquiry into the Circumstances Surrounding the
Death of Kennedy McFarlane, d.o.b. 17 April 1997*. Edinburgh: Dumfries & Galloway
Child Protection Committee.

Hammond, S. (2008) *Gang Busters: States Respond to Rising Gang Violence*. Washington,
DC: States Legislatures.

Handley, G. and Doyle, C. (2012) Ascertaining the wishes and feelings of young children.
Child and Family Social Work. DOI: 10.1111/cfs.12043.

Handy, C. (1993) *Understanding Organisations* (4th edition). Harmondsworth: Penguin.

Happer, H., McCreadie, J. and Aldgate, J. (2006) *Celebrating Success: What Helps Looked
After Children Succeed*. Edinburgh: Social Work Inspection Agency.

Harris, P.L. (1989) *Children and Emotion*. Oxford: Blackwell.

Hart, S.N., Germain, R.B. and Brassard, M. (1987) The challenge to better understand and
combat psychological maltreatment of children and youth. In M. Brassard, R.B. Germain
and S.N. Hart (eds), *Psychological Maltreatment of Children and Youth*. New York:
Pergamon Press, pp. 3–24.

Haslam, N. and Loughnan, S. (2012) Prejudice and dehumanization. In J. Dixon and M. Levine
(eds), *Beyond Prejudice*. Cambridge: Cambridge University Press, pp. 89–104.

Healy, K. and Mulholland, J. (2012) *Writing Skills for Social Workers*. London: Sage.

Hearing, S.D. (2004) Refeeding syndrome is underdiagnosed and undertreated, but treatable.
British Medical Journal 328: 908–909.

Hearn, J. (2011) Unmet needs in addressing child neglect: should we go back to the drawing
board? *Children and Youth Services Review* 33(5): 715–722.

Henrichs, J., Bongers-Schokking, J.J., Schenk, J.J., Ghassabian, A., Schmidt, H.G., Visser, R.J.
et al. (2010) Maternal thyroid function during early pregnancy and cognitive functioning
in early childhood. *Journal of Clinical and Endocrinology and Metabolism* 95(9): 4227–
4234.

Heuschkel, R., Salvestrini, C., Bettlie, R.M., Hildebrand, H., Walters, T. and Griffiths, A.
(2008) Guidelines for the management of growth failure in childhood inflammatory bowel
disease. *Inflammatory Bowel Disease* 14(6): 839–849.

Hicks, M.I. and Elston, D.M. (2009) Scabies. *Dermatologic Therapy* 22: 279–292.

Hogg, C. and Warne, T. (2012) Ordinary people, extraordinary voices: the emotional labour
of lay people caring for and about people with a mental health problem. *International
Journal of Mental Health Nursing* 19: 297–306.

Holland, S. (2010) *Child and Family Assessment in Social Work Practice* (2nd edition).
London: Sage.

Holland, S., Tanock, S. and Collicott, H. (2011) Everybody's business? A research review of
the informal safeguarding of other people's children in the UK. *Children & Society* 25(5):
406–416.

Hollingsworth, J., Glass, J. and Heisler, K.W. (2008) Empathy deficits in siblings of severely scapegoated children. *Journal of Emotional Abuse* 7(4): 69–88.

Homes, M.M. (2000) *A Terrible Thing Happened*. Washington, DC: American Psychological Association.

Hooper, L.M., Doehler, K., Jankowski, P.J. and Tomek, S.E. (2012) Patterns of self-reported alcohol use, depressive symptoms, and body mass index in a family sample. *Family Journal* 20(2): 164–178.

Horwath, J. (2013) *Child Neglect* (2nd edition). Basingstoke: Palgrave.

Houston, S. and Griffiths, H. (2000) Reflections on risk in child protection: is it time for a shift in paradigms? *Child and Family Social Work* 5: 1–10.

Howe, D. (2008) *The Emotionally Intelligent Social Worker*. Basingstoke: Palgrave Macmillan.

Howe, D. (2009) *A Brief Introduction to Social Work Theory*. Basingstoke: Palgrave Macmillan.

Howe, D. (2011) *Attachment Theory across the Lifespan: A Brief Introduction*. Basingstoke: Palgrave Macmillan.

Howie, G.J., Sloboda, D.M., Kamal, T. and Vickers, M.H. (2009) Maternal nutritional history predicts obesity in adult offspring independent of postnatal diet. *Journal of Physiology* 587(4): 905–915.

Hussain, F. and Raczka, R. (1997) Life-story work for people with learning disabilities. *British Journal of Learning Disabilities* 25: 73–76.

Hutson, J.R., Stade, B., Lehotay, D.C., Collier, C.P. and Kapur, B.M. (2012) Folic acid transport to the human fetus is decreased in pregnancies with chronic alcohol exposure. *PLoS One* 7(5), e38057: 1–6.

Ino, T. (2010) Maternal smoking during pregnancy and offspring obesity: meta-analysis. *Pediatrics International* 52: 94–99.

Iwaniec, D. (2006) *The Emotionally Abused and Neglected Child: Identification, Assessment and Intervention*. Chichester: John Wiley & Sons.

Iwaniec, D., Larkin, E. and Higgins, S. (2006) Research review: risk and resilience in cases of emotional abuse. *Child and Family Social Work* 11: 73–82.

Jacobs, M. (2003) *Sigmund Freud* (2nd edition). London: Sage.

Jahromi, L.B., Gulsrud, A., Kasari, C. and Dykens, E. (2008) Emotional competence in children with Down syndrome. *American Journal on Mental Retardation* 113(1): 32–43.

James, A.C., James, G., Cowdrey, F.A., Soler, A. and Choke, A. (2013) Cognitive behavioural therapy for anxiety disorders in children and adolescents. *Cochrane Database of Systematic Reviews* 2013, Issue 6. Art. No.: CD004690. DOI: 0.1002/14651858.CD004690.pub3.

James, P.D. (1999) *Time to be in Earnest*. London: Faber and Faber

Jernberg, A.M. (1988) Theraplay for the elderly tyrant. *Clinical Gerontologist* 8(1): 76–79.

Johnstone, M. (2007) *I Had a Black Dog*. London: Constable & Robinson.

Jones, A. (2010) *Haringey Local Safeguarding Board: Serious Case Review, Child 'A'*. London: Department of Education.

Jones, A., Jeyashingham, D. and Rajasooriya, S. (2002) *Invisible Families: The Strengths and Needs of Black Families in which Young People have Caring Responsibilities*. York: Joseph Rowntree Foundation.

Jones, R. (2012) Child protection, social work and the media: doing as well as being done to. *Research, Policy and Planning* 29(2): 83–94.

Jones, R., Everson-Hock, E.S., Papaioannou, D., Guillaume, L., Goyder, E., Chilcott, J. et al. (2011) Factors associated with outcomes for looked-after children and young people. *Child Care Health Devopment* 37(5): 613–622.

Jones, T.B., Bailey, B.A. and Sokol, R.J. (2013) Alcohol use in pregnancy: insights in screening and intervention for the clinician. *Clinical Obstetrics and Gynecology* 56(1): 114–123.

Jones, K.L. and Smith, D.W. (1973) Recognition of the fetal alcohol syndrome in early infancy. *Lancet* 2: 999–1001.

Kampusch, N. (2010) *3,096 Days*. Trans J. Kreuer. London: Penguin.

Kanner, L. (1943) Autistic disturbances of affective contact. *The Nervous Child* 2: 217–250.

Karmiloff-Smith, A. (2010) Neuroimaging of the developing brain: taking 'developing' seriously. *Human Brain Mapping* 31: 934–941.

Kempe, C.H. and Helfer, R.E. (eds) (1968) *The Battered Child*. Chicago, IL: Chicago University Press.

Kennedy, L. (2010) Benefits arising from lay involvement in community-based public health initiatives: the experience from community nutrition. *Perspectives in Public Health* 130: 165–173.

Kennedy, M. and Wonnacott, J. (2005) Neglect of disabled children. In J. Taylor and B. Daniel (eds), *Child Neglect*. London: Jessica Kingsley, pp. 228–248.

Kennedy, S. (2013) White woman listening. In A. Bartoli (ed.), *Anti-racism in Social Work Practice*. St Albans: Critical Publishing, pp. 83–102.

Khan, I.Y., Taylor, P.D., Dekou, V., Seed, P.T., Lakasing, L., Graham, D. et al. (2003) Gender-linked hypertension in offspring of lard-fed pregnant rats. *Hypertension* 41: 168–175.

Kim, Y.K. (2011) The effect of group Theraplay on self-esteem and depression of the elderly in a day care centre. *Korean Journal of Counselling* 12(5): 1413–1430.

Kim-Cohen, J. and Turkewitz, R. (2012) Resilience and measured gene–environment interactions. *Developmental Psychopathology* 24: 1297–1306.

Kinns, H., Housely, D. and Freeman, D.B. (2013) Munchausen syndrome and factitious disorder: the role of the laboratory in its detection and diagnosis. *Annals of Clinical Biochemistry* 50(3): 194–203.

Kinsey, D. and Schlösser, A. (2012) Interventions in foster and kinship care: a systematic review. *Clinical Child Psychology and Psychiatry*. DOI: 10.1177/1359104512458204.

Kirkwood, A. (1993) *The Leicestershire Inquiry, 1992*. Leicester: Leicestershire County Council.

Klein-Tasman, B.P., Mervis, C.B., Lord, C. and Phillips, K.D. (2007) Socio-communicative deficits in young children with Williams Syndrome. *Child Neuropsychology* 13(5): 444–467.

Knutson, J.F., Taber, S.M., Murray, A.J., Valles, N.-L. and Koeppl, G. (2010) The role of care neglect and supervisory neglect in childhood obesity in a disadvantaged sample. *Journal of Pediatric Psychology* 35(5): 523–532.

Kolb, B., Mychasiuk, R., Williams, P. and Gibb, R. (2011) Brain plasticity and recovery from early cortical injury. *Developmental Medicine & Child Neurology* 53 (Suppl. 4): 4–8.

Kolb, B. and Teskey, G.C. (2012) Age, experience, injury, and the changing brain. *Developmental Psychobiology* 54: 311–325.

Kopp, C.B. (2011) Development in the early years: socialization, motor development, and consciousness. *Annual Review of Psychology* 62: 165–187.

Koprowska, J. (2010) *Communication and Interpersonal Skills in Social Work* (3rd edition). Exeter: Learning Matters.

Koramoa, J., Lynch, M. and Kinnair, D. (2002) A continuum of child rearing. *Child Abuse Review* 11(6): 415–421.

Korosi, A. and Baram, T.Z. (2010) Plasticity of the stress response early in life. *Developmental Psychobiology* 52: 661–670.

Kriz, K. and Skivenes M. (2010) Lost in translation. *British Journal of Social Work* 50: 1353–1367.

Kroll, B. and Taylor, A. (2003) *Parental Substance Misuse and Child Welfare*. Chichester: Jessica Kingsley.

Kucuker, H., Demir, T. and Oral, R. (2010) Pediatric condition falsification (Munchausen syndrome by proxy) as a continuum of maternal factitious disorder (Munchausen syndrome). *Pediatric Diabetes* 11: 572–578.

Kuijvenhoven, T. and Kortleven, W.J. (2010) Inquiries into fatal child abuse in the Netherlands. *British Journal of Social Work* 40(4): 1152–1173.

Kuleshnyk, I. (1984) The Stockholm syndrome. *Social Action and the Law.* 10(2): 37–42.

Kwong, W.Y., Wild, A.E., Roberts, P., Willis, A.C. and Fleming, T.P. (2000) Maternal undernutrition during the preimplantation period of rat development causes blastocyst abnormalities and programming of postnatal hypertension. *Development* 127: 4195–4202.

La Fontaine, J. (ed.) (2013) *The Devil's Children*. Farnham: Ashgate.

Lahr, J. (2002) *Prick Up Your Ears: The Biography of Joe Orton*. London: Bloomsbury.

Laird, S.E. (2008) *Anti-oppressive Social Work*. London: Sage.

Laming, H. (2003) *The Victoria Climbié Inquiry*. London: The Stationery Office.

Laming, H. (2009) *The Protection of Children in England*. London: The Stationery Office.

Lancy, D.F. (2013) 'Babies aren't persons': a survey of delayed personhood. In H. Keller and H. Otto (eds), *Different Faces of Attachment*. Cambridge: Cambridge University Press.

Landreth, G.L. (2012) *Play Therapy* (3rd edition). New York: Routledge.

Langan, M. (2011) Parental voices and controversies in autism. *Disability & Society* 26(2): 193–205.

Laslett, A.-M.L., Room, R.G.W., Dietze, P.M. and Ferris, J. (2012) Alcohol's involvement in recurrent child abuse and neglect cases. *Addiction* 107: 1786–1793.

Lazenbatte, A. (2013) Fabricated or induced illness in children: a narrative review of the literature. *Child Care in Practice* 19(1): 61–77.

Le Sage, L. and De Ruyter, D. (2008) Criminal parental responsibility: blaming parents on the basis of their duty to control versus their duty to morally educate their children. *Educational Philosophy and Theory* 40(6): 789–802.

Leeson, C. (2010) The emotional labour of caring about looked after children. *Child and Family Social Work* 15: 483–491.

Levendosky, A.A. and Graham-Bermann, S.A. (2000) Trauma and parenting in battered women. *Journal of Aggression Maltreatment and Trauma* 3(1): 25–35.

Levendosky, A.A., Bogat, G.A. and Martinez-Torteya, C. (2013) PTSD symptoms in young children exposed to intimate partner violence. *Violence against Women* 19(2): 187–201.

Levy, A. and Kahan, B. (1991) *The Pindown Experience and the Protection of Children*. Stafford: Staffordshire County Council.

Lewin, L.C. and Farkas, K.J. (2012) Living with the loss of a child. *Palliative and Supportive Care* 10: 265–272.

Lewin, S., Munabi-Babigumira, S., Glenton, C., Daniels, K., Bosch-Capblanch, X., van Wyk, B.E. et al. (2010) Lay health workers in primary and community health care for maternal and child health and the management of infectious diseases. *Cochrane Database of Systematic Reviews*, Issue 3. Art. No.: CD004015. DOI: 10.1002/14651858.CD004015.pub3.

Leyens, J.-P., Paladino, P.M., Rodriguez-Torres, R., Vaes, J., Demoulin, S., Rodriguez-Perez, A. and Gaunt, R. (2000) The emotional side of prejudice: the attribution of secondary emotions to ingroups and outgroups. *Personality and Social Psychology Review* 4(2): 186–197.

Lieberman, A.F., Chu, A., Van Horn, P. and Harris, W.W. (2011) Trauma in early childhood. *Developmental Psychopathology* 23: 397–410.

Lindon, J. (2010) *Understanding Child Development* (2nd edition). London: Hodder Education.

Littlechild, B. (2012) Working with resistant parents in child protection. Paper presented at the 2012 World Congress IASSW/IFSW/ICD Stockholm, July.

Logan, B.A., Brown, M.S. and Hayes, M.J. (2013) Neonatal abstinence syndrome. *Clinical Obstetrics and Gynecology* 56(1): 186–192.

Lok, W., Anteunis, L.J.C., Meesters, C., Chenault, M.N. and Haggard, M.P. (2012) Risk factors for failing the hearing screen due to otitis media in Dutch infants. *European Archives of Oto-Rhino-Laryngology* 269(12): 2485–2496.

London Borough of Bexley and Bexley Area Health Authority (1982) *Linda Gates and Her Family*. London: London Borough of Bexley.

London Borough of Hillingdon (1986) *Report of the Review Panel into the Death of Heidi Koseda*. London: London Borough of Hillingdon.

Long, T., Murphy, M., Fallon, D., Livesley, J., Devitt, P., McLoughlin, M. and Cavanagh, A. (2012) *Four Year Longitudinal Evaluation of the Action for Children UK Neglect Project*. Manchester: University of Salford.

Losel, F., Pugh, G., Markson, L., Souza, K.A. and Lanskey, C. (2012) *Risk and Protective Factors in the Resettlement of Imprisoned Fathers with their Families*. Cambridge: University of Cambridge/Ormiston.

Lu, J., Huang, Z., Yang, T., Li, Y., Mei, L., Xiang, M. et al. (2011) Screening for delayed-onset hearing loss in preschool children who previously passed the newborn hearing screening. *International Journal of Pediatric Otorhinolaryngology* 75: 1045–1049.

Lupien, S.J., McEwen, B.S., Gunnar, M.R. and Heim, C. (2009) The effects of stress throughout the lifespan on the brain, behaviour and cognition. *Nature Reviews Neuroscience* 10: 434–445.

Lutman, E. and Farmer, E. (2012) What contributes to outcomes for neglected children who are reunified with their parents? *British Journal of Social Work* 43(3): 559–78.

Macdonald, G. (2005) Intervening with neglect. In J. Taylor and B. Daniel (2005) *Child Neglect*. London: Jessica Kingsley, pp. 279–290.

Macpherson, W. (1999) *The Stephen Lawrence Inquiry*. Norwich: The Stationery Office.

Madan, A., Mrug, S. and Windle, M. (2011) Brief report: Do delinquency and community violence exposure explain internalizing problems in early adolescent gang members? *Journal of Adolescence* 34: 1093–1096.

Madeley, R. (2008) *Fathers & Sons*. London: Simon & Schuster.

Mah, A.Y. (2002) *Chinese Cinderella*. Harlow: Pearson Education.

Maier, E. (2009) Ten reasons why social workers must speak to the media. Available from: www.communitycare.co.uk/blogs/social-work-media/2009/04/ten-reasons-social-workers-must-speak-to-the-media.html (accessed 02/02/13).

March, S., Spence, S. and Donovan, C.L. (2009) The efficacy of an internet-based cognitive-behavioural therapy intervention for child anxiety disorders. *Journal of Pediatric Psychology* 34(5): 474–487.

Maritz, G.S. and Mutemwa, M. (2012) Tobacco smoking. *Global Journal of Health Science* 4(4): 62–75.

Martin, R. (2010) *Social Work Assessment*. Exeter: Learning Matters.

Maslow, A. (1987) *Motivation and Personality* (3rd edition). New York: Addison-Wesley.

Masson, J. (2012) What are care proceedings really like? *Adoption & Fostering* 36(1): 5–12.

Masten, A.S. (2011) Resilience in children threatened by extreme adversity. *Developmental Psychopathology* 23: 493–506.

Masten, C.L., Guyer, A.E., Hodgdon, H.C., McClure, E.B., Charney, D.S., Ernst, M. et al. (2008) Recognition of facial emotions among maltreated children with high rates of posttraumatic stress disorder. *Child Abuse and Neglect* 32: 139–153.

Mathieu, F. (2012) *The Compassion Fatigue Workbook*. New York: Routledge.

Maurer, D. and Hensch, T.K. (2012) Amblyopia: background to the special issue on stroke recovery. *Developmental Psychobiology* 54: 224–238.

McCreight, B.S. (2004) A grief ignored: narratives of pregnancy loss from a male perspective. *Sociology of Health & Illness* 26(3): 326–350.

McCrory, E., De Brito, S.A. and Viding, E. (2011) The impact of child maltreatment: a review of neurobiological and genetic factors. *Frontiers in Psychiatry* 2(48): 1–14.

McCutcheon, J.E. and Marinelli, M. (2009) Age matters. *European Journal of Neuroscience* 29: 997–1014.

McGee, R.A. and Wolfe, D.A. (1991) Psychological maltreatment. *Developmental Psychopathology* 3: 3–18.

McGoron, L., Gleason, M.M., Smyke, A.T., Drury, S.S., Nelson, C.A., Gregas, M.C. et al. (2012) Recovering from early deprivation. *Journal of theAmerican Academy of Child and Adolescent Psychiatry* 51(7): 683–693.

McMurray, I., Connolly, H., Preston-Shoot, M. and Wigley, V. (2011) Shards of the old looking glass. *Child and Family Social Work* 16: 210–218.

Meggitt, C. (2006) *Child Development: An Illustrated Guide* (2nd edition). Oxford: Heinemann Educational.

Mehanna, H.M., Moledina, J. and Travis, J. (2008) Refeeding syndrome: what it is, and how to prevent and treat it. *British Medical Journal* 336: 1495–1498.

Melhuish, J. (2011) Crack cocaine use and parenting. *Practice* 23(4): 201–213.

Mellor, D.L., Carne, L., Shen, Y.-C., McCabe, M. and Wang, L. (2012) Stigma toward mental illness. *Journal of Cross-Cultural Psychology*, 20 July. DOI: 0022022112451052.

Mendis, S., Puska, P. and Norrving, B. (eds) (2011) *Global Atlas on Cardiovascular Disease Prevention and Control*. Geneva: World Health Organization.

Mercer, J. (2012) Deliverance, demonic possession, and mental illness. *Mental Health, Religion and Culture* 16(6). DOI:10.1080/13674676.2012.706272.

Mercer, J., Sarner, L. and Rosa, L. (2003) *Attachment Therapy on Trial*. Westport, CT: Praeger.

Mignon, S.I. and Ransford, P. (2012) Mothers in prison. *Social Work in Public Health* 27(1–2): 69–88.

Millam, R. (2011) *Anti-discriminatory Practice: A Guide for Those Working with Children and Young People* (3rd edition). London: Continuum International.

Miller, P.H. (2010) *Theories of Developmental Psychology* (5th edition). New York: Worth Publishers.

Mills, E. and Kellington, S. (2012) Using group art therapy to address the shame and silencing surrounding children's experiences of witnessing domestic violence. *International Journal of Art Therapy* 17(1): 3–12.

Mills, H. (2003) *Meeting the Needs of Black and Minority Ethnic Young Carers*. London: Barnado's Policy, Research and Influencing Unit.

Minty, B. (2005) The nature of emotional child neglect and abuse. In J. Taylor and B. Daniel (eds), *Child Neglect*. London: Jessica Kingsley, pp. 57–72.

Miscarriage Association (2013) After the miscarriage. Available from: www.miscarriageassociation.org.uk/information/management-of-miscarriage/after-the-miscarriage/ (accessed 15/02/13).

Mishna, F., Morrison, J., Basarke, S. and Cook, C. (2012) Expanding the playroom: school-based treatment for maltreated children. *Psychoanalytic Social Work* 19(1–2): 70–90.

Monk, C., Georgieff, M.K. and Osterholm, E.A. (2013) Research Review: Maternal prenatal distress and poor nutrition – mutually influencing risk factors affecting infant neurocognitive development. *Journal of Child Psychology and Psychiatry* 54(2): 115–130.

Monds-Watson, A., Manktelow, R. and McColgan, M. (2010) Social work with children when parents have mental health difficulties. *Child Care in Practice* 16(1): 35–55.

Morgan, N. (2007) *Blame My Brain: The Amazing Teenage Brain Revealed.* London: Walker Books.

Morland, L.A., Hynes, A.K., Mackintosh, M.-A., Resick, P.A. and Chard, K.M. (2011) Group cognitive processing therapy delivered to veterans via telehealth. *Journal of Traumatic Stress* 24(4): 465–469.

Morrell, B. and Tilley, D.S. (2012) The role of nonperpetrating fathers in Munchausen syndrome by proxy. *Journal of Pediatric Nursing* 27: 328–335.

Morris, K. (2012) Thinking family? The complexities for family engagement in care and protection. *British Journal of Social Work* 42: 906–920.

Morris, S. (2012) Woman jailed for faking son's illness to claim £85,000 in benefits. *The Guardian*, Tuesday 13 November. Available from: www.guardian.co.uk/uk/2012/nov/13/woman-jailed-faking-sons-illness (accessed 10/07/13).

Morrongiello, B.A., Schwebel, D.C., Bell, M., Stewart, J. and Davis, A.L. (2012) An evaluation of *The Great Escape. Health Psychology* 31(4): 496–502.

Morrongiello, B.A., Zdzieborski, D., Sandomierski, M. and Munroe, K. (2013) Results of a randomized controlled trial assessing the efficacy of the Supervising for Home Safety program. *Accident Analysis and Prevention* 50: 587–595.

Mujtaba, T. and Furnham, A. (2001) Cross-cultural study of parental conflict and eating disorders in a non-clinical sample. *International Journal of Social Psychiatry* 47: 24–35.

Muller, U., Carpendale, J.I.M. and Smith, L. (eds) (2009) *Cambridge Companion to Piaget.* Cambridge: Cambridge University Press.

Munns, E. (2008) Theraply with zero to three year olds. In C.E. Schaefer, S. Kelly-Zion, J. McCormick and A. Ohnogi (eds), *Play Therapy for Very Young Children.* Lanham, MD: Jason Aronson, pp. 157–172.

Munro, E. (2011) *The Munro Review of Child Protection: Final Report.* Norwich: The Stationery Office.

Murphy, C. (2011) *Serious Case Review in Respect of Child S: Executive Summary.* Leeds: Leeds Safeguarding Board.

Murphy, Y. (2011) *Commission of Investigation, Dublin Archdiocese, Catholic Diocese of Cloyne.* Available from: www.justice.ie/en/JELR/Cloyne_Rpt.pdf/Files/Cloyne_Rpt.pdf. (accessed 31/08/13).

Myers, J. (2003) Exercise and cardiovascular health. *Circulation* 107: e2–e5.

Nandy, S. and Selwyn, J. (2012) Kinship care and poverty. *British Journal of Social Work*, 1–18. DOI: 10.1093/bjsw/bcs057.

Napolitano, A., Theophilopoulos, D., Seng, S.K. and Calhoun, D.A. (2013) Pharmacologic management of neonatal abstinence syndrome in a community hospital. *Clinical Obstetrics and Gynecology* 56(1): 193–201.

Navarre, E.L. (1987) Psychological maltreatment. In M. Brassard, R. Germain and S. Hart (eds), *Psychological Maltreatment of Children and Youth.* New York: Pergamon Press, pp. 45–58.

Newcastle Safeguarding Children Board (2011) *Serious Case Review Regarding Child B.* Newcastle: Newcastle Safeguarding Children Board.

NICE (2005) *The Management of PTSD in Adults and Children in Primary and Secondary Care.* Manchester: National Institute for Health and Care Excellence.

NICE (2010) *Looked-after Children and Young People.* Manchester: NICE.

Nichols, J. (2012) *Conducting the Home Visit in Child Protection.* Maidenhead: Open University Press.

Norfolk County Council (1975) *Report of the Review Body Appointed to Enquire into the Case of Stephen Meurs.* Norwich: Norfolk County Council.

Nouwen, E., Decuyper, S. and Put, J. (2012) Team decision making in child welfare. *Children and Youth Services Review* 34: 2101–2116.

Novotny, C.N. (2010) *Treating Traumatized Children through Puppet Play Therapy.* Available from: www.alfredadler.edu/sites/default/files/Novotny%20MP%202012.pdf. (accessed 12/07/13).

Nowinski, S.H. and Bowden, E. (2012) Partner violence against heterosexual and gay men. *Aggression and Violent Behavior* 17: 36–52.

Oates, M.R. (2003) Perinatal psychiatric disorders: a leading cause of maternal morbidity and mortality. *British Medical Bulletin* 67: 219–229.

Oates, M.R., Cox, J.L., Neema, S. Asten, P., Glangeaud-Freudenthal, N., Figueiredo, B. et al. (2004) Postnatal depression across countries and cultures: a qualitative study. *British Journal of Psychiatry* 184: s10–s16.

Obadina, S. (2012) Witchcraft accusations and exorcisms. *British Journal of School Nursing* 7(6): 287–291.

Oberlander, T.F., Warburton, W., Misri, S., Riggs, W., Aghajanian, J. and Hertzman, C. (2008) Major congenital malformations following prenatal exposure to serotonin reuptake inhibitors and benzodiazepines using population-based health data. *Birth Defects Research (Part B)* 83: 68–76.

O'Brien, C.P. (2005) Benzodiazepine use, abuse, and dependence. *Journal of Clinical Psychiatry* 66 (Suppl 2): 28–33.

O'Brien, V. (2012) The benefits and challenges of kinship care. *Child Care in Practice* 18(2): 127–146.

O'Donohue, W.T. and Ferguson, K.E. (2001) *The Psychology of B.F. Skinner.* Thousand Oaks, CA: Sage.

Ofsted (2011) *The Voice of the Child.* Manchester: Ofsted.

O'Hagan, K. (2006) *Identifying Emotional and Psychological Abuse.* Maidenhead: Open University Press.

O'Loughlin, M. and O'Loughlin, S. (2012) Substitute care for children. In M. O'Loughlin and S. O'Loughlin (eds), *Social Work with Children and Families* (3rd edition). London: Learning Matters/Sage, pp. 121–149.

Onyefulu, O. and Safarewicz, E. (1994) *Chinye: A West African Folk Tale.* London: Frances Lincoln.

Ovesen, P., Rasmussen, S. and Kesmodel, U. (2011) Effect of prepregnancy maternal overweight and obesity on pregnancy outcome. *Obstetrics and Gynecology* 118: 305–312.

Owusu-Bempah, K. (1995) Information about the absent parent as a factor in the well-being of children of single-parent families. *International Social Work* 38: 253–275.

Ozonoff, S., Losif, A.M., Baguio, F., Cook, I.C., Hill, M.M., Hutman, T. et al. (2010) A prospective study of the emergence of early behavioral signs of autism. *Journal of the American Academy of Child and Adolescent Psychiatry* 49(3): 256–266.

PACT Parents and Children Together (2013) Adoption – fostering – therapeutic services – community projects. Available from http://www.pactcharity.org/about_us/history (accessed 04/03/13)

Padget, L.S., Stickland, D. and Coles, C.D. (2006) Case study: using a virtual reality computer game to teach fire safety skills to children diagnosed with fetal alcohol syndrome. *Journal of Pediatric Psychology* 31(1): 65–70.

Pala, E., Erguven, M., Guven, S., Erdogan, M. and Balta, T. (2010) Psychomotor development in children with iron deficiency and iron-deficiency anemia. *Food and Nutrition Bulletin* 31(3): 431–435.

Papalia, D.E. and Milton, J.S. (2003) *Child Development*. New York: McGraw-Hill.

Parton, N. (2011) Child protection and safeguarding in England. *British Journal of Social Work* 41: 854–875.

Pawson R., Boaz, A. and Sullivan, F. (2004) *Mentoring Relationships*. Working Paper 21. Leeds: ESRC.

Pearce, C. (2009) *A Short Introduction to Attachment and Attachment Disorder*. London: Jessica Kingsley.

Pearce, T. (2012) Identifying children at risk of abuse linked to belief. *British Journal of School Nursing* 7(6): 270–271.

Peek, L. and Stough, L.M. (2010) Children with disabilities in the context of disaster. *Child Development* 81(4): 1260–1270.

Pemberton, C. (2012) *Eastenders*' portrayal of social work left me in tears. Available from: www.communitycare.co.uk/blogs/childrens-services-blog/2012/10/eastenders-portrayal-of-social-work-left-me-in-tears.html (accessed 03/02/13).

Perkins, D.F. and Jones, K.R. (2004) Risk behaviors and resiliency within physically abused adolescents. *Child Abuse and Neglect* 28(5): 547–563.

Plummer, D.M. and Harper, A. (2007) *Helping Children to Build Self-esteem* (2nd edition). London: Jessica Kingsley.

Pollack, K.M., Austin, W. and Grisso, J.A. (2010) Employee assistance programs. *Journal of Women's Health* 19(4): 729–733.

Pomeroy, E.C. (2012) The bully at work. *Social Work* 58(1): 5–8.

Potter, J. and Hepburn, A. (2003) 'I'm a bit concerned': early actions and psychological constructions in a child protection helpline. *Research on Language and Social Interaction* 36(3): 197–240.

Radford, J. (2010) *Serious Case Review under Chapter VIII 'Working Together to Safeguard Children' in Respect of the Death of a Child*. Case Number 14. Birmingham: Birmingham Safeguarding Board.

Radford, L., Corral, S., Bradley, C., Fisher, H., Bassett, C., Howat, N. and Collishaw, S. (2011) *Child Abuse and Neglect in the UK Today*. London: NSPCC.

Razzell, P. and Spence, C. (2007) The history of infant, child and adult mortality in London, 1550–1850. *London Journal* 32(3): 271–292.

Reder, P. and Duncan, S. (1995) Closure, covert warnings, and escalating child abuse. *Child Abuse and Neglect* 19(12): 1517–1521.

Reder, P., Duncan, S. and Gray, M. (1993) Child protection dilemmas in a 'not-existing' pattern of abuse. *Journal of Family Therapy* 15: 57–64.

Rees, C.D., Williams, T.N. and Gladwin, M.T. (2010) Sickle-cell disease. *Lancet* 376: 2018–2031.

Rees, G., Stein, M., Hicks, L. and Gorin, S. (2011) *Adolescent Neglect*. London: Jessica Kingsley.

Reupert, A.E., Maybery, D.J. and Kowalenko, N.M. (2012) Children whose parents have a mental illness. *Medical Journal Australia Open* 1(Suppl 1): 7–9. DOI: 10.5694/mjao11.11200.

Ridge, T. (2011) The everyday costs of poverty in childhood. *Child & Society* 25(1): 73–84.

Rocque, B. (2010) Mediating self-hood. *Disability & Society* 25(4): 485–497.

Rogers, C. (1961) *On Becoming a Person*. London: Constable.

Roth, G. and Assor, A. (2010) Parental conditional regard as a predictor of deficiencies in young children's capacities to respond to sad feelings. *Infant and Child Development* 19(5): 465–477.

Rothbaum, B.O. (2009) Using virtual reality to help our patients in the real world. *Depression and Anxiety* 26: 209–211.

Rubble, N.M. and Turner, W.L. (2000) A systemic analysis of the dynamics and organization of urban street gangs. *American Journal of Family Therapy* 28(2): 117–132.

Ruiz-Casares, M., Rousseau, C., Currie, J.L. and Heymann, J. (2012) 'I hold on to my teddy bear really tight': children's experiences when they are home alone. *American Journal of Orthopsychiatry* 82(1): 97–103.

Rutter, M. (1972) *Maternal Deprivation Reassessed*. Harmondsworth: Penguin.

Rutter, M. (1981) Stress, coping and development: some issues and some questions. *Journal of Child Psychology and Psychiatry* 22(4): 323–335

Rutter, M. (1985) Resilience in the face of adversity: protective factors and resistance to psychiatric disorder. *British Journal of Psychiatry* 147: 598–611.

Rutter, M. (2006) Implications of resilience concepts for scientific understanding. *Annals of the New York Academy of Science* 1094: 1–12.

Rutter, M. (2012a) Annual Research Review: Resilience: clinical implications. *Journal of Child Psychology and Psychiatry* 54(4): 474–87. DOI: 10.1111/j.1469-7610.2012.02615.x.

Rutter, M. (2012b) Resilience as a dynamic concept. *Developmental Psychopathology* 24(2): 335–344.

Rutter, M., Beckett, C., Castle, J., Colvert, E., Kreppner, J., Mehta, M. et al. (2007) Effects of profound early institutional deprivation. *European Journal of Developmental Psychology* 4(3): 332–350.

Rutter, M., Kreppner, J. and Sonuga-Barke, E. (2009) Emanuel Miller Lecture: Attachment insecurity, disinhibited attachment, and attachment disorders. *Journal of Child Psychology and Psychiatry* 50(5): 529–543.

Rutter, M. and Quinton, D. (1984) Long-term follow-up of women institutionalized in childhood. *British Journal of Developmental Psychology* 2(3): 191–204.

Ryan, S. (2009) *The Commission to Inquire into Child Abuse*. Available from: www.childabusecommission.com/rpt/ExecSummary.php (accessed 31/07/13).

Sambrooks, P. (2009) *Dennis Duckling*. London: British Association for Adoption and Fostering.

Samek, D.R. and Rueter, M.A. (2011) Considerations of elder sibling closeness in predicting younger sibling substance use. *Journal of Family Psychology* 25(6): 931–941.

Sanders, R. (2004) *Sibling Relationships*. Basingstoke: Palgrave Macmillan.

Sanger, C. (2012) The birth of death: stillbirth certificates and problem for the law. *Californian Law Review* 100: 269–312.

Sapienza, J.K. and Masten, A.S. (2011) Understanding and promoting resilience in children and youth. *Current Opinion in Psychiatry* 24: 267–273.

Scaife, J. (2012) *Deciding Children's Future*. Hove: Routledge.

Schwebel, D.C., Morrongiello, B.A., Aaron, L., Davis, A.L., Stewart, J. and Bell, M. (2012) The Blue Dog. *Journal of Pediatric Psychology* 37(3): 272–281.

Scottish Government (2012) *Statistical Bulletin: Children's Social Work Statistics Scotland* (No.1, 2012 edition). Edinburgh: Scottish Government Statistician Group.

Scourfield, J. and Walsh, I. (2003) Risk, reflexivity and social control in child protection. *Critical Social Policy* 23(3): 398–420.

Seymour, C. and Seymour, R. (2011) *Courtroom and Report Writing Skills for Social Workers* (2nd edition). Exeter: Learning Matters.

Sharkey, J.D., Shekhtmeyster, Z., Chavez-Lopez, L., Norris, E. and Sass, L. (2011) The protective influence of gangs. *Aggression and Violent Behavior* 16: 45–54.

Sharp, C., Aldridge, J. and Medina, J. (2006) *Delinquent Youth Groups and Offending Behaviour*. London: Home Office.

Sheehan, K.A., Thakor, S. and Stewart, E. (2012) Turning points for perpetrators of intimate partner violence. *Trauma Violence Abuse* 13(1): 30–40.

Sheiham, A. (2006) Dental caries affects body weight, growth and quality of life in pre-school children. *British Dental Journal* 201: 625–626.

Shemmings, D. and Shemmings, Y. (2011) *Understanding Disorganised Attachment*. London: Jessica Kingsley.

Sheridan, M., Sharma, A. and Cockerill, H. (2008) *From Birth to Five Years* (3rd edition). New York: Routledge.

Sherman, J. (2009) Father and son group thereaplay. In E. Munns (ed.), *Applications of Family and Group Theraplay*. Lanham, MD: Jason Aronson, pp. 237–247.

Sidebotham, P., Bailey, S., Belderson, P. and Brandon, M. (2011) Fatal child maltreatment in England, 2005–2009. *Child Abuse and Neglect* 35: 299–306.

Silverstein, D.N. and Livingston-Smith, S. (eds) (2009) *Siblings in Adoption and Foster Care*. Westport, CT: Praeger.

Singh, S. (2013) Anti-racist social work education. In A. Bartoli (ed.), *Anti-racism in Social Work Practice*. St Albans: Critical Publishing, pp. 25–47.

Singhal, A., Cole, T.J., Fewtrell, M., Deanfield, J. and Lucas, A. (2004) Is slower early growth beneficial for long-term cardiovascular health? *Circulation* 109: 1108–1113.

Sithisarn, T., Bada, H.S., Charnigo, R.J., Legan, S.J. and Randall, D.C. (2013) Effects of perinatal oxycodone exposure on the cardiovascular response to acute stress in male rats at weaning and in young adulthood. *Frontiers in Physiology* 4(85): 1–9.

Siu, A.F.Y. (2009) Theraplay in the Chinese World. *International Journal of Play Therapy* 18(1):1–12.

Smit, B.J., Kok, J.H., Vulsma, T., Briet, J.M., Boer, K. and Wiersinga, W.M. (2000) Neurologic development of the newborn and young child in relation to maternal thyroid function. *Acta Paediatrica* 89: 291–295.

Smith, A. (2012) Guide to evaluation and treatment of anaemia in general practice. *Prescriber* 23(21): 25–42.

Somerville, J.W., Swanson, A.M., Robertson, R.L., Arnett, M.A. and McLin, O.H. (2009) Handling a dog by children with attention-deficit/hyperactivity disorder. *North American Journal of Psychology* 11(1): 111–120.

Sonuga-Barke, E.J., Beckett, C., Kreppner, J., Castle, J., Colvert, E., Stevens, S. et al. (2008) Is sub-nutrition necessary for a poor outcome following early institutional deprivation? *Developmental Medicine and Child Neurology* 50(9): 664–671.

South, J., Meah, A. and Branney, P.E. (2012) Think differently and be prepared to demonstrate trust. *Health Promotion International* 27(2): 284–294.

Spencer, N. and Baldwin, N. (2005) Economic, cultural and social contexts of neglect. In J. Taylor and B. Daniel (eds), *Child Neglect*. London: Jessica Kingsley, pp. 26–42.

Spinney, A. (2012) Safe from the start? *Children & Society* 27(5): 397–405.

Spratt, T. and Devaney, J. (2009) Identifying families with multiple problems. *British Journal of Social Work* 39(3): 418–434.

Squires, J.E. and Squires, R.H. (2013) A review of Munchausen syndrome by proxy. *Pediatric Annals* 42(4): 67–71.

Srivastava, O.P., Stewart, J., Fountain, R. and Ayre, P. (2005) Common operational approach using the 'Graded Care Profile' in cases of neglect. In J. Taylor and B. Daniel (eds), *Child Neglect*. London: Jessica Kingsley, pp. 131–146.

Stanley, N. (2011) *Children Experiencing Domestic Violence*. Dartington: Research in Practice.

Stanley, N., Miller, P. and Foster, H.R. (2012) Engaging with children's and parents' perspectives on domestic violence. *Child and Family Social Work* 17: 192–201.

Stanley, N., Miller, P., Foster, H.R. and Thomson, G. (2011a) A stop–start response. *British Journal of Social Work* 41: 296–313.

Stanley, N., Miller, P., Foster, H.R. and Thomson, G. (2011b) Children's experiences of domestic violence. *Journal of Interpersonal Violence* 26(12): 2372–2391.

Stein, Z.A., Susser, M., Saenger, G. and Marrolla, F. (1975) *Famine and Human Development: The Dutch Hunger Winter of 1944–1945*. New York: Oxford University Press.

Stevenson, O. (2007) *Neglected Children and their Families* (2nd edition). Oxford: Blackwell.

Stiles, J. (2012) The effects of injury to dynamic neural networks in the mature and developing brain. *Developmental Psychobiology* 54: 343–349.

Stobart, E. (2009) Child abuse linked to accusations of 'possession' and 'witchcraft'. In J. La Fontaine (ed.), *The Devil's Children: From Spirit Possession to Witchcraft*. Farnham: Ashgate, pp. 151–172.

Stokes, J. and Schmidt, G. (2011) Race, poverty and child protection decision making. *British Journal of Social Work* 4(6): 1105–1121.

Storr, A. (2001) *Freud: A Very Short Introduction*. Oxford: Oxford University Press.

Stothard, K.J., Tennant, P.W.G., Bell, R. and Rankin, J. (2009) Maternal overweight and obesity and the risk of congenital anomalies. *Journal of the American Medical Association* 301(6): 636–650.

Strentz, T. (1980) The Stockholm Syndrome. *Annals of the New York Academy of Science* 347: 137–150.

Strong, M. and Johnstone, P. (2010) Interventions for treating scabies. Cochrane Database Systematic Review. In: *The Cochrane Library, Issue 10, 2010*. Chichester: John Wiley & Sons.

Sturman, D.A. and Moghaddam, B. (2011) The neurobiology of adolescence. *Neuroscience and Biobehavioural Reviews* 35: 1704–1712.

Stutts, J.T., Hickey, S.E. and Kasdan, M.L. (2003) Malingering by proxy: a form of pediatric condition falsification. *Journal of Developmental and Behavioral Pediatrics* 24(4): 276–278.

Sunderland, M. (2003) *Teenie Weenie in a Too Big World: A Story for Fearful Children*. Milton Keynes: Speechmark Publishing.

Talge, N.M., Neal, C. and Glover, V. (2007) Antenatal maternal stress and long-term effects on child neurodevelopment: how and why? *Journal of Child Psychology and Psychiatry* 48(3/4): 245–261.

Taylor, J. and Daniel, B. (eds) (2005) *Child Neglect*. London: Jessica Kingsley.

Tedam, P. (2013) Developing cultural competence. In A. Bartoli (ed.), *Anti-racism in Social Work Practice*. St Albans: Critical Publishing, pp. 48–65.

Theraplay Institute (2013) Professional Training. Available from: www.theraplay.org/index.php/training (accessed 01/08/13).

Thoburn, J., Wilding, J. and Watson, J. (2000) *Family Support in Cases of Emotional Maltreatment and Neglect*. Norwich: The Stationery Office.

Thompson, E.H. (2011) The evolution of a children's domestic violence counseling group. *Journal for Specialists in Group Work* 36(3): 178–201.

Thompson, E.H. and Trice-Black, S. (2012) School-based group interventions for children exposed to domestic violence. *Journal of Family Violence* 27(3): 233–241.

Thompson, N. (2012) *Anti-discriminatory Practice: Equality, Diversity and Social Justice* (5th edition). Basingsoke: Palgrave Macmillan.

Thompson, R.S., Strong, P.V. and Fleshner, M. (2012) Physiological consequences of repeated exposures to conditioned fear. *Behavioural Scences* 2: 57–78.

Timms, C., Chan, D., Kang, J.-Y., Forton, D. and Poullis, A. (2013) Social media use by inflammatory bowel disease and viral hepatitis patients and potential application for healthcare. *Gut* 62(Suppl 1): A240–A241.

Tiplady, C.M., Walsh, D.B. and Phillips, C.J.C. (2012) Intimate partner violence and companion animal welfare. *Australian Vetinary Journal* 2(90): 48–53.

Tomlinson, B. and Blome, W.W. (2012) Hold the presses. *Journal of Public Child Welfare* 6(3): 243–254.

Tomoda, A., Sheu, Y.-S., Rabi, K., Suzuki, H., Navalta, C.P., Polcari, A. and Teicher, M.H. (2011) Exposure to parental verbal abuse is associated with increased gray matter volume in superior temporal gyrus. *NeuroImage* 54: S280–S286.

Tucker, C.J. and Updegraff, K. (2009) The relative contributions of parents and siblings to child and adolescent development. In L. Kramer and K.J. Conger (eds), *Siblings as Agents of Socialization: New Directions for Child and Adolescent Development*, 126. San Francisco, CA: Jossey-Bass, pp. 13–28.

Turner, H.A., Finkelhor, D. and Ormrod, R. (2007) Family structure variations in patterns and predictors of child victimization. *American Journal of Orthopsychiatry* 77(2): 282–295.

Ulrich-Lai, Y.M. and Herman, J.P. (2009) Neural regulation of endocrine and autonomic stress responses. *Nature Review: Neuroscience* 10: 397–409.

Ungar, M. (2009) Overprotective parenting: helping parents provide children with the right amount of risk and responsibility. *American Journal of Family Therapy* 37(3): 258–271.

Ungar, M. (2012) Researching and theorizing resilience across cultures and contexts. *Preventive Medicine* 55: 387–389.

UNODC (United Nations Office on Drugs and Crime) (2010) *Compilation of Evidence-based Family Skills Training Programmes*. Available from: www.unodc.org/docs/youthnet/Compilation/10-0018_Ebook.pdf (accessed 09/02/13).

Unwin, P. and Hogg, R. (2012) *Effective Social Work with Children and Families*. London: Sage.

Urh, S. (2011) Ethnic sensitivity: a challenge for social work. *International Social Work* 54 (4): 471–484.

Uzun, S., Kozumplik, O., Jakovljević, M. and Sedić, B. (2010) Side effects of treatment with benzodiazepines. *Psychiatria Danubina* 22(1): 90–93.

VanFleet, R. and Faa-Thompson, T. (2010) The case for using animal assisted play therapy. *British Journal of Play Therapy* 6: 4–18.

VanFleet, R., Sywulak, A.E. and Sniscak, C.C. (2010) *Child-centred Play Therapy*. New York: Guilford Press.

Verbanck, P. (2009) Drug dependence on benzodiazepines and antidepressants. *Review medicale de Bruxelles* 30(4): 372–375.

Vernig, P.M. (2011) Family roles in homes with alcohol-dependent parents: an evidence-based review. *Substance Use and Misuse* 46(4): 535–542.

Vida, M.D., Vingilis-Jaremko, L., Butler, B.E., Gibson, L.C. and Monteiro, S. (2012) The reorganized brain: how treatment strategies for stroke and amblyopia can inform our knowledge of plasticity throughout the lifespan. *Developmental Psychobiology* 54: 357–368.

Vina, J., Sanchis-Gomar, F., Martinez-Bello V. and Gomez-Cabrera, M.C. (2012) Exercise acts as a drug: the pharmacological benefits of exercise. *British Journal of Pharmacology* 167: 1–12.

Vincent, S. and Petch, A. (2012) *Audit and Analysis of Significant Case Reviews*. Edinburgh: The Scottish Government.

Vygotsky, L.S. (1978) *Mind in Society*. Cambridge, MA: Harvard University Press.

Wager, F., Hill, M., Bailey, N., Day, R., Hamilton, D. and King, C. (2010) The impact of poverty on children and young people's use of services. *Children & Society* 24(5): 400–412.

Walker, D.F., Reid, H., O'Neill, T. and Brown, L. (2009) Changes in personal religion/spirituality during and after childhood abuse. *Psychological Trauma* 1(2): 130–145.

Walker, G.J. and Johnstone, P.W. (2000) Interventions for treating scabies. Cochrane Database Systematic Review. In *The Cochrane Library, Issue 2, 2000*. Chichester: John Wiley & Sons.

Walters, T.D., Gilman, A.R. and Griffiths, A.M. (2007) Linear growth improves during infliximab therapy in children with chronically active severe Crohn's disease. *Inflammatory Bowel Diseases* 13: 424–430.

Wampler, R.S., Downs, A.B. and Fischer, J.L. (2009) Development of a brief version of the Children's Roles Inventory (CRI-20). *American Journal of Family Therapy* 37(4): 287–298.

Watt, J. (2013) *Report Writing for Social Workers*. London: Learning Matters/Sage.

Watts-English, T., Fortson, B.L., Gibler, N., Hooper, S.R. and De Bellis, M.D. (2006) The psychobiology of maltreatment in childhood. *Journal of Social Issues* 62(4): 717–736.

Wedl, M. and Kotrschal, K. (2009) Social and individual components of animal contact in preschool children. *Anthrozoös* 22(4): 333–396.

Wegscheider-Cruse, S. (1989) *Another Chance: Hope and Health for the Alcoholic Family* (2nd edition). Palo Alto, CA: Science and Behavior Books.

Weinstock, M. (2008) The long-term behavioural consequences of prenatal stress. *Neuroscience and Biobehavioural Reviews* 32: 1073–1086.

Welsh Government (2012) *Adoptions, Outcomes and Placements for Children Looked After by Local Authorities, Wales, 2011–12*. Cardiff: Knowledge and Analytic Services.

Werner, E.E. and Smith, R.S. (1982) *Vulnerable but Invincible: A Study of Resilient Children*. New York: McGraw-Hill.

Westmarland, N. and Kelly, L. (2012) Why extending measurements of 'success' in domestic violence perpetrator programmes matters for social work. *British Journal of Social Work*, 1–19. DOI: 10.1093/bjsw/bcs049.

Wettig, H.H.G., Coleman, A.R. and Geider, F.J. (2011) Evaluating the effectiveness of Theraplay in treating shy, socially withdrawn children. *International Journal of Play Therapy* 20(1): 26–37.

White, S. (2009) Arguing the case in safeguarding. In K. Broadhurst, C. Grover and J. Jamieson (eds), *Critical Perspectives on Safeguarding Children*. Chichester: John Wiley & Sons, pp. 93–110.

White, S., Hall, C. and Peckover, S. (2009) The descriptive tyranny of the common assessment framework: technologies of categorization and professional practice in child welfare. *British Journal of SocialWork* 39: 1197–1217.

Widen, S.C. and Russell, J.A. (2008) Young children's understanding of others' emotions. In M. Lewis, J.M. Haviland-Jones and L.F. Barrett (eds), *Handbook of Emotions* (3rd edition). New York: Guilford Press, pp. 348–362.

Wiegerink, D.J.H.G., Roebroeck, M.E., Donkervoort, M., Stam, H.J. and Cohen-Kettenis, P.T. (2006) Social and sexual relationships of adolescents and young adults with cerebral palsy. *Clinical Rehabilitation* 20: 1023–1031.

Wilber, K. (1998) *The Essential Ken Wilber*. Boston, MA: Shambhala.

Wildeman, C., Schnittker, J. and Turney, K. (2012) Despair by association? The mental health of mothers with children by recently incarcerated fathers. *American Sociological Review* 77(2): 216–243.

Wilson, K.R., Hansen, D.J. and Lu, M. (2011) The traumatic stress response in child maltreatment and resultant neuropsychological effects. *Aggression and Violent Behavior* 16: 87–97.

Winter, K. (2011) *Building Relationships and Communicating with Young Children*. Abingdon, Oxon: Routledge.

Wood, D., Bruner, J. and Ross, G. (1976) The role of tutoring in problem solving. *Journal of Child Psychology and Psychiatry* 17: 89–100.

Wood, J. and Alleyne, E. (2010) Street gang theory and research: where are we now and where do we go from here? *Aggression andViolent Behavior* 15: 100–111.

World Health Organization (1996) *The ICD-10 Classification of Mental and Behavioural Disorders*. Geneva: WHO.

Wright, C.M. (2005) What is weight faltering (failure to thrive) and when does it become a child protection issue. In J. Taylor and B. Daniel (eds), *Child Neglect*. London: Jessica Kingsley, pp. 166–187.

Yamawaki, N., Ochoa-Shipp, M., Pulsipher, C., Harlos, A. and Swindler, S. (2012) Perceptions of domestic violence. *Journal of Interpersonal Violence* 27(16): 3195–3212.

Yorke, J. (2010) The significance of human–animal relationships as modulators of trauma effects in children. *Early Child Development and Care* 180(5): 559–570.

Young, B.J., Bunnell, B.E. and Beidel, D.C. (2012) Evaluation of children with selective mutism and social phobia. *Behavior Modification* 36(4): 525–544.

Young, S., McKenzie, M., Schjelderup, L. and More, C. (2012) The rights of the child enabling community development to contribute to a valid social work practice with children at risk. *European Journal of Social Work* 15(2): 169–184.

Zaidi, M.A., Griffiths, R., Newson-Smith, M. and Levack, W. (2012) Impact of stigma, culture and law on healthcare providers after occupational exposure to HIV and hepatitis C. *Culture, Health and Sexuality* 14(4): 379–391.

Zugazaga, C.B., Surette, R.B., Mendez, M. and Otto, C.W. (2006) Social worker perceptions of the portrayal of the profession in the news and entertainment media. *Journal of Social Work Education* 43(3): 621–636.

Index